THE INNER GAME

DOMINIC LAWSON

THE
INNER GAME

M

MACMILLAN

LONDON

First published 1993 by Macmillan London Limited

a division of Pan Macmillan Publishers Limited
Cavaye Place London SW10 9PG
and Basingstoke

Associated companies throughout the world

ISBN 0 333 60949 2

1 3 5 7 9 8 6 4 2

A CIP catalogue record for this book is available from
the British Library

Typeset by CentraCet Limited, Cambridge
Printed and bound in Great Britain by
Mackays of Chatham plc,
Chatham, Kent

For Rosa,
who understands another,
more important, language

CONTENTS

PREFACE

This is, in part, an adventure story. It is the story of how a young Englishman with no formal education in chess, and without a penny of support from the state, succeeded in becoming only the second man in almost sixty years to challenge the Russian hegemony over the world chess championship.

Unlike Bobby Fischer in 1972, Nigel Short's challenge failed at the last and steepest hurdle. But then Bobby Fischer never had to play Garri Kasparov, deservedly considered the strongest chessplayer in the history of our oldest game. And while the strange American contents himself with rematches against his old chopping block, Boris Spassky, Nigel Short is even now preparing his second expedition to conquer Mount Kasparov.

This, though, is the inside account of Short's first assault on the summit, over the three years it took to beat the best of the rest, including Kasparov's predecessor as world champion, the awesome Anatoly Karpov. That victory alone was worthy of a book. Indeed, one or two have been written about it, but only in Russian. Here, I am afraid, it merely forms part of one chapter.

That is because I have attempted to describe much more than just the moves that the greatest chessplayers make on the board. I have also tried, with the privilege of complete access to all of Nigel Short's preparation and training, to reveal the psychological tricks of the grandmaster's trade, and how such men set up their defences in advance against the low mental blows of their enemies.

This is also an account of the political manoeuvrings behind the scenes of the world chess championship, which, during Short's challenge to Kasparov, erupted into an as yet unresolved battle for control between the top players and the bureaucrats who have ruled the game for almost half a century. To the extent that I was intimately involved in that battle at its outset, this book might be seen as *parti pris*. I can only say that I have told it as I saw it happen.

I might also be accused of a bias in favour of Nigel Short and against Garri Kasparov. To this I plead guilty. First, Nigel is a good friend, and good friends deserve support. Second, I had long dreamt that one day Britain would produce a great chess-player with not just the skill, but also the will to wrest the world championship from the Russians. Nigel Short had the same wild dream, and it was the most extraordinary experience of my life to be closely involved in the attempt to render that fantasy a fact. I hope that some of the excitement, joy, chaos and sheer nervous tension of that experience comes across in the telling of it.

I have also tried to explain the strange tricks of the mental light which pass between the likes of Garri Kasparov and Nigel Short as each attempts, under the constraints of time and nervous energy, to outwit the other at the board. The moves of the games between those two men appear at the back of the book. But the true nature of the chess struggle lies only partly in the moves themselves; it lies also in the attempts to read the opponent's thoughts and emotions, the attempts to camouflage the most dangerous plans through bluff and acting, and the attempts to hide the deepest wounds by similar means. This is something which Garri Kasparov taught Nigel Short over two months in London in the autumn of 1993. By teaching him that lesson (among many others), he will have made Short an even more lethal player. How much more lethal we – and his opponents – will discover over the next few years.

Finally, I have done my best to reveal the inner lives and characters of those men who, 'escaping madness, can unremit-tingly devote all of [their] mental energy during ten, twenty, thirty, forty years to the ludicrous effort to corner a wooden king on a wooden board'.

It is obvious that this book could not have been attempted, let alone written, without the help of Grandmaster Nigel Short over a number of years. Among others who gave me generous access to their strange world of abstract thought and bitter competitiveness were Grandmasters Lubomir Kavalek, Robert Hübner, Jon Speelman and Michael Stean.

Roland Philipps at Macmillan has been the editor every author should have: a man who changes nothing, including deadlines. Without his encouragement this would have been a much less enjoyable book to write; and without Ed Victor, my far from secret agent, I would never have pursued the idea in the first place.

I was allowed to desert my post at the *Spectator* for two months, in order to research and write *The Inner Game*. That was a kind favour from Conrad Black, whose concept of time and motion within the Telegraph Group is not always so indulgent. I am grateful to Simon Heffer for editing the *Spectator* while I was gravitating among grandmasters.

Theirs is a man's world. But it is to two women that I owe a special debt of gratitude. Rea Short saw little enough of her husband during his campaign of the past three years; her tolerance of my presence, at times when she must have wanted nothing more than to be alone with her family, bordered on the saintly.

Above all I am grateful to Rosa, my wife. It follows that, if I was spending far too much time with Nigel Short, I was spending far too little time with Rosa. Yet she never once complained at becoming a chess widow, even when, on some rare evening at home, I tactlessly spoke of nothing but the game. Rosa has also been a marvellous editor. She read every page of this book before its final setting, and her suggestions have improved the flow of the text immeasurably. Any remaining infelicities are my responsibility alone.

31 October 1993
Alice's Cottage
Duntisbourne Leer
Gloucestershire

I had never before had the chance to know a great chess player personally, and the more I now sought to familiarize myself with the type, the more incomprehensible seemed a lifelong brain activity that rotated exclusively about a space composed of 64 black and white squares.

Children can learn its simple rules, duffers succumb to its temptation, yet within this immutable tight square it creates a particular species of master not to be compared with any other – persons destined for chess alone, specific geniuses in whom vision, patience and technique are operative through a distribution no less precisely ordained than in mathematicians, poets, composers, but merely united on a different level.

It stands to reason that so unusual a game, one touched with genius, must create out of itself fitting matadors. This I always knew, but what was difficult and almost impossible to conceive of was the life of a mentally alert person whose world contracts to a narrow, black-and-white one-way street; who seeks ultimate triumphs in the to-and-fro, forward and backward movement of thirty-two pieces; a being who, by a new opening in which the knight is preferred to a pawn, appreciates greatness and the immortality that goes with casual mention in a chess handbook – of a man of spirit who, escaping madness, can unremittingly devote all of his mental energy during ten, twenty, thirty, forty years to the ludicrous effort to corner a wooden king on a wooden board!

STEFAN ZWEIG, *The Royal Game* (1942)

CHAPTER ONE

The women had left the room and it was time for boys' talk. I asked the tough-looking man to my right if Nigel Mansell was a genius. Jackie Stewart, the former motor-racing world champion, sighed quietly. 'Do you know about Formula One?' No, I didn't. 'What sport do you know about?' Chess, I said. 'Well,' said Stewart, 'how many people in the world play chess?' Oh, millions, I said. 'How many of those play in clubs and championships?' Hundreds of thousands, I thought. 'And how many are so good that they can make money out of it?' A few thousand, I guessed. 'And how many of those make it to be a grandmaster?' About three hundred, I supposed. 'And how many of those grandmasters have what it takes to be a world champion?' At the moment, one. Perhaps two. 'So he or they are very special people. Would you call them geniuses?' I would. 'Well, you might call them the Nigel Mansells of chess,' said Mr Stewart, and I had my answer.

I had known Nigel Short for about ten years, and, although I have never met the other Nigel, I liked Jackie Stewart's comparison. It seemed to me that both men were a certain type, if genius can be a type, of British sporting hero. A bland, almost inhibited exterior convincingly hides not just the turmoil of genius, but also the inner rage of the demonically competitive. Such a carapace used to be described as the stiff upper lip. In Nigel Short's case we should call it the stiff upper cerebral cortex.

As for Garri Kasparov, I knew him much less well, although I first encountered him, strangely enough, on the day of my first meeting with Nigel Short. I was on the organization committee of Kasparov's world championship semi-final match in London against the Soviet defector Viktor Korchnoi. It was October 1983; Kasparov was nineteen years old, and already the most stellar body in the chess firmament.

The body then liked to wear black leather jackets, and, thus attired, it burst into our little committee room in the

1

appropriately named Great Eastern Hotel. Its owner ranted away in Russian: it was angry about some details of the match arrangements. That much could be gleaned from the desperately diplomatic translations of its interpreter and minder, an elegant woman called Valentina Fominikh, whom the *Daily Mail* subsequently described as a colonel in the KGB (this was, after all, 1983). 'Colonel' Fominikh could not keep up with the eruption of words from her young charge – Kasparov has always found anger a great spur to verbosity – so I just sat and stared.

I think everyone in that room would have noticed two things about this strange young man. First, he did not look like a young man. Even then his frizzy black hair had the metallic tinge of the prematurely grey. Second, he possessed an energy to which the word demonic scarcely does justice. It seemed as though he did not sit in his chair, but somehow was hovering about two inches above it, like a human humming bird. I instantly connected these two first impressions and concluded that the man would burn out within a few years, like a star imploding under the stress of its own energy. I felt even surer of this when 'Colonel' Fominikh, with a candour which belied her supposed profession, later told me that Kasparov was frequently woken up at night by sudden heart palpitations, suffered from 'rheumatic carditis' and had to have injections for the condition.

Subsequent events, of course, cast doubt on my theories and 'Colonel' Fominikh's diagnosis: that month Kasparov, famously, went on to beat the durable Korchnoi, and then, two years later, the world champion himself, Anatoly Karpov. Less well remembered is that Nigel Short was playing on the same bill as Kasparov–Korchnoi. It seemed a good idea at the time: Short had just returned from a sensational victory in a grandmaster tournament in Kasparov's home town of Baku and we, the organizers, had arranged a match between Short and the US junior champion Joel Benjamin.

A few hours after my encounter with Kasparov I bumped into the seventeen-year-old Short as he loped – Nigel has always loped – through the dusty corridors of the Great Eastern Hotel. He muttered something about not having a room for the night, though not in a tone of voice which suggested that he cared very much one way or the other. I gave him the room allotted to me as a member of the organizing committee – as a resident Londoner I hardly needed it.

There could not have been a much greater contrast between Kasparov's hysterics over some minor point of organizational detail and Nigel's blithe unconcern about sleeping rough. Unfortunately there could also not have been a greater contrast between their chessboard performances in London in October 1983. While Kasparov showed astonishing maturity in his dissection of the weak points in Korchnoi's game, Short lost horribly to a player he should have trounced. Perhaps there was something to be said for Kasparov's neurotic perfectionism. At the end of the event, while Kasparov was firmly grabbed by his ever-present and even more neurotic mother Klara, Short was loping around in the company of a dreamy-eyed blonde woman, rumoured to be one of Denmark's most promising young players of her sex. Perhaps there was something to be said for the seventeen-year-old Nigel's unneurotic unperfectionism too.

In recent years Short has stigmatized his teens as a period when he hardly worked on his chess at all. He is painfully aware that Kasparov's intensive and unremitting training in the Soviet School, notably under the tutelage of the first Soviet world champion, Mikhail Botvinnik, has given him a lead in chess knowledge that Short, however talented, can never recover. In chess, as in politics, knowledge is power.

It was, however, understandable that the young Short should have thought that his talent and determination, once at the board, would be enough. At three he was able to solve six jigsaw puzzles simultaneously. At eight he beat Korchnoi in an exhibition game. At twelve he qualified for the British chess championship, where he beat the ten-times British chess champion Dr Jonathan Penrose – after cockily turning down the great doctor's magnanimous offer of a draw. At seventeen he became the world's youngest grandmaster.

Not surprisingly these exploits came to Kasparov's attention, and, even before becoming champion himself, Kasparov brooded over the idea that one day he would face a challenge from Short for the world chess championship. In the 1987 edition of his autobiography Kasparov wrote, 'Nigel Short, the British player, is destined, in my opinion, to become the leading Western grandmaster. . . . in fact, his career has closely paralleled my own. All that now seems to stand between Nigel and the prospect of the world crown is the unfortunate fact that fate brought him into this world only two years after Kasparov.' Kasparov's perception of chess ability has only ever been matched by his lack of any false, or indeed genuine, modesty.

(It was remarks like that which began to create in Nigel's mind an antipathy against Kasparov which grew with each new example of the new champion's braggadocio. The first – scarcely noticed – public outing for this antipathy came when in 1987 I asked Nigel to review Kasparov's autobiography for the *Spectator*. Quoting Kasparov's self-portrait – 'Many a player who has become World Champion and has scaled the Mount Olympus of chess, realizes that he can go no higher and begins to descend. . . . I see no danger of this for myself. I see only new peaks before me and no descent' – Nigel observed, 'Unashamed conceit runs like a connecting thread throughout the book. We have repeated references to Kasparov's brilliant memory, which he imagines knows no limits. My own experience is different. I witnessed a game between Kasparov and ex-world champion Boris Spassky, where the younger man tried and failed miserably to recall his own previous analysis. . . . Another facet of Kasparov's personality is his ability to manipulate a set of circumstances into a simplistic theory, to suit his emotional needs. Of course, this defence mechanism is present in us all, but in Kasparov it seems to be in permanent overdrive.' Kasparov, concluded Short, was a 'Grandmaster of self-delusion'.)

Three years after his victory against Viktor Korchnoi, Kasparov was back in London, this time to defend his newly acquired world title from the previous, very careful owner, Anatoly Karpov. With Kasparov came his chief second, the former captain of the Red Army chess team, Grandmaster Josef Dorfman. I became quite friendly with 'Joe', though I still wince at the memory of his pulverizing handshake, acquired, I liked to imagine, in regimental arm-wrestling competitions.

I greatly enjoyed Joe Dorfman's rather disloyal evocations of working for Garri Kasparov. 'Do you know, when we go on walks, he insists on keeping at least four paces ahead of the rest of us. He's from the Middle East of the Soviet Union, you know, and he behaves as if he was some sheikh. And the way he eats! He tears at his food, like an animal. I can't bear to eat in the same room as him any more!'

Entertaining as all this was, I was more interested in knowing Dorfman's opinions about Nigel's chances of reaching a match against Kasparov, of becoming the first Westerner since Bobby Fischer to challenge the post-war Russian chess hegemony. After all, earlier that year, in Brussels, Nigel had scored his first tournament victory over Kasparov. Over a lunch in a gloomy and obscure City steak-house – it was not altogether a healthy thing at that time for Joe to be seen talking to a Western journalist – I asked Dorfman: can Nigel Short take on Kasparov? can he even become world champion?

Joe's forkful of best Angus rump steak stopped suddenly on its path towards a good Soviet set of silver-capped molars. From that mouth came a low gurgle, which turned into almost uncontrollable laughter. After a while Grandmaster Josef Dorfman recovered his composure, and answered the apparently hilarious question. 'No Westerner will become world champion. All your players are on their own. They have no support from the state. Who do you think pays me – and two other grandmasters – full-time to help Kasparov? Who makes sure that we say yes when we are asked to help? Who do you think paid for Kasparov's chess education from childhood? Nigel Short is very talented – I've studied his games, of course. But one man cannot beat a system. Forget it.' I did – for a time.

The Soviet system of chess did not die with the Soviet Union – indeed Kasparov is its greatest achievement. Strictly in political terms it was started by Lenin's colleague Nikolai Krylenko, who commandeered the trade union movement to spread chess throughout the new socialist state. Strictly in chess terms it was founded by Kasparov's tutor Mikhail Botvinnik, world chess champion, with one or two unwelcome interruptions, from 1948 to 1963. Botvinnik introduced into chess the total dedication which became characteristic of the Soviet players. It was not just that they were backed by the state, and could concentrate on the game full-time, unlike virtually all their Western opponents. It was their attitude to the game.

Botvinnik, when preparing for a match against an opponent who smoked, would play secret training matches in sealed rooms against specially selected grandmasters ordered to blow smoke into his face. Under the Botvinnik influence, the Soviet players developed a style of total warfare, deliberately dragging out games to exhaust their less physically well-trained Western opponents, and, whenever possible, manipulating results among themselves so as to deny prizes to their Western rivals. It was this attitude which prompted Bobby Fischer to write an article in 1963 entitled 'The Russians Have Fixed World Chess'.

But twenty years later they were still at their old tricks, with the result that Nigel Short, Fischer's ultimate successor as the great Western hope, had come to despise the Soviets. He always described them to me as 'commies', and has turned down one or two lucrative invitations to tournaments on discovering that he was the one non-Russian invitee. As an example of unscrupulous Russian – and Kasparovian – chess conduct, Nigel will allude to the big Moscow tournament of 1992, organized by Kasparov himself. Kasparov had secured an invitation for his chief second, the Georgian Grandmaster Zurab Azmaiparashvili. 'Azmai', according to Nigel, had the black pieces against the American Grandmaster Nick de Firmian and desperately wanted a draw. Nigel told me, 'Azmai offered Nick a draw and $2000 if he took it. Nick declined. Kasparov went up to Nick and was very angry with him. He said that $2000 was a very generous offer for a draw and that he should accept. Of course he's a friend of Azmaiparashvili and wanted to help him. But he was also the tournament organizer, and this was something really shady.'

One of the other achievements of the Soviet school was to license, if not encourage, the aggressive stare at the board. Mikhail Tal, world champion fleetingly in the early 1960s, was the most famous exponent of this practice. Kasparov himself – clearly impressed – described Tal's gaze as 'intimidating, hypnotic'. To be fair to the hard-drinking Latvian, his bulging-eyed bullying was more sardonic than sadistic: in a world championship tournament in 1962, his American opponent, Benko, attempted to deflect the evil eye by donning dark glasses. For their next encounter Tal, whose university thesis was 'Satire', arrived at the board wearing tinted spectacles of a grotesqueness not usually seen outside the dressing room of Dame Edna Everage. He won the game.

Anatoly Karpov, world champion from 1975 to 1985, was another great Soviet starer, although his gaze was designed to chill rather than bully. An intense, strangely yellowish colour, his eyes would flicker 'like a snake's tongue', observed one shaken opponent. It is difficult to appreciate the power of such tactics, unless the gaze is aimed in your direction. I recall such a moment when Nigel Short was playing Karpov in their world championship eliminator in Spain. Nigel played a move which offered to repeat a position which earlier in the match had been much to Karpov's advantage. Bluff? Or a trap? I was sitting in the front row of the audience, and Karpov knew I was in the Short camp. He also knew that Nigel's face was not the sort which gives anything away, even under the most intimidating pressure. Suddenly Karpov swivelled round and locked his eyes on to mine. I had two impressions: first, that a torch was casting its beam into the darkest recesses of my mind, and, second, that it was just as well that I didn't really know whether Nigel was bluffing either.

Viktor Korchnoi, Karpov's opponent in two matches for the world championship in the early 1980s, sought to turn Karpov's evil eye against its owner by wearing reflector glasses. Contrary to Korchnoi's hopes, Karpov did not hypnotize himself, although he seemed somewhat irritated to observe his own snake eyes emerging from the rabbit's side of the board.

It is Kasparov, however, who has developed the intimidating stare into something approaching an art form. His technique differs from that of his Soviet predecessors. While Tal specialized in straightforward aggression, and Karpov in 'look no hands' brain-scans, Kasparov's gaze is designed to humiliate.

The best example, or rather the worst, that I actually witnessed was during the eleventh game of his 1987 world championship match against old snake-eyes himself, Anatoly

Karpov. Karpov fell for a sinister little one-move trap which allowed Kasparov to turn a terrible position into a winning one. When Karpov fell into it, Kasparov could have flashed out his prepared winning reply instantly. But he did not. Instead he gazed across the board with undisguised contempt. At that moment Karpov must have realized what he had done: his right hand, which was just writing down his own last move, suddenly froze in mid-hieroglyphic. Kasparov, savouring the moment, slowly lifted his own right hand from the table, and with a sweeping gesture, like a matador putting on a cape, played the killing reply. He then sat and stared at Karpov, while clapping his now free right hand over his mouth, as if to stifle a giggle.

Nigel's first taste of this sort of behaviour from Kasparov came in the Linares international grandmaster tournament of 1991, and as tastes go it was not a very pleasant one. Playing Black against one of Kasparov's most aggressive openings, Nigel uncorked an innovation of startling originality, advancing a pawn in front of his own king's position, in contravention of the most basic of chess principles. Kasparov, who at that time was experimenting with spectacles, stared wide-eyed at the miscreant pawn, whipped out his glasses and ostentatiously peered through them at the board. Then he laughed out loud. This, as it was designed to do, attracted the attention of other players, including Karpov, to Nigel's peculiar move. 'I wanted to say something, but decided Kasparov wasn't worth it,' Nigel said at the time.

But weeks later, over dinner at my home, Nigel was still smarting at what he described as Kasparov's 'insulting behaviour', although I suspect he would have felt less sore about it had not Kasparov demolished his innovation with even more than his customary brutality.

By 1993, when it became clear that Nigel was likely to be the challenger for the world title, Kasparov seemed to have singled him out for special treatment. In the England–Russia match in the 1993 world team championships in Hungary, Kasparov once again beat Nigel. But his off-the-board tactics shook even seasoned observers. Grandmaster Michael Stean, the non-playing captain of the English team, told me, 'Kasparov's behaviour during the game was something else. He was pounding up and down the stage like a raging bull. He was actually snorting, I swear it. I found it intimidating just as a spectator. I can't imagine what it must have been like at the board.' It was at around this time that Nigel began to describe Kasparov to me as 'an animal'.

Kasparov himself dismisses Short's accusation that he deliberately uses physical and facial gestures to humiliate: 'People think that this is all an act designed to frighten and intimidate my opponent, like Tal's famous glare. This is not so, though I admit that it may sometimes have that effect on a weak or impressionable opponent. It is all for my own benefit really, to force myself to dig deep inside my mind for the right combinations.'

The truth is that grandmaster chess is a game of extreme psychic aggression: when Bobby Fischer said, famously, on the *Johnny Carson Show*, 'I like to crush the other guy's ego,' he was thought to be uniquely crass, unpleasant even. He was in fact saying with his customary childlike openness what most chess grandmasters feel. Even Nigel Short, with his cool, almost detached manner at the chessboard, is not different in this respect. On numerous occasions before a big game he would describe to me, in gory detail, what he would do to his opponent. 'I'm going to give it to him good and hard' or 'I'm going to give the guy a good rogering' are two particular favourites.

On another occasion I remember standing beside Nigel and Yasser Seirawan, the top American grandmaster, as they analysed their game from the 1987 Barcelona world chess cup tournament. Nigel, who had won the game, described his winning process as 'TDF'. At first I said nothing, thinking that this was the name of a variation I should know well. But the winning process 'TDF' kept cropping up, so I asked what it stood for. Almost in unison the two grandmasters chanted 'Trap. Dominate. Fuck.'

At the same event Seirawan, who had been on the receiving end of some of Kasparov's contemptuous glares, advised Nigel on the correct response: 'I gave Kasparov a look which meant "Buster, you do that one more time, and I'll rip your lungs out and feed them to you." He hasn't bothered me since.' Seirawan, to be fair, has the Californian swimmer's physique which makes such a threat believable. But Nigel's response was simply: 'I don't want to sink to the level of the animal to beat the animal.'

Nigel, as the Jewish saying has it, should have been so lucky. In that tournament he played with the mixture for which he was becoming all too well known in the chess world: brilliant wins against the world's best interspersed with horrible defeats to lesser players. And, of course, he lost again to Kasparov. On paper, Nigel's ranking had risen to fifth in the world. In practice, he was losing far too many games through sheer carelessness to be considered as a contender for the world championship. On the flight back from Barcelona I sat next to Rea, Nigel's wife of a few months. I asked her what could be done to help her husband gain the results that his talent seemed to warrant. It seemed too soon to write off Nigel Short as just another example of that most poignant of chess careers: the child prodigy who failed to make the grade.

CHAPTER TWO

I t is not necessarily true that behind every man there is a great woman. It is equally not necessarily true that behind every great chessplayer there is a great psychotherapist. But it certainly helps. At any event, it might not be a coincidence that the two most successful Western chess grandmasters, Nigel Short and the Dutchman Jan Timman are both married to psychotherapists.

The chess grandmaster puts himself under a mental strain that can become overwhelming in two distinct ways. First, the game itself is of a depth that requires fantastic feats of calculation. Yet even the greatest players are merely scratching the bark of the analytical tree: chess, as has been written before, is more than a match for the human mind. After the first three moves by each player, the position on the board is one of more than nine million that could have arisen. After that the game starts to become complicated: it has been estimated that there are vastly more possible chess games than atoms in the known universe.

The second area of intense strain is the competitive. While a mathematician might tax his nerves in trying to solve a theoretical problem, he does not have another mathematician in the room attempting to change the problem whenever he looks like solving it. Nor does he have a clock ticking, timing his every thought and banning all ideas of relaxation until victory or defeat is realized.

The professional scientist or mathematician, moreover, tends to live and work in an institution, with all the security and collegiate atmosphere that goes with it. The chess grandmaster has no sinecure, he has no fixed salary; indeed he has no fixed abode. Like most international sportsmen he rushes from tournament to tournament, from city to city, from hotel to hotel, from time-zone to time-zone. A loner by nature, the professional chessplayer's sense of social isolation is all the greater because the only people he sees regularly are the same people who wish to take the bread from his mouth – his rivals. It is hardly surprising that the grandmaster population is dense with the difficult, the misanthropic and the plain crazy. England's first ever grandmaster, world junior champion and Nigel Short's predecessor as the great hope of English chess, Tony Miles, spent some months in an institution in 1988 following a complete mental collapse. (At one point he had to be restrained by four policemen after he vaulted over the barrier at the entrance to Downing Street and was advancing on Number 10.)

Interestingly, this occurred just at the time when Nigel Short was usurping Miles's treasured position as the top British player and was beginning to crush the older man in tournament after tournament. Following the break-up of his marriage – to England's top woman chessplayer, as it happened – Miles did not have the domestic security to cope with the strains of top-flight chess or with the sudden realization that he was no longer even the first choice of his own country. Shortly after his release from observation, Tony Miles left England – briefly – and took up American citizenship.

Miles is by no means the first great chessplayer to have suffered profound mental breakdown at a time of crisis in his chess career. The two strongest players of the last century, Paul Morphy and Wilhelm Steinitz, both suffered from extreme paranoid delusions, although Steinitz, in one of his visits to the sanatorium, was able to point out with admirable objectivity: 'Like all lunatics I imagine that the doctors are crazier than I am.' Steinitz's psychotic episode, like Miles's, occurred at a time of painful defeat: in his case the ultimate one of losing a world championship match.

To most people, the highly strung, almost fissile, characters of the chess world are distinctly unnerving. To Rea Karageorgiou, an elegant, russet-haired Greek woman with a professional interest in the problems and potential of the human mind, they were fascinating. In November 1984, she decided to observe the phenomenon at first hand: she travelled to the Greek city of Thessaloniki, which that year was the host of the annual chess Olympiad. There, as she engaged in her first scientific study of the mental fauna and flora of grandmasterdom, Rea saw her future husband, Nigel Short, although to this day he cannot believe that she noticed the eighteen-year-old English third string amid the thousands of milling chessplayers from around the world.

Rea once told me that she found chessplayers as a breed 'very strong individualists, with very forceful and developed personalities'. I said I thought that 'strange' was a better description. 'Strange?' retorted the psychotherapist. 'That, for me, does not exist. What is "strange"? What is "not strange"? What you call strange, I would describe as sharply defined.'

In late 1985, at the home in Solingen of one of the most 'sharply defined' characters in the chess world, the German champion Dr Robert Hübner, Rea and Nigel met for the first time. Nigel immediately decided he had met the woman he wanted to marry. Some years earlier Short, discussing the attributes he most looked for in a partner, had said, 'The most important thing for anyone close to me to understand is how much enjoyment I get from playing chess, and not ever to think of it as some little game to make money at.' Rea understood that as well as any woman could who was not herself a chessplayer. For two years Nigel pursued her, while Rea attempted to maintain her independence and an intellectual relationship with the chess world as a whole, rather than an intimate one with Nigel Short. 'I kept telling him over and over again that he couldn't be the most important person in my life, but he always believed that he would win in the end. There was something he wanted. I was it. And he had to do whatever had to be done to get it.'

Rea, as a result, is one of the few people who were not surprised by Nigel's single-minded assault on the world chess championship. 'I knew he could withstand all sorts of blows and defeats, because he had already proved to himself – with me – that he could get what he most wanted, if only he persevered. I was the testing ground.'

Rea is still a fiercely independent woman, but following her marriage to Short in the summer of 1987 she has become Nigel's muse, in a way which other chess grandmasters comment on with something close to envy. During his games she sits watching his every move, in a place in the auditorium where he can see her clearly. It is, for her, nothing less than a torment. She is desperately nervous about the result, but, scarcely understanding the moves, she is unable to calm herself by analysing the position. Worse, Nigel's posture and demeanour at the board is so carefully calculated not to give anything away that Rea herself cannot tell from looking at her husband whether he is winning, drawing or losing. 'During the game,' Rea once told me, 'I am doing nothing but suffering. I hate it. But Nigel says he needs my presence there. Some of his opponents think I'm there attempting to radiate positive energy towards him, but that's not what's happening. I'm there just because he thinks it matters to him. It's something of a ritual for both of us, and I just give myself up to it.'

Nigel never seems to look up at Rea at any point, no matter how many hours he is at the board. As Rea says, rather contemptuously, 'We don't sit there giving each other encouraging little glances.' But on one occasion, during the eighth hour of a particularly gruelling game in Nigel's final world championship eliminator against Jan Timman, Rea weakened, and for a few minutes surreptitiously looked away from the board and flicked over a few pages of a book. I was sitting next to her at the time and Nigel seemed to be completely engrossed in the position on the board. But after the game he was most put out, and complained that Rea had taken her attention away from the game. What's more, he lost.

That was, as it happens, a critical game. By losing it, Nigel allowed his opponent to claw his way back into a match which had seemed all but over. That night, as we sat around the dining table contemplating the next day's game, Nigel seemed exhausted. He had blundered in a drawn position, one, moreover, which he had previously analysed. He still needed just three draws from the last three games to win the match, and the right to challenge Kasparov, but could not decide whether to play safe or go for the kill in the next game.

It was obvious, as he pushed his food around on his plate, that he absolutely could not make up his mind on his strategy for the following day. Rea was watching him, clearly trying to come up with the words which would help clear the air. She also knew that the one sure way of losing a game is to enter it without knowing whether one wants a win or a draw. She pushed her own plate of food to one side, uneaten, and glared across at her husband. 'Nigel,' Rea intoned like some Greek oracle, 'for tomorrow's game I will give you the advice my Spartan countrywomen gave their men as they left for battle: "Come back either with your shield or upon it."'

Nigel gave a fair impression of a man in the electric chair receiving the first 10,000 volts. And the shock worked. The next day he plunged into one of the sharpest and most complicated of all opening lines, and emerged with a winning position. I turned to Rea, as we were watching the game, from the private box allotted to her by the match organizers. 'He's playing chess like a Spartan,' I whispered. 'But how did you think that one up?' Rea laughed. 'I don't know. It was just that he had lost his energy through disappointment, and, when that happens, he must take it from me.'

Know the child, and you understand the man. This is as true of Nigel Short and Garri Kasparov as it is of many less complex characters. Short is the second of three brothers born in the Lancashire town of Leigh, whose biggest company is famed for its willingness to dig holes in the ground and dump industrial quantities of waste in them. His earliest memory is of walking with his mother and elder brother Martin, who steps into a puddle and soaks his trousers. Martin asks Nigel to take his clean, dry trousers off so that he can wear them. No, says little Nigel. His mother Jean, rightly wanting to avoid a fight, tells Nigel he must take off his trousers and give them to his big brother. Nigel is a quiet, uncomplaining child, who will not make a fuss. He silently agrees, silently rages, and silently never forgets. For that little boy, the chessboard becomes the place where he can assert himself, where silence is not a weakness but a strength, and where size and age count for nothing.

Garik Weinstein is an only child, born in the Soviet Middle Eastern oil city of Baku to a Jewish father and an Armenian mother. Kim Weinstein, an engineer, declares that his little boy 'has a fine analytical brain' but never discovers just how fine: he dies of lymphatic sarcoma when Garik is seven. His mother, Klara Kasparova, the senior scientific associate of the Azerbaizhani Electrical Engineering Research Institute, gives up her career, devotes herself entirely to her son and, in due course, as the son gratefully wrote, 'entirely to my chess career.' Young Garri Kasparov is the only man in his ambitious mother's life. He is praised, protected and promoted. Klara does not remarry. Recently she said of her son, 'Every move he makes is part of my life.' To which observation, if there were any room for doubt about the nature of their relationship, the world champion added his own: 'We are one unit.'

In 1986 a German psychologist, Dr Reinhard Munzer, travelled to Seville to study Kasparov at close quarters during his second world championship defence against Anatoly Karpov. Kasparov reminded Dr Munzer of nothing so much as Freud's description of Goethe: 'If you have been mother's undisputed darling, then you will retain for life that feeling for conquest and confidence in success which not infrequently begets success.'

Freud also suggested that single traumatic events in childhood have the power to determine the course of lives. In the case of Nigel Short and Garri Kasparov, born two continents and two years apart, that event, quite possibly was the same one: in 1972 Bobby Fischer, by beating Boris Spassky in Iceland, became the first Westerner since the war to wrest the world chess championship from the Soviet Union.

The Soviet Union, or at least its political élite, was certainly traumatized by the loss of the title it had held for a quarter of a century. In the true spirit of communist self-criticism, the Soviet chess authorities confessed that they – by which they meant their grandmasters – had become complacent. It was necessary to create once again the spirit of Stakhanovite effort and enthusiasm which had brought the title to the motherland in 1948. So Mikhail Botvinnik, the man responsible for that triumph of socialism, was dusted down from his Stalinist attic and increased state funding was directed into the Botvinnik Chess School, which, it was hoped, would create a new generation of Soviet world champions. His star pupil was little Garri Weinstein – soon to become Kasparov. In 1975, the year in which Fischer abandoned his title, Botvinnik declared publicly of Kasparov, 'The future of chess is in the hands of this young man.' This young man was immediately assigned a full-time professional trainer in the form of Grandmaster Nikitin, who remained his coach up to the time that Kasparov won the world title.

(Nowadays, as is the fashion, Kasparov is reluctant to acknowledge the peculiarly Soviet nature of his achievement. But, in the first edition of his autobiography, he laid great stress on his adoption of the 'investigative' chess style which, Botvinnik claimed, distinguished Soviet players from the lazy, undialectical intuitiveness of the Western school. More pointedly, he cast scorn on Westerners who refused to believe that he could still be a communist as well as a millionaire. Kasparov was a member of the Communist Party, a mark of conformity which had been studiously avoided by some other Soviet world champions, such as Mikhail Tal and Boris Spassky. Kasparov has made much of his battle against the old Soviet political establishment and against the arch-conformist Karpov. But Kasparov's mentor was Geidar Aliev, the former head of both the Communist Party and the KGB in Azerbaizhan. Kasparov added a special dedication to the communist leader Gorbachev in the first edition of his autobiography. By the time of the second edition he had become a supporter of the new Russian leader, Boris Yeltsin. But according to Nigel Short, 'Kasparov will always have a Soviet cast of mind. Those who were brought up under that system all have the same warped outlook: "You fuck with my wife – I kill you. I fuck with your wife – you keep quiet if you know what's good for you."')

For the seven-year-old Nigel Short, the victory of Bobby Fischer over the Soviets in 1972 was galvanizing. He had been playing chess for two years with a skill which had astounded his parents, but which meant nothing to him. It never occurred to Nigel that it was odd to beat adults at chess, if only because he had been playing for scarcely any length of time before that began to happen. Then came the Fischer–Spassky match, and a sudden craze for chess which temporarily overtook the English-speaking world, including, fortunately, the Lancashire town of Leigh.

There, Nigel began playing over the moves of Fischer vs. Spassky, as they appeared every morning in the newspapers, and he was amazed. 'I felt', Nigel told me twenty years later, 'there and then, that I could be world champion. Not just that I wanted to be, but that I could be. The point was, I understood the games, or thought that I did. And I felt that, if I could understand the games now, as a child, what could I not achieve as an adult?' At the same time, and for the same reason, Nigel also decided, at the age of seven, that he wanted to become a chess professional.

By the age of ten Nigel was playing 180 tournament games a year – 'about three times as many as I do now' – and at the age of twelve he received that least sought-after mark of professional recognition, a demand for income tax from the Inland Revenue ('It came as a bit of a shock, actually'). There was some criticism at the time that Nigel was being pushed too hard by his father, a public relations man who, when Nigel was twelve, produced a book called *Nigel Short: Chess Prodigy*. One British grandmaster, with whom Nigel travelled abroad for his first overseas tournament, recalls with some displeasure receiving a call from Mr Short in which 'all he wanted to know was how high Nigel had finished in the tournament and how much money he had won'. But, Nigel insisted to me, 'I was never pushed into doing anything I didn't want to do.' This, remember, was a child who, at the age of ten, defeated Viktor Korchnoi in a game which lasted nine and a half hours. The boy couldn't play enough chess.

The real problem was that this extraordinary talent was never given any sort of direction. While Kasparov was instructed daily by grandmasters in the theory and practice of professional chess, Nigel, as far as he can recall, 'had just half a dozen sessions with the Lancashire junior chess coach, Mike Conroy. Apart from that, I was entirely self-taught, which is not enough, particularly for a child. Chess is like any other discipline: you need order and method, and that can only be supplied by a teacher. I believe that had I had some good training in my teens, correcting some simple errors that I made time and time again, then I would have been phenomenally good.'

In 1977 and then again in 1980 Nigel encountered Kasparov at junior chess representative tournaments. 'At the time I thought he was a nice guy. He was still a human then. But I felt a little sorry for him. He was incredibly serious, seemed much older than the rest of us, and spoke only about chess. Pop music, girls – the things I was interested in – forget it! But the point is that he had already been taught things about chess which even now I am learning for the first time. I wasted my teenage years doing nothing. I played chess for fun and I spent a lot of time lying in bed. It was only when I got to twenty I realized I should have been studying chess. At the time I didn't mind. But now I resent enormously the fact that I didn't receive a proper chess education. I would have become a much stronger player: there are some things you can never catch up.'

One could come to a quite different conclusion: that Nigel's straightforward down-to-earth qualities, his lack of eccentricity, stem precisely from not being treated as a chess machine as a child. His playfulness and sense of humour – qualities which one does not immediately associate with Kasparov – are, to some degree, functions of having been allowed a childhood, albeit a somewhat unusual one. Kasparov himself has observed with a certain wistfulness, 'The loss of my childhood was the price of becoming the youngest world champion in history. When you have to fight every day from a young age, your soul could become contaminated. I lost my childhood. I never really had it. Today I have to be careful not to become cruel, because I became a soldier too early.'

In the Soviet Union, where hundreds of chessplayers lived – more comfortably than most of their fellow citizens – off state stipends, Kasparov would have been marked out at a very early age as one who would always do nothing but play chess. While he was an extraordinary talent, there was nothing extraordinary in Kasparov's becoming a chess professional in a country which contained many more full-time chessplayers than the rest of the world combined.

But in Britain, for even such a talent as Nigel Short, a decision to become a professional chessplayer was an oddity. There was absolutely no tradition of chess, as a career, in Britain.

All its greatest players of the past had been amateurs, and proud of it. At the time, 1983, when the seventeen-year-old Short left home to live off his wits as a chessplayer, there were probably no more than three or four Britons who could be said to be earning their living from chess. In Nigel's first year as a professional, he made £5000 – and that was counted a great success.

Financial security aside, in other, even more important, respects the Soviet system of state planning treated Kasparov more kindly than English laissez-faire treated Nigel. Kasparov was gradually introduced into the far-from-childlike world of top-flight grandmaster chess. The Soviet chess authorities liked to wean their young stars slowly from junior tournaments on to obscure Eastern European adult events in which, if necessary, some ageing and hard-up Czech or Bulgarian grandmaster could be persuaded to throw the odd game to the young Russian master, *pour encourager*. Kasparov was never entered for an event he was not expected to win: and he never disappointed.

Grandmaster John Tisdall sums up the different backgrounds of Short and Kasparov very well: 'Western players have a tendency to mature more slowly than their Eastern counterparts. Minor distractions like general education and a near infinite assortment of more appealing professions start the process of delay. The relatively meagre opportunities for training and playing also play a part, though breaking through to the elite eventually guarantees a player the chance to complete his chess education. Nigel, though a prodigy and a professional, certainly followed this pattern. Another reason why Westerners in general, and Nigel in particular, had a hard time being taken seriously at the highest level is that they tended to receive more psychological knocks at the board than the chosen few who have taken the title of late. Karpov never experienced anything resembling professional adversity until he was world champion, and Kasparov's only knowledge of failure is as a theoretical concept. Then again, perhaps he defines it as something which happens to others. Short has had to endure the customary speculation about wasted talent and fading promise. . . .'

Nigel has had to live with those accusations since, at the age of fourteen, he was casually thrown into the crocodile-infested deep end of professional chess, and entered for the 1980 Phillips & Drew grandmaster tournament. It was the strongest chess event ever to be held in Britain, with the top players not just of the host country, but also of America, Yugoslavia and, of course, the Soviet Union, represented by the world champion Anatoly Karpov. The hopelessly under-prepared Short managed to scramble to a draw against Karpov, but lost almost every other game. It was not a matter of ability. Nigel simply did not yet have the mental toughness to play three consecutive weeks of chess against the best in the world. It was a débâcle.

Even as he was preparing for his match with Kasparov thirteen years later, Nigel was still reluctant to talk to me about it. 'It was incredibly traumatic, and not just because my parents' divorce was happening at about the same time. I lost all my appetite for chess, and all my confidence for a very long time. That effect is still with me, and emerges from time to time. I've never totally been able to eradicate it.' (Some who knew Nigel well in those days say that he developed a stammer at that time, and that his curiously stilted style of speech is the legacy of that double trauma.)

In all sports, confidence is the key to success. When it goes, often for no very obvious reason, everything else collapses. The top tennis-player double-faults on set point, the international cricketer bowls a series of no-balls, the golfing superstar gets the yips, the £5 million football-player misses the penalty. But in chess, a game which, unlike all those others, is entirely in the mind, with no trained limbs to take over when the brain is in crisis, a collapse of confidence is terminal. Above all, across the board the opponent can sense this mental bleeding, as clearly as a boxer can see blood oozing from his adversary's head.

Ultimately, the contest between Nigel Short and Garri Kasparov, the culmination of a decade's arm's-length rivalry, would be decided by the balance of confidence at the time of greatest crisis. It could not be otherwise in such a battle of wills.

Talent, in chess, as in all other sports, is not enough. Not even genius is enough. Indeed, it might not even be necessary. The conventional wisdom is that people like Kasparov and Short are both geniuses, and it is that which separates them from us.

This is something with which Short, at least, profoundly disagrees. Kasparov does sometimes talk about 'inspiration from heaven' when discussing some of his most brilliant moves. Short dismisses such language as 'bollocks'. 'I am not a genius,' he insists. 'I simply studied chess for up to fifteen hours a day at a very early age.' But what about his ability, which I have myself observed frequently at first hand, to visualize the most extraordinarily complicated variations in a twinkling of his mind's eye? 'Visualization too is easily learnt, providing you have half a brain. Kasparov is possibly better at visualization than I am, but I do not consider him to be a genius. He is a trained dog.' (This remark is calculatedly mischievous, being a quote from Kasparov's own bedside book of insults: when he was asked his opinion of the chessplaying talent of the Hungarian girl prodigy Judit Polgar, who was taught nothing but chess from infancy by an obsessive father, Kasparov described her as 'a trained dog'. Nigel now refers to Judit merely as 'Lassie'.)

Short does not deny the possibility of natural chess genius. Indeed he describes his friend, the Indian Grandmaster Vishwanathan Anand, as one. Anand, entirely self-taught, is the quickest player in the history of the game, and regularly defeats strong grandmasters using only half an hour for all his moves. 'Vishy', says Nigel, 'has a speed of thought which is simply incredible. He lacks Kasparov's acquired knowledge and will to win, but, when it comes to talent, his is vastly bigger.'

Perhaps the different claims by Short and Kasparov about the importance of genius simply reflect their different characters both at and away from the chessboard. Kasparov is a very highly strung, volatile, aggressive personality, some would say a typical product of the part of the world he comes from. The idea of genius is an extreme one, and appeals to the extremist in Kasparov. It also appeals to the man that Kasparov believes himself to be: 'Deep down inside,' he wrote in his autobiography, 'I am a romantic.' He has also described himself as 'an artist'. And how could the world's greatest artist, albeit on a canvas of just sixty-four squares, be anything other than a genius?

Nigel Short, however, comes from a part of the world, the industrial north-west of England, where the virtues of common sense, industriousness and phlegmaticism are the most highly prized. Even today, Nigel Short, if asked what characteristic he most admires, will say without hesitation, 'Toughness.'

He is a taciturn man, often described by other chessplayers, a touch irritably, as 'aloof'. This is not, I think, a manifestation of superiority, still less of snobbery. It is just that, while Kasparov is a talker, Short is a listener. He likes to suck knowledge out of people, and is quite prepared to be thought uninteresting if that is the price of receiving more information than he gives.

When he does speak freely, even on subjects on which he is well informed, the words tend to come out slowly, and with intense deliberation, as if he was trying to give directions to a lost foreign tourist. Partly that is because for Nigel, as Richard Reti famously wrote of Capablanca, 'Chess is his mother tongue.' Partly it is because he is an intensely self-controlled individual.

This is where the link between Short the chessplayer and Short the human being becomes most clear. Nigel views chess as a game of control. The winner is not necessarily the one who has the most brilliant ideas, but the one who manages to impose his vision of how the game should go both on his own unruly pieces and on those of his opponent. In Short's best games there is a tremendous sense of harmonious yet powerful order being applied to an inherently unstable region. (By contrast, in Kasparov's games there is a tangible feeling of volcanic energy sweeping aside the order which the opponent is attempting to construct, of the irresistible force overcoming the immovable object.)

In his personal life, Nigel exhibits a similar passion for order. He is a compulsively neat parker of cars. His clothes, however casual, always look as if they were being worn for the first time, and he is inclined to brush away specks of dust from the clothes of close friends, if they are within flicking range. At home, there is never a book or a magazine out of place, particularly if it is about chess. While Kasparov is apt to lose his temper at the least provocation, I have never heard Nigel raise his voice in anger, even at times of great stress or setback. While this is nowadays frowned on by psychiatrists as a sign of repression, I think that in Nigel's case it is genuinely that he has a very high level of tolerance for stress, that he is profoundly unneurotic.

This is a very important aspect of Nigel Short's success at chess, particularly in the fierce cockpit of world championship matchplay. The ability of a great chessplayer to remain calm under extreme pressure of time and position is not unlike that of a fighter pilot able to keep up a steady flow of observation and information while under intense anti-aircraft fire. The appearance of coolness and control is not enough. It is necessary actually to be cool and self-controlled. Otherwise the hand on the trigger is unsteady . . . the fatal blunder is committed.

Grandmaster Michael Stean is now Short's manager, but when Nigel was in his early teens he acted as his coach in representative tournaments such as the world junior championship in 1979 (Nigel came second to Kasparov in a clash of the adolescent titans): 'Nigel has changed since those days. I always thought he had the talent to challenge for the world championship, but in those days he lacked the steel which Kasparov had even as a kid. Then, if Nigel lost a game, he would lose another, and another. Nowadays, if he loses a game, he fights back savagely to win the next one. Rea is responsible for this, because she has put steel in his backbone.'

Rea herself thinks that such an assessment is wide of the mark: 'I'm not averse to taking credit, but I simply don't believe that one person can change the character of another. You can't put steel into a person. But you can unsheathe it.'

It would in any case be wrong to see the relationship between Nigel and Rea Short purely in terms of chess. Indeed, according to Rea, the main difference between Nigel and Garri Kasparov is that her husband has an emotional hinterland beyond chess, whereas Kasparov has not. In the run-up to the world championship match, we often discussed how each player would measure up to defeat, and how much it would matter psychologically.

Not surprisingly Rea had considered the matter deeply: 'Nigel and Garri are antitheses. They are both very deep people, but in Garri's case that strength and depth is centred exclusively on chess. Nigel is very capable of emotional understanding. For him, chess is one thing in a complex life. For Garri, chess is everything, with a bit of life tacked on the end. With Garri everything just erupts through chess in a blind, unconscious way. He has to win, or he's nothing. His sense of self is so connected with being champion; without that there would be a gaping hole where his ego is. It's what holds him together.'

Among Rea's clients in her practice in Athens are schizophrenics and psychotics, and I once asked her if, with her professional hat on, she considered Kasparov to be in any way psychotic. The answer, after some hesitation, was 'No. I would say he is predominantly neurotic, like most men who have had too close a relationship with a dominant mother. In any event I'm sure he'd be a very interesting client.'

At the time we had that conversation, in the summer of 1989, it had seemed as likely that Kasparov would become a client of Rea as that he would be an opponent for Nigel in a world championship match. In the previous three-year world championship cycle, Nigel, despite his then ranking as the third-strongest player in the world, behind only Kasparov and Karpov, lost in the quarter-finals to his friend, fellow resident of Hampstead and British number two Jonathan Speelman.

To add insult to elimination, Garri Kasparov, alone in the chess world, had predicted the result. 'Nigel Short', he opined, 'has not got the character to fight such matches. He cannot stand the tension. If he wishes to progress further,' the world champion concluded, 'he must change his character.' Perhaps Kasparov meant that Nigel should become as monomaniacal as himself, a rather bleak prospect for both his family and his friends.

But, if Kasparov meant that Nigel did not care enough about winning or losing, he should have been with us as we walked away from the Barbican Centre just after Nigel had conceded final defeat to Speelman. He suddenly ran on ahead and, at what he thought was a safe distance, stopped, bent double and let out a long, high-pitched scream of anguish. For some months after the loss in the quarter-finals to Speelman, Nigel was dazed. A loss in a match against a Karpov or a

Kasparov was something he could comprehend. But to lose to another Englishman, and moreover one whom he regarded as a pleasant companion rather than a threat, was not so easy to come to terms with.

Nigel Short had plenty of time to brood about the defeat. The world chess championship is a pitiless three-year cycle, in which the world champion sits it out, while his rivals exhaust and destroy each other in a series of knock-out tournaments and matches. Nigel knew that the next world championship cycle would be resolved in 1993, when he was likely to be at his peak, but before the current generation of monstrously talented Russian teenagers had reached their own full potential.

It was at this stage, while Nigel was slowly recovering from his defeat by Hampstead's number-two player, that I asked Rea what could be done to help Nigel, if not to win the world championship, at least help him to justify the hope that British chess fans had held for so long. They – we – did not expect Nigel to become world champion, but even Kasparov had publicly acknowledged that Short ought to have been the greatest Western threat to the continued Russian domination of the world chess championship.

Rea's reply came almost before I had finished asking the question. What Nigel needed, she said, with even more than her usual emphasis, was a grandmaster assistant, and not just any grandmaster, but one with vast experience, who could accelerate Nigel's understanding of chess by passing on that wisdom in distilled form. And such a person, if he existed, should be available whenever Nigel needed him. In essence, Rea was making the same point that Kasparov's second, Josef Dorfman, had made to me some years earlier: that one man alone, however talented, could not hope to take on the Russian chess machine, with all its state-sponsored trainers and tuition. Dorfman's boss certainly shared that opinion in 1987. He was given a scare by Short in a closely fought six-game quickplay match. 'Nigel is a hugely talented player,' Kasparov conceded after the event (which he won 4–2), 'but he lacks the back-up resources, such as a budget for trainers and assistance, which are available to Soviet grandmasters.' The problem for Nigel was precisely that the British state had never been prepared to put anything into chess, and for one professional grandmaster to employ another out of earnings for any length of time was an impossibility.

The solution could only be to find some private sponsor willing to pay whatever it took to get the best man for the job. I approached one or two firms, who let it be known that, even if we were not in a recession, their shareholders might find it an odd use of funds to start up a chess grandmaster job-creation scheme. I had attempted to sell the idea to them on the basis that it was to finance a British assault on the world chess championship: but it was hard to break down the preconception that this was an event which was only settled between two hatchet-faced Russians in a draughty hall in Moscow.

Finally, I approached Sir Patrick Sheehy, the chairman of the tobacco multinational BAT. Cigarette companies seemed to enjoy backing indoor sports. If snooker, why not chess? Sir Patrick responded that there was nothing in it for his tobacco businesses, but he had a financial services company, Eagle Star Insurance, which might just be interested. And, following a call from Sir Patrick's office, Eagle Star was very interested. All Nigel had to do in return for the lolly was to play a number of simultaneous chess games each year against Eagle Star's brightest and best. Insurance actuaries, it turned out, were mad-keen chess fiends almost to a man.

The next step was to find the best chess coach that Eagle Star's money could buy. Nigel's instant first choice was Boris Spassky. It seemed a very good idea. The two men were close friends, at least as close as grandmaster rivals ever get, and their styles were also similar: both played classical, direct chess. As a former world champion Spassky knew as well as anyone could what was involved in training and preparing for matches at the highest level, and, of course, had an intimate knowledge of the workings of the Russian chess mind. Best of all, he now lived almost next door – in Paris with his third wife, a Frenchwoman.

But, after a few months of London-to-Paris commuting, it was clear that Boris was not the solution. First, he had acquired a Lebanese manager who saw it as a challenge to charge as much as possible per hour of Spassky thinking time. Second, Boris himself had become lazy, and did not any longer enjoy – if he ever had – the intense strain of generating new and challenging ideas. Like many much less gifted grandmasters, he had become deeply dogmatic in middle age. I recall once watching Spassky going over a game of Nigel's from the Barcelona world cup. At one point he rejected one of Nigel's moves and substituted one of his own. With a resounding thump he placed a knight on a certain square. 'In such positions,' he pronounced, 'one must always place the knight here.' Nigel asked why. Spassky waved his arms in an expansive manner. 'That is how one plays such positions.' Probably Spassky was absolutely right. But Nigel knew that the 'how' without the 'why' was an intellectual dead-end, a recipe for imitation rather than inspiration.

There were other reasons for welcoming an end to the professional relationship between Spassky and Nigel. The Russian ex-world champion, in common with many lesser men of his age and race, was a thoroughgoing anti-Semite, and there were occasions when he seemed to be teaching Nigel how this could be applied to chess. Following this expert tuition Nigel would pronounce a certain opening, such as the Grünfeld Defence, to be a 'Jewish' opening. (It was, incidentally, the then favourite opening of Garri Kasparov. And Garri Kasparov was born Garri Weinstein, only taking his mother's surname upon the death of his father, a Jew.) Under the Spassky influence, Nigel even began to refer to a 'Jewish' style of playing chess. This, I gathered, was an indirect, modernist style of almost wilful complexity – as practised by the likes of Garri Kasparov and Jonathan Speelman, and not at all like the classically direct play of Boris Spassky and Nigel Short. Fortunately, with the dropping of Boris Spassky, Nigel also dropped his racial theories of chess.

The problem remained: who could be relied upon to give Nigel the best chance of succeeding in his quest to become the first non-Russian to challenge for the world chess championship since Bobby Fischer in 1972? The answer, when it came, was obvious: the man who had acted as Fischer's second in that earlier, successful assault on Russian chess hegemony. His name was Lubomir Kavalek, a fifty-year-old Czech-born grandmaster who had fled to the United States in the wake of the Soviet invasion of his country (but not before putting on a black armband in the 1968 Chess Olympiad, when he represented Czechoslovakia against the USSR). For Kavalek – whose father had worked for Radio Free Europe – usurping Russians from positions of power is a potent mixture of duty and pleasure. In the first few years after he left Czechoslovakia, his printed letter headings consisted of a drawing of a chessboard with White pieces facing Black enemy tanks.

Kavalek – Lubosh to his friends – was also a very, very strong chessplayer. After Fischer's retirement he became the dominant American grandmaster, winning the US championship on three occasions. According to Kavalek, in an article he wrote for the *Washington Post*, Nigel turned up on his doorstep in the small Virginia town of Reston and said, 'Lubosh, I want you to make me world champion like you made Bobby Fischer world champion.' Nigel denies he said exactly that, and indeed, for all Kavalek's skills, no one made Bobby Fischer champion apart from Bobby Fischer.

Fischer was completely dedicated to chess, and did not require lessons from anyone on the need for hard work. Nigel Short, however, while capable of fantastic concentration at the chessboard even as a nine-year-old, had never been what one might call a swot. There were some good reasons for this: his talent was so outrageous that he did not need to do any homework to beat most of his likely opponents. And as Rea pointed out to me, he is interested in many things other than chess. Nevertheless, I remember being surprised when we went on a holiday together in Spain in 1989, just before he was due to play in a big tournament there, that Nigel did not appear even to have packed a chess set.

By taking on Kavalek, an intense and methodical man, Nigel was making a decision to work as he had never done before. He knew, following his defeat in the previous world championship cycle, that in modern grandmaster chess genius without discipline is just a way of failing elegantly.

The first thing many people notice about Kavalek is that he

is short and almost bald. But I was most immediately struck by the size of his forearms. He is a keen tennis-player, but I liked to imagine that this unusual muscular development stemmed from his dragging from tournament to tournament his specially designed 120-megabyte computer, which contains upwards of one million games of chess. Here the games of the modern era are logged and coded, sorted and categorized according to player, date, opening variation and result. So if Nigel wanted to know whether, for example, Grandmaster Salov has played a Nimzo-Indian defence within the past six months, it would take Kavalek about ten seconds to come up with the answer. Then the game would be replayed on the computer screen.

And at what speed! It was impossible for me to keep up with the pirouettes of the pieces as they flickered across the screen at the rate of a move every half-second. Occasionally, his face oddly illuminated by the oscillating black-and-white light of the screen, Nigel would mutter, 'Let me see that in slow motion,' Kavalek would press a button and the pieces would cease their St Vitus' dance and move at a pace which I could follow.

The crucial point about such a database is the speed and comprehensiveness with which it is updated. Thirty years ago the rate of change in chess theory was leisurely. The same opening variations, accepted as 'best', would be played over and over again. But in grandmaster chess today, as in so many other fields, the growth of information and knowledge has become almost exponential. If Kavalek's King's Indian Defence database is two weeks out of date, then it is probably useless, or worse than useless, since it will not have the latest theoretical develop-ment, one which might have refuted an important subvariation that had been the height of fashion in the previous month's Baden-Baden grandmaster tournament.

While Nigel was at the board playing, Kavalek would often be on the telephone ringing up participants in tournaments in progress, to find out all the moves of that day's games. If there was a brilliant new idea, Nigel would know about it before he sat down to play his next match-game. Equally important, he could not be taken by surprise if his opponent were to use an idea which was new twelve hours before.

Nigel had good reason to be very sensitive on this point. He had been eliminated from the previous world championship cycle precisely by being caught out in this way. In a crucial game of his world championship quarter-final match with Jonathan Speelman, his opponent played a startling new move against Short's favourite variation of the Queen's Gambit Declined. It astounded the audience, and, worse, astounded Nigel, who quickly succumbed to the novel attack. After the game Speelman revealed that the move was not entirely new, nor even his own: his second, the American Grandmaster John Tisdall, had 'lifted it' from a game played three days before in the Russian championships.

Speelman had gone on to lose to Jan Timman in the semi-finals. Timman in turn lost to Karpov in the final eliminator. And, in December 1990 Karpov yet again failed to wrest back his title from Kasparov, who thereby guaranteed himself at least another three years of unchallenged supremacy.

Now, as the next world chess championship cycle began and those who aspired to win it made their dispositions, Nigel Short had decided that, if he were to fail again, it would not be for want of preparation.

CHAPTER THREE

In July 1990, sixty-four chess masters, exactly as many as there are squares on the chessboard, gathered in Manila. They were the qualifiers from a worldwide series of eliminating chess tournaments known as zonals. Manila, logically enough, was called the interzonal. It was also the chess equivalent of musical chairs. After thirteen rounds in which players were pitted against those who had the same running score, the eleven with the highest number of points when the music stopped – the 'candidates' – would go through to a series of knock-out matches. Their number would be augmented by the five most successful participants in the previous world championship cycle, to provide a pool of sixteen grandmaster piranhas.

Thereafter sixteen would become eight, would become four, would become two. Those two would, if they still had the stomach for the fight, play each other for the undoubted right, and the doubtful pleasure, of contesting a world championship match in 1993 against the most successful player in the history of chess: Garri Kasparov. This system of determining the best chessplayer in the world, devised by the Fédération Internationale des Echecs, can perhaps best be seen as a mixture of the spirit of the United Nations and that of the most ruthless Darwinism.

Nigel Short was to take part in the Manila interzonal barely three months after he had formed his partnership with Lubosh Kavalek. That first outing for the team came within a single game of being its last. Two losses by Nigel in the first three rounds put him at the back of a galloping field. Even a late series of victories, including a burst of three successive wins against grandmaster opponents, looked insufficient to qualify. In the last round Nigel was paired against Mikhail Gurevich of the Soviet Union, then ranked the fourth strongest player in the world. Gurevich had the advantage of the White pieces. He needed only a draw to qualify. Nigel needed to win.

The night before the game I spoke to Nigel on the telephone.

He seemed strangely tranquil, even as he informed me that, earlier in the day, the hotel he was staying in had been shaken both by an earthquake and by a terrorist's bomb which had devastated the car of the leading Filipino Grandmaster.

Gurevich, however, according to one of his co-nationals, arrived at the board 'with a deep sense of foreboding'. Perhaps he had been more distressed than the deeply phlegmatic Short by the events of the previous day. Perhaps he was simply unnerved by the sense of calm purpose emanating from the other side of the board. In any event, Gurevich made the classic error of playing for the draw from the start. He exchanged pieces frantically, in an attempt to drain all possible tension from the position. But as the men on the board grew fewer and fewer, Nigel's grip on the position, paradoxically, increased. By the end, with only two pieces each, Gurevich had simply run out of moves; Short had a hatful, and they all won. After four and a half hours' play, Gurevich extended his hand and offered his congratulations. 'He behaved like a gent,' Nigel said immediately afterwards, 'because it must have hurt like hell.' Just how much became obvious only later. Since that single game threw him out of the world championship cycle, Gurevich has not won a major tournament, and his world chess ranking over the succeeding three years dropped precipitately. 'It's strange', Nigel mused later as we discussed the fate of Mikhail Gurevich, 'how one game can destroy a man's career.' His words hung in the air slightly awkwardly. I suppose we were both thinking about what would have happened if Nigel had lost, instead of his now obscure opponent. We could both recall what had happened to Nigel following his defeat by Speelman in the previous world championship cycle. His world ranking dropped from third to eighteenth, where it was still languishing at the time of the Manila interzonal.

In these circumstances, the draw for the first round of the world championship candidates' matches could hardly have been more unfortunate, at least from Nigel's point of view. He had been paired off with Jon Speelman yet again. The fact that Nigel had the higher rating was absolutely irrelevant. He was still psychologically wounded from their previous match, and in the only game which they had played since then, in the chess world cup in Barcelona, Speelman had won without seeming to strain a single synapse.

Nigel had a particular problem playing Speelman. They were good friends. They regularly visited each other in Hampstead, where their homes are barely five minutes' walk apart. This was a fine basis for a match, as far as the thirty-four-year-old Speelman was concerned. He is a gentle, pacific vegetarian and the only grandmaster I have met who actually feels sorry for his opponents when he beats them. He therefore felt quite at ease playing someone he liked. A more hostile atmosphere would have been distressing for him. For Nigel, the reverse is the case. While not, like Kasparov, an initiator of emotional tension, he is never so motivated as when he senses hostility from the opponent. He was deeply confused by Speelman's apparent ambivalence, a man who didn't seem to burn with the desire to win, but, in his own mysterious way, managed it all the same.

The peculiarly domestic nature of the event was compounded by its being held in a single room of the office of a firm of solicitors in the City of London. For Nigel, who had become used to playing in large theatres in front of rows of foreign chess fans, it hardly felt like a match between two of the last sixteen in the world chess championship.

After five games of the best-of-eight event, Speelman was leading by two wins to one, and Short sank into a deep depression. He seemed almost resigned to losing the match, and with it all his cherished hopes of getting back at those who had, since the first loss to Speelman, claimed that Nigel Short was a man whose ambitions exceeded his abilities. On the rest day after the fifth game, Rea, who was by now heavily pregnant with their first child, stepped in. As she told me, 'I got very angry with him. He was so listless, almost fatalistic. So I said, "Stop feeling so sorry for yourself. Do you want to win the match or not? Do you want to take part in the world championship or not? Because if you don't, just resign the match here and now, and save us all a lot of trouble."'

The effect of this rather brutal pep-talk was evident the very next day. Nigel ground his Hampstead neighbour down remorselessly, allowing the normally resourceful Speelman not the faintest hint of counterplay from move one to move forty-three, when resignation came. Scores were level. By the end of the scheduled eight games they were still level. Under the rules of the competition two more games were to be played in the same afternoon, with a time-limit of one hour for all moves. In the first of the two play-off games, Nigel had the advantage of the White pieces, but blundered into a draw when on the verge of victory.

Nigel, Rea, Lubosh and I gathered silently in the rest room during the half-hour break before the next play-off game. There was a sense that a vital opportunity had been missed, that Speelman now had the psychological ascendancy. It was Kavalek who broke the silence with his deep and sonorous voice. 'You are all right, Nigel. Speelman is tired. That is why you managed to get a winning position so easily. Now you must put him away.' And he did.

As Nigel stood up at the end of the final game, while the match arbiter, with a fine sense of anticlimax, simply plonked the now discarded pieces back into their box, I tried to offer my congratulations. But then I saw that Nigel's eyes were full of tears, and he was shaking. I stood aside, and he rushed towards Rea, who consoled him, wordlessly. And the winner did need consoling. Like a child after escaping from a dark room into the light, Nigel was still terrified about what might have happened if he had never emerged. I looked around for Jon Speelman. But he had gone. We seemed, apart from the security guard, to be the last people in the building. And so we left. Outside, the City was suddenly covered in snow, and flakes were still falling. Nigel peered into the murky whiteness. 'I don't think I can remember where I parked the car,' he said, and then laughed.

It was February 1991 then, and Nigel had six months to prepare for his opponent in the quarter-finals, Grandmaster Boris Gelfand. Gelfand, at twenty-four, was two years younger than Nigel. But he was already ranked third in the world and had been publicly proclaimed that year by Kasparov to be his most likely challenger, after a game in which Gelfand had traded blow for blow with the champion and had not been worsted.

Gelfand, whom Nigel nicknamed 'Bob', came from what was now becoming known as Belarus. But, as far as Nigel was concerned, 'Bob' was still the archetypal Soviet player: 'These guys are so predictable, so diligent, so well prepared. But talented?' Nigel would give a dismissive wave of the hand.

Earlier that year Nigel had played a game against Gelfand in which having been 'caught' in a piece of classic Soviet opening preparation he was on the verge of resignation, a whole rook down. But he somehow bluffed 'Bob' into confusion and then actually checkmated him, in broad daylight. Kasparov, who was playing in the same tournament, walked past the board as the mate suddenly materialized from nowhere and, recalls Nigel, stared at the position 'goggle-eyed with astonishment'. After that, the champion spoke rather less of Gelfand's great prospects and began to worry rather more about Short's.

Factors other than chess, however, were making Nigel less confident about victory. Three weeks before the match was to start, his daughter, to be named Kyveli, was born. The Shorts' small two-bedroom flat in Hampstead was transformed from a place of study into an echo chamber for Kyveli's screams. Nigel complained to me that he would go to the supermarket to shop and then stay there, 'because it was so wonderfully quiet'. As he lingered over the supermarket shelves he would be calculating opening variations for use in the match, which he was unable to do at home. I'm not sure who then said what to whom, but, only a week after Kyveli was born, Rea left with her for Greece. Perhaps it was an assertion of priorities on both sides.

When the four quarter-final matches began, in Brussels in August, Nigel was still dazed by the sudden change in his life. In the first game of another eight-game event, he managed to establish a lost position as White within eighteen moves. This time Gelfand did not allow any swindles and forced resignation on move twenty-four. Nigel had played atrociously. Watching the game, Anatoly Karpov, who was playing his own quarter-final on the same stage, turned to Kavalek and, in his nasal, high-pitched voice, sneered, 'You have had six months to prepare, and this is the best you can come up with?' Kavalek nobly refrained from laying out the sardonic ex-world champion. Besides, he was even angrier with his own player. This time, though, Nigel required no pep-talks from wife or coach: 'They couldn't have been angrier with me than I was. I was yelling at myself, I was so livid.'

The self-criticism seemed to work. Nigel won the next two games, and by the final game required only to draw with the Black pieces to qualify for the semi-final round of the world championship. Anticipating triumph, Rea flew with the month-old Kyveli from Athens to Brussels.

The game did not go according to plan. Gelfand built up a massive attack which ought to have won the game and forced the match into another play-off. But in a desperate position Nigel again and again found the only move to stay alive. It should not have been enough to hold the game, but the strain began to tell on Gelfand. Like the boxer who has been on the attack for round after round, the Belorussian was beginning to be exhausted by his own punches. On the thirty-ninth move, just one before the end of the first session, Gelfand finally blundered, in a winning position he no longer had the intellectual stamina to exploit. Suddenly Nigel could force a draw with a perpetual checking motion. And the draw would mean he had won the match.

It was here that Nigel signalled not just to Boris Gelfand, but to all his future opponents, what sort of player he had become – 'a grimly determined bastard with nerves of steel', according to Jon Speelman's rueful second, Grandmaster John Tisdall. Spurning the draw which guaranteed victory, Nigel coldly and deliberately played a different continuation. Eventually he drove Gelfand's king into the open and mated it, as chessplayers like to say, 'up a tree'.

Afterwards Nigel explained to me his reasons for killing his opponent, rather than accepting his surrender: 'I've got nothing against Bob Gelfand personally. But you should never, ever miss a chance to stick it to these guys.' Should Nigel have had any doubts about his approach, it would have been dispelled by Kavalek's words to him at the closing ceremony. 'From now on,' said Lubosh, 'it will get dirty.'

*

Whatever the methods, Nigel had to 'stick it' to only two more of 'these guys' to become the first Briton ever to contest a world championship chess match. His potential opponents were Jan Timman, the Dutch champion, and one of two Russians: either Artur Yusupov or Anatoly Karpov, the former world champion, and the most successful tournament player in the long history of chess. Short was paired against Karpov in the semi-final, and no one gave him more than the ghost of a chance.

Karpov had been world champion for ten years until 1985, when he lost his title to Kasparov. But in several matches with Kasparov over the following six years, Karpov had never lost by more than a very narrow margin. At forty, he was still a chess strangler with the grip of a python, his famed hardness and competitiveness only enhanced by the loss of the title, which he in any case considered merely to be on loan to Kasparov. As far as the chess world was concerned Nigel was merely something small and furry for Karpov to asphyxiate before the main meal of the day walked along.

Nigel, however, was quite happy to play Karpov. When I called him to commiserate at his bad luck in the draw, he replied that, if he wanted to play a match for the world title, he would almost certainly have to play a match with Karpov at some stage. It was only a question of when. And, he pointed out, he had never found the ex-world champion a particularly difficult opponent. Over many games since they had first met in 1980, the older man had only slightly the better score, with most of their encounters hard-fought draws. Also, he had become increasingly aware of certain weaknesses in Karpov's opening repertoire which could be exploited in a match. He did not elaborate.

Above all Nigel had developed a marked antipathy to Anatoly Karpov, which seemed to imbue him with a positive relish for the battle. In particular the Englishman had become enraged by Karpov's habit, after they had finished a game, of insisting on a post-mortem in which the Russian would cast aspersions on all of Nigel's favourite moves and, whirling his pieces around the board, explain how, by this . . . and this . . .

and this . . . which he had of course *seen* at the board at the time he should *obviously* have beaten Short, who was *incredibly* lucky to have escaped with a draw. The fact that Karpov – as I pointed out to Nigel – did this to all his opponents scarcely diminished Nigel's dislike of the Russian. If anything it strengthened his antipathy. 'So, Dominic, what you are saying is that he does not just lie to me, but he lies all the time. Well, I'll tell you one thing: I won't be having any post-mortems with Karpov after the games in our match. Win or lose, I'm just going to get up from the table and walk away. If he wants, he can tell himself that he was winning every game, but I'm not going to be around to listen.'

Normally it would not be clear why anyone should want to stay in Linares, a bleak southern Spanish mining town of self-assured ugliness and some slight prosperity. But the most successful entrepreneur in this Andalusian eyesore, Sr Luis Rentero, is a chess fanatic, who put up the 300,000 Swiss francs laid down by Fidé as the appropriate prize fund for the two semi-finals of the world chess championship candidates' matches. The matches were to be held in April 1992 in Sr Rentero's very own hotel, the Anibal. And there, with a nice sense of drama, Sr Rentero installed Anatoly Karpov and Nigel Short in two adjoining rooms separated by the sort of wall through which light breathing, let alone the heavy variety, could easily be heard.

So when I first walked into Nigel's room, after arriving at the Anibal, he put his finger to his lips. 'Just talk in whispers,' he whispered. 'Otherwise Karpov might hear everything we say.' 'But he's probably bugged the room anyway,' I joked – or thought I did. 'No,' Nigel replied, 'I've swept the room, and there are no bugs, at least not of the electronic variety.' Catching my look of bemusement, Nigel exclaimed, 'Get serious, Dominic! This is the world chess championship!'

I wondered whether, in the adjoining room, Karpov was whispering prepared opening variations to his seconds, Grandmasters Epishin and Podgaets, just as Nigel and Lubosh were on our side of this improvised Anglo-Russian border. Try as I might, I could hear no Slavic susurrations. Perhaps they were using Cyrillic sign language.

If there was any spooking going on, it would have been the function of one Rudolf Zagainov, who was officially described as Karpov's parapsychologist. Karpov seemed very proud of this arrangement, most particularly because Zagainov's previous employer was Garri Kasparov. During the six-hour sessions on game days, Zagainov would sit in the front row of the auditorium gazing at Nigel, and occasionally writing down notes on a pad. Once I peered over his shoulder. Quite pointless really, since I don't understand Russian. But I was curious to see what 'Short takes sip of coffee. This is most significant' would look like in that language. Instead I saw such English phrases as 'I love you' and 'Would you like a drink?' It later transpired that Zagainov had been smitten by Nigel's twenty-two-year-old cousin Jayne, who was in Linares to help Rea look after Kyveli. Evidently Zagainov was hoping to engage the lissom Jayne in a romantic conversation, but he never plucked up the courage. Perhaps he was even more afraid of what Karpov might do to him if he found out that his parapsychologist was fraternizing with the enemy nanny.

It's quite possible that, even had such a bizarre encounter actually taken place, Nigel would have known nothing about it. His concentration on the chess was total, and routine, as dictated by Kavalek, was the key. Up at the same time every morning, followed by the same walk around the town, followed by the same lunch at the same restaurant. Then would come the game, and it was only at the board that Nigel would exercise any discretion. That, of course, was Kavalek's idea: to ensure that all of Nigel's intellectual energies would be concentrated on the grim business of pushing pieces. He would even instruct Nigel when to go to the loo, usually about half an hour before the game. 'Now you must have piss,' Kavalek would intone, and Nigel would do as he was told.

Occasionally, the routine would appear on the verge of interruption, when Rea, Jayne and Kyveli would turn up for lunch at the same restaurant where Nigel had his unvarying fodder. But Nigel, Lubosh and I would continue to sit at our reserved table in monkish isolation, and in a silence that bordered on the Trappist.

Over the board things were not exactly a barrel of laughs either. In the very first game Anatoly Karpov demonstrated just how formidable an opponent he could be. Nigel played a very rare opening gambit, never seen before in chess at this level, which he and Kavalek had devoted two full weeks to preparing. When the gambit, known to cognoscenti as the Budapest, was played, Karpov merely arched his eyebrows – a favourite mannerism of his – and, after a brief pause, proceeded to rattle off a series of moves which reduced Nigel's preparation to rubble.

Still wobbling, Nigel had the worst of a draw in the second game. But in the third some of the homework of the previous few months finally came off. Another brand-new opening variation from the Kavalek–Short laboratory caught the former world champion somewhere soft and undefended. By the adjournment, after six hours and sixty moves, Nigel had an overwhelming position, and was ready to level the scores.

'If I can't win this position against Karpov,' Nigel excitedly remarked to me that night, 'then I can't win any position. It's as good as that.' Just to make sure, he and Lubosh spent much of the night analysing every possible continuation by Karpov, and satisfied themselves that they all lost. The next day the match referee opened the envelope containing Karpov's sealed move. It was one Short's team had completely missed.

Nigel is normally adept at concealing his emotions at the chessboard. Not on this occasion. His face instantly changed colour to a greenish white. Rea, sitting in the audience, muttered under her breath, 'My God, Nigel must be losing.' Karpov's move, in fact, was entirely random, and did not make the position any the less winning for Nigel. But it was an astute psychological coup by the Russian. Confused by the very purposelessness of Karpov's move, Nigel panicked and completely mishandled the new position. Four hours, and thirty moves later Karpov instantly accepted Nigel's offer of a draw, and almost pranced out of the hall, followed by two beaming grandmaster assistants and one much happier parapsychologist.

For the next two hours, as they walked up and down the tiny park outside the playing hall, Rea fought to keep Nigel in the match. He bitterly recalled his earlier pronouncement that, if he couldn't win the adjourned position, then he couldn't win any game against Karpov. Then he reached into his pocket, pulled out a good-luck charm that a friend had given him for the match, and hurled it into the bushes.

'Why did Karpov play a rubbish move against you, that he knew didn't draw?' Rea demanded. 'Because he wanted to confuse you. He succeeded. Now what does he want? He wants you to doubt everything. He wants you to feel you can't win any position against him, even when he plays rubbish. Now, do you want to limit your loss to half a point, which you have already conceded, or a whole match, which has barely started?' By the time darkness fell, Nigel was over the worst and began to talk about what he would do to Karpov in the next day's game: 'I'm going to give it to him good and hard, right up him.' Later that night when Nigel was asleep, dreaming perhaps of some act of controlled and obscene violence against Karpov, Rea went back out into the park with a torch and searched for the discarded good-luck charm. She never found it.

And the next game Nigel really did 'stick it right up' Karpov. Or, to be more precise, Karpov stuck it up himself. In a position of complete equilibrium, with both players having only a minute left on their clocks for a handful of moves, Karpov brusquely declined an offer of a draw, played on and went down with all pawns.

Afterwards, in his room, Nigel forgot all about the thinness of the wall between him and Karpov. Or perhaps he wanted the Russian to hear his triumphant whoops: 'He gambled! He just threw the dice! He wanted to win the match there and then! He couldn't wait! He threw the dice, and he lost!' In a way, one had to admire Karpov's courage: he really was just throwing the dice, gambling that Nigel would be so demoralized by the disaster of the previous game that he would crack in the last frenetic minute before the time-control. But, for once, Karpov's characteristic – and feared – willingness to put the psychology of conflict before purely chessboard considerations failed. In twenty-five years of tournament play it had broken the spirit of some pretty tough customers. But on this occasion he had underestimated his opponent, or, just possibly, his opponent's wife.

The psychological initiative, which, as Karpov had always surmised, meant more than the balance of the chess pieces, had in fact changed hands. The incubus of doubt, the emotion most feared by chessplayers, settled on the shoulders of the ex-world champion. In a way, it was horrible to see his torment. Karpov began muttering moves to himself obsessively during the games, as if he was checking and double-checking variations. This is a sign of real trouble. The average chessplayer is allowed to go over the same moves in his head again and again. The grandmaster should check each variation only once: if he needs to check more often, then he is not playing like a grandmaster.

Karpov's sudden indecision meant that he ran fearfully short of time in every game that remained of the match. Then his mental agonies were made physically manifest. He would twitch uncontrollably in his seat, sometimes plunging his thumb in his mouth, as he must have done as a child in distress. Karpov had once defined the essence of a chess champion as 'someone with very strong nerves'. His had gone.

Nigel did not need a psychotherapist wife to see what was happening, and his mood became buoyant. Putting on the discarded Lancashire accent of his youth, he would chortle before the game, 'Ayoop! Looks like trouble at t'mill for yoong Anatowly.' Or ''Appen ah've got 'im on sticky wicket!' Kavalek was at first bemused by these expressions, and even more by the hilarity which they seemed to cause. But by the end of the match the Czech was fully conversant with Lancashire sayings, if not the accent. 'Dere's trouble at der mill' or 'Dat is a sticky vicket' he would say as Karpov slid into further difficulties.

The lightheartedness spilt over into the chess, which can only have confused Karpov further. In the fifth game Nigel played an invented new opening line of almost absurd cheekiness. He dubbed it the 'Beck's Beer variation' because he had discovered it while under the influence of a few cans of the stuff. Karpov thought for almost three-quarters of an hour over one move in an attempt to find the refutation of his opponent's intoxicated imagination. It existed, but Karpov failed to find it. Now it was Nigel who was rolling the dice, and winning.

By the last game of the scheduled ten, Nigel had won two more games to Karpov's one, and required only a draw with the White pieces. This time the psychological onslaught began before the game. Ten minutes before the players were due to leave their rooms for the tournament hall Nigel grabbed his faithful and well-travelled guitar from its corner of the room and began to strum violently a punk rock song whose only lyrics were, *fortissimo*, 'I don't care!' Probably this was designed merely to work off some of Nigel's tension, but I can't imagine it did much for the peace of mind of the man next door.

Karpov emerged wearing what had become known in the chess world as his 'executioner's suit'. A shiny navy-blue cotton and silk mix, it was certainly a cut above the usual Karpov couture, which owes more to Moscow than Milan. Karpov used to bring this Italian suit out of his wardrobe when he had to win, notably for the final game of his 1985 match against Kasparov. He lost that game, but did not blame the suit.

Against Nigel Short's tracksuit bottoms and T-shirt, Karpov's undoubted sartorial supremacy was no substitute for good moves. Five hours after the final game began, Karpov was staring at a lost position. Five hours and twenty-five minutes later, he was still staring at exactly the same lost position. Why didn't he move, or resign? Could he just not face the now unavoidable truth, that he had lost a match to a player he was supposed to crush, and to an Englishman at that? What else could he be thinking about?

Finally, after Nigel had sat waiting for half an hour, Karpov extended his hand. 'Congratulations,' he said, in a clear, loud voice. Then he added, 'But what would you have done if I had, in this position,' and the Russian hastily rearranged the pieces, 'played my queen here?' And he thumped his queen down on a square which, indeed, would have threatened mayhem. So that was what Karpov had been thinking about for the past half-hour. 'My God!' said Nigel, 'I don't know what I would have done.' Karpov gave a thin smile. He had had his little victory after all. Nigel, in the first afterglow of triumph, had forgotten his pre-match vow never to allow Karpov to indulge in his favourite game of post-mortem humiliation. Or perhaps, in the words of the song, Nigel didn't care.

What perhaps bothered Nigel more was the fact that, on a day when an Englishman had gone further than any other in the world chess championship, and had beaten a former champion to boot, there was only one representative of the English press present, and not a single English chess fan. At the moment of Britain's greatest chess triumph, the only applause came from the many foreign journalists present in the auditorium. As the winner left the hall, Russians, Spaniards, Dutchmen gathered around him with their microphones poised to capture some words of triumph. But Nigel was laconic, merely remarking that Karpov was 'still a great player. He shouldn't be written off.'

We slammed Nigel's hotel door on the pursuing pack, and he subsided into the room's solitary sofa. Suddenly he leapt up, and began a series of splay-legged jumps beloved by rock guitarists: 'Yeah! I've beaten Karpov! I've beaten Karpov! Yeah!' Then Nigel leapt on to the bed where Kyveli was lying, sending her trampolining into the air. She giggled. He jumped again on to the bed and again his daughter bounced and giggled.

I thought that it was not possible for a man to be happier than Nigel was at that instant. The next morning my wife called to tell me that she was pregnant with our first child, and I was no longer envious.

For beating Karpov, Nigel won five-eighths of a prize fund of 150,000 Swiss francs. For the final round of the candidates' matches, against Jan Timman of Holland, the prize fund would be 300,000 Swiss francs, as laid down by the rather arbitrary rules of Fidé. This was nothing to be sneered at, but nor was it a great incentive. By playing chess tournaments outside the Fidé world championship system, players like Short and Timman could comfortably earn £80,000 a year. As the top two Western players they were much in demand, and could command large fees just for showing up at tournaments. But suddenly both grandmasters were on the verge of earning from the world championship cycle alone the sort of money which would secure their families' future; the sort of money which meant that, if they never played chess again, they could still comfortably live off their investment income.

The German chess computer company Mephisto had guaranteed a prize of one million Swiss francs to the first non-Soviet player since Bobby Fischer to qualify for a match for the world championship. When the offer had first been made several years earlier, Mephisto had gained much publicity, with the added pleasure that it seemed most unlikely that any Western player would so qualify. Kasparov and Karpov seemed set to battle out the world championship for the rest of the century, and behind them was an avalanche of frighteningly gifted young ex-Soviets: Boris Gelfand from Belorussia, Alexei Shirov from Latvia, Vassily Ivanchuk from the Ukraine, and, most tipped of all, especially by Kasparov, Vladimir Kramnik of mother Russia.

When it became clear that there would be a Western challenger, Mephisto attempted to back out of the award of one million Swiss francs by claiming that with the fall of communism the terms 'Western' and indeed 'Soviet' no longer had any meaning, and so neither did the award. Short and Timman promptly threatened to sue, and Mephisto restored the offer. But there was far more at stake than one million Swiss francs for the winner.

For the world championship itself there was likely to be a prize fund of around $4 million. That had been on offer from a Los Angeles consortium led by a businessman called Jim McKay. Although that seemed to have collapsed following the LA riots, there were reports that the Olympic city of Barcelona was on the verge of offering 400 million pesetas – about £2.5 million – for the match between Kasparov and his ultimate challenger. Add to that the endorsement income a Western challenger could expect, and it was clear that the stakes in Nigel Short's match against Jan Timman could be counted in the millions of pounds.

As anyone who has played or watched poker knows, the tension of the game is in direct proportion to the amount of money at stake. The same is true of chess: the players might seem more monk-like, less worldly than the average poker professional: but they care about money just the same. This is certainly true of Nigel, who once told me that 'Poverty is the biggest fear of my life.' Like most self-made men, he is haunted by the prospect that he might slip down the ladder he has laboriously climbed. And he still had enormous difficulties in getting even small amounts of credit from a bank: what sort of security of income could a self-employed chessplayer offer? There is nothing wrong, let alone abject, in starting life in a small terraced house in the former mining area of Leigh, Lancashire, but it is a long way from the world of Swiss bank accounts and superstardom.

Even leaving the money aside, which it is hard to do, chess at the final stages of the world championship is far more concerned with psychology and strength of character than it is with the mere moves on the board. At stake is more than a game, more even than financial security for life: it is the prospect of becoming immortal, to have one's name listed alongside those other world champions such as Capablanca, Alekhine, Fischer and, yes, Kasparov. To win the world championship is to gain something that can never be taken away from you: the knowledge that you proved yourself the best in the world and that future generations of chessplayers, not just in Leigh, but in Moscow, New York and Peking, will associate your name with chess triumph for as long as the game is played and studied.

These thoughts of fame and money plagued both Nigel Short and Jan Timman when they met to play their final eliminator match in the Spanish royal city of San Lorenzo del Escorial, fifty miles from Madrid. When they shook hands before the first game each noticed that the other's hand was clammy and shaking.

Each player, in his own way, attempted to find some method to avoid falling victim to terminal nervous tension. With Jan it was the bottle. Most nights, even before a game, he would have dinner at some fine restaurant in the town, and choose extensively from the wine list. Nigel, by contrast, remained immured in his hotel, making great demands only upon the place's supply of mineral water. One North American commentator, who boisterously joined Timman on one or two of his bouts, opined that the Dutchman was a well-rounded character, a credit to the chess world, whereas Short was 'a tight-arsed Englishman' who was 'interested in nothing beyond the sixty-four squares of the chessboard'. In fact, of course, both players were simply counter-ing the strain of the event in their own different ways.

Even before the match Nigel had attempted to attain a state of supreme calmness by spending a fortnight in meditation at the monastery on Mount Athos. And, once ensconced in San Lorenzo, he would insist on going with me and Lubosh every day to the Church of the Escorial, Philip II's characteristically austere monument to his austere God. There, at twelve o'clock, exactly three hours before the start of the game, Nigel would pray for victory. I was surprised by this, since I had always counted Nigel an atheist. 'So I am,' he said after one of our trips to the church, 'but I am also an opportunist.' I asked him what his prayers consisted of. 'Please God, let me beat this shit-head,' he said. Naturally, we cannot know what God thought of this request from the Church of the Escorial, but it probably made a change from the usual prayers for a win in the Spanish state lottery.

Nigel's trips to the church were not in the least religious: they had become just a part of an atmosphere of increasing superstition. Despite the apparent, or even actual, rationality of their pursuit, chessplayers at the highest level are often intensely superstitious. I think the reason is linked to the nature of the life of a chess professional. It is all about the attempt to control something which is beyond human control: the 'abysmal depths', as Nabokov put it, of chess itself. The chessplayer knows intuitively, but cannot bear to admit openly, that chance or, more correctly, good fortune plays as much a part in the struggle as skill and planning. So, to feel supremely confident before a game, it is necessary for him to feel not just that he has the best moves, but that, at the stage in a game where chaos takes over, the luck of not making the final mistake will be with him.

So, in San Lorenzo, Nigel, in all other respects the most rational and analytical man I have ever known, became convinced that Jan Timman's wife was attempting to practise what he called 'voodoo' against him. Ilse Timman is a handsome and formidable black Surinamese, and I suppose Central Casting could conceivably have allotted her the part of a voodoo priestess. But in real life, like Rea Short, she is a successful practising psychotherapist, and, so far as is known, the techniques she applies in her clinic in Amsterdam do not include the use of waxen images or the pouring of chicken's blood over her clients.

Mrs Timman would, however, enter the Carlos III Theatre where the match was being played and, in the early games, take up a position in a box which enabled her to stare directly into Nigel's eyes. And when, as the rules demanded, the players switched chairs with each game, she would switch her position accordingly, giving Nigel what he thought was the 'evil eye' from the other end of the auditorium.

Having started the match badly, losing ineptly with the White pieces in the second game, Nigel was prepared to believe that something fishy was going on. The solution he suggested was that Rea should get into the theatre before Mrs Timman, and herself take the box which most directly came within Nigel's field of vision. After a few undignified scrambles, the two wives came to an unspoken agreement that each would take a certain box for the duration, and not move from there. Thus their husbands could alternate the discomfort of seeing their opponent's wife glaring with the pleasure of seeing their own wife beaming sympathetically. This seemed to reassure Nigel greatly, although he still insisted that Ilse Timman had been attempting voodoo on him. And the visits to the Church of the Escorial would have been viewed, at least in Philip II's day, as appropriate behaviour for a chessplayer in Nigel's predicament: in *The Game of Chess*, produced by the Sicilian priest Pietro Carrera in 1617, the prospective match player is advised 'to confess his sins and receive spiritual absolution just before sitting down to play in order to counteract the demoniacal influence of magic spells'.

As so often in chess matches, a single game can, in retrospect, be seen as the decisive moment, the turning point. In San Lorenzo del Escorial it was the ninth game in a match to be played over fourteen. The scores were level, but Nigel seemed to be in crisis. In the fifth game, when a point ahead, he had offered a draw in a position which almost everyone, including his opponent, assessed as winning for Short. Nigel later explained to me that he had been too tense to sleep the previous night, and after six hours' play felt so exhausted that he could no longer calculate a single variation: 'I felt, across the board, that Jan was getting stronger with every move, while I felt my strength ebbing away. If I had played on, I could even have lost.' But this let-off was an enormous encouragement to Timman, who felt that his opponent had lost his famed 'bottle'.

In game six Nigel narrowly avoided defeat, and in the seventh he was caught out by a rare move in a familiar opening. What made it worse was that the move ought to have been in Kavalek's databank, but somehow the relevant game had either been 'wiped' or not entered at all. Surprised and disoriented, Nigel was swept from the board, losing his queen within twenty-five moves.

In the eighth game, Nigel wanted to seek quick revenge with the White pieces but Kavalek sternly told him to 'take a breather' and so he headed tamely for a position devoid of tension. Timman misinterpreted that as another sign of weakness, rather than as a deliberate gathering of strength. So in the ninth game, the forty-one-year-old Dutchman decided to put the boy away. He unveiled a prepared variation of fantastic originality and complexity, studded with sacrifices and traps.

Kavalek, no slouch in these matters himself, told me afterwards that the prepared variation was 'a work of genius'. Unfortunately for Timman it had a hole in it. And after only seven minutes' thought at the board Nigel found the refutation. It was not all calculation, of course. The position was far too complex for that. When I asked Nigel why he had not played the obvious move that Timman expected, that everyone in the hall expected, but which probably would have lost, he said, 'I never considered it. It didn't smell right.' It is the sort of answer which explains why the top human chessplayer is still more than a match for the computer, why instant human judgement in chess is still to be treasured more than the tireless calculations of the artificial brain.

Timman was punctured after that, although the air came out of the Dutchman sufficiently slowly so that he did not finally deflate until the thirteenth game. Afterwards it became clear how much the ninth game had affected him and continued to play on his mind. In his own chess magazine, *New in Chess*, he immediately published reams of analysis to prove that his new opening line was good, and that, after Short's much praised reply, the Englishman should in fact have lost the critical ninth game. When I discussed this article with Nigel later, he said that Timman's published analysis was 'disgracefully bad: it assumes that I have to play only bad moves'. But Nigel did not publicly engage in dispute with Timman. After all, he had proved to be the stronger where it counted: over the chessboard. Like Karpov before him, Timman could be allowed the only consolation for the loser's ego: scoring futile points in a private post-mortem.

The match finally ended with the thirteenth game, on a Friday, and it turned out to be unlucky for Timman. Nigel needed only a draw, which he obtained by playing a most peculiar new idea in the hoary old Queen's Gambit Declined. It didn't look very sound, but had obviously been specially prepared for the game. I caught up with Kavalek as he prowled around outside the theatre. 'What is Nigel playing?' I asked. Lubosh grinned. 'Crap,' he said. 'But very good crap.' It was good enough for Timman, at any rate. By move thirty-nine he had no choice but to concede the draw and the match.

This time, as we fled back to Nigel's suite at the Victoria Palace Hotel, there were actually British journalists among the pursuing press pack. A BBC team entered the room for a brief interview, and Nigel told them, with a straight face, that he 'felt nothing'. Almost as soon as the camera crew left, he began leaping about the room. Last time, when he had beaten Karpov, he had leapt on to the bed, sending Kyveli giggling through the air. This time, anaesthetized by triumph, he crashed a few times on to the floor, while Kyveli just stared in the way that children do when they think an adult is making a fool of himself. Then Kyveli's dad grabbed his guitar and launched into one of Jimi Hendrix's more drug-crazed numbers: 'Purple haze, through my brain . . .'

The next morning, not so many hours after the festivities in Nigel's suite had ended, I was heading back towards the same room. Kyveli wanted to say hello to her father, and she couldn't wait. Rea gave me the keys to the suite – during matches she never shares a room with her husband – and I opened the door with Kyveli by my side. Nigel was lying on the bed and his body stirred slightly. I remember thinking that I had never before noticed what a very large head sat on top of that gangling body. It seemed completely out of proportion, almost a caricature of an egghead.

Suddenly the egghead awoke. 'I thought I'd better remind you,' I said, 'in case you thought it was just a dream: you are the official challenger for the world chess championship. In eight months' time, it's you against Kasparov.'

'Eight months? Is that all? There's so much work to be done. I'd better start now.' And the challenger reached out for his round, wire-framed spectacles, as a boxer would for his gloves. Except, of course, in world championship chess, the gloves tend to come off. And Garri Kasparov has never heard the one about not hitting guys wearing glasses.

CHAPTER FOUR

Professional boxers have long known that the public demands more than just a fight between two great exponents of the pugilistic art. The public also wants to believe that the two men hate each other. And the boxers, artfully aided by their promoters, have always been willing to oblige: 'I'll moider da bum' is one of the oldest phrases in the commercial fight game.

So, when, on the day after Nigel Short's victory against Jan Timman, I published an article in the *Sunday Telegraph* containing a coruscating attack by Nigel on the character of Garri Kasparov, a number of commentators remarked that the challenger was merely attempting to increase the public's interest in his forthcoming match with the champion. It is a new sort of cynicism this, which refuses to believe that one man can honestly dislike another.

For my part, I had heard Nigel too often in private castigating the behaviour and morals of Kasparov to doubt that what he was now telling me for public consumption was not characteristically sincere. Nigel started with an attack on Kasparov's manners at the board, and went on to denounce his entire character: 'The world champion, whoever he is, should behave with decorum. But Kasparov does all this staring. He paces up and down the tournament hall, like a baboon, deliberately in my field of vision. . . . Kasparov can't deal with human beings at all. He has no normal relationships. It's master–slave; that's all he can understand. He behaves badly on purpose. He doesn't even mind being seen as a complete arsehole. But I don't want to sink to the level of the animal to beat the animal.'

Three weeks later, on 17 February 1993, Kasparov arrived in London for a simultaneous chess display which had been arranged before it was known that Short would be the official challenger. A press conference was hastily arranged, in part to enable Kasparov to answer Short's charges. While Nigel was probably right that Kasparov did not mind if his fellow grand-masters thought him 'an arsehole' – that he could put down to professional jealousy – he would obviously rather not have had this revealed to the wider public, who hitherto had seen him simply as the enlightened new Russian 'good guy' who had fought and beaten the 'bad' old Brezhnevite Karpov.

'My response to Short's remarks will be in my moves at the board,' Kasparov retorted, 'but I can say now that my match with Short will not be much of a contest. There will be no fight about the title. Nigel has less chance of becoming world champion than Luke McShane.' (The English boy Luke McShane was at the time the world under-ten chess champion: aside from the calculated insult to Nigel, Kasparov was subtly insinuating that it would be the best part of twenty years before anyone could challenge his supremacy.)

While Nigel had not been attacking Kasparov merely in order to solicit high bids for their match, he was still outraged by the effect Kasparov's remarks might have on potential bidders when I reported them back to him. 'I know he thinks I'll be a walk-over and I'm happy for him to go on thinking that. But he's an idiot to announce to possible sponsors that the match will be a non-event. I never thought his arrogance would get the better of his greed, but I should have known better.'

Nigel's concern at the dwindling financial attractions of the match were well founded. He had not been so worried at the earlier collapse of the $4 million bid from Los Angeles, backed by several ex-White House lawyers led by Jim McKay. That bid had been solicited by Kasparov himself, who, according to Nigel, had 'arranged several side-deals' with the Los Angelenos. As far as Nigel was concerned LA was Kasparov territory, and the financial earthquake which hit it after the riots was Kasparov's problem, not his.

The Fédération Internationale des Echecs gratefully pocketed the $400,000 deposit that McKay's group had been obliged to lodge with its bid and offered the Kasparov–Short match up to new bidders, with a deadline of 8 February, barely a week after the conclusion of the Short–Timman match. When the bidders' sealed envelopes were opened in the Lucerne office of Florencio

Campomanes, the Fidé president, there was no sign of the much vaunted 400 million peseta offer from Barcelona. The only Spanish offer was 1 million Swiss francs (nearly £900,000), the minimum reserve stipulated by Fidé, from Santiago de Compostela. There was one other offer: $5 million from the Yugoskandic Corporation, run by a thuggish Serbian financier called Jezdemir Vasilievic. Mr Vasilievic's company, essentially an unregulated bank which acted as a clearing house for illicit Serbian foreign currency accounts, had already spent $5 million of its depositors' money on subsidizing the UN-sanctions-busting Fischer–Spassky rematch in Belgrade.

Nigel had high hopes of Mr Vasilievic. He didn't know where Yugoskandic's money was coming from, and he didn't particularly care. All he knew was that his friend Boris Spassky had left Belgrade with millions of genuine greenbacks, paid out on the nail by an apparently grateful Serb. In the case of an official world title match between Kasparov and Short, Mr Vasilievic generously conceded that Belgrade would be a politically unacceptable venue, and proposed Bucharest instead.

Two days later I invited Nigel out to dinner. He was already mentally packing his bags for Romania. 'No, I'll pay for dinner this time. It's not every day that I'm offered a share of $5 million.'

It was not inconceivable that Fidé would take the Serbian's offer. Despite posturing as a kind of mini-United Nations and glorying in the motto of 'Gens una sumus', Fidé had in the previous year taken Vasilievic's money in order to fund the European team chess championships. That caused trouble when it transpired that one of Vasilievic's conditions was that a Serbian team be allowed to take part, although he backed down when all the other national sides threatened to boycott the event. Only the chess press noted the incident.

The individual world chess championship, however, was far too prominent and public for Fidé to be able to take Serbian money without great embarrassment. Fidé promptly and primly declared that the Serbian bid, 'due to the existing United Nations embargo, could not comply with Fidé regulations'.

(As it turned out, Nigel could have no quarrel with Fidé, on

this matter at least. In April, Jezdemir Vasilievic fled to Israel
with several large briefcases, narrowly avoiding a lynching from
thousands of his dispossessed Belgrade depositors. One of those
dispossessed, it turned out, was Bobby Fischer, who had stayed
on in Belgrade after his match with Spassky and had not taken
the Russian's precaution of removing his prize money *in toto*
from his numbered Yugoskandic bank account.)

So, once again, Fidé reopened the bidding for the world
chess championship, this time specifying a deadline for sub-
missions of Monday, 22 February. By this stage it had finally
dawned on corporate Britain that an Englishman was involved,
and that Nigel Short might be a property worth investing in.
The city of Manchester, already involved in a bid for the 2000
Olympics and well aware of Short's Lancastrian origins, prepared
to bid. One of its advisers was a solicitor called David Anderton,
who had been appointed to high office within Fidé by President
Campomanes, and who for many years had been the most
powerful man in the British Chess Federation. Channel Four
also entered the lists, as did the London Chess Group, a
syndicate of companies assembled by a sports-sponsorship pro-
moter called Matthew Patten.

Under Fidé's own rules, it was obliged to consult the
players before deciding which bid to accept. Nigel, however,
was on a long-planned holiday with Rea, driving down through
France and Italy, and booked on to a thirty-four-hour ferry
journey from Ancona to the Greek port of Patras at the time
that the bids were to be delivered and opened. He had, though,
held detailed conversations with Manchester's sponsorship advisers, a company called Stanniforth. According to Nigel they
had given him 'many assurances that if Manchester were going
to bid they would bid high. All along they spoke to me of
£3 million.'

On 19 February, fully three days before the close of bidding,
the city of Manchester announced that it had made a bid for the
Fidé world chess championship. Most unusually, it publicly
revealed the size of its bid, a disappointing 2.185 million Swiss
francs, the currency in which Fidé, prudently, requested that all

bids were made. I was puzzled about this at the time. How could Manchester be so confident of victory that it should announce its – not especially knock-out – offer price (£977,000) before the end of an open bidding period?

On 22 February Fidé revealed that it had received two other bids. One from the London Chess Group, the syndicate put together by Matthew Patten, was for 2.3 million Swiss francs (£1,050,000). A third, worth 2.6 million Swiss francs (£1,188,000), came in from Channel Four, but the company attached the condition that this would include all television rights. Fidé had always insisted that it should be free to sell world championship television rights separately and divide the revenues as it saw fit between the players and itself.

Fidé also announced Manchester's bid. It had been deftly raised from 2.185 million Swiss francs (£977,000) to 2.538 million (£1,160,000), fortuitously just above the only other unconditional offer, from the London Chess Group. Had Manchester simply responded to the prospect of another bigger bid? Or could Fidé have alerted Manchester, the bidder supported by one of its own officials, to the size of the offer from the London Chess Group? Timed faxes of the bids, subsequently supplied to me by Nigel Short, show that the hastily revised second Manchester bid came several hours after the bid from the London Chess Group had arrived at Fidé headquarters.

Three days before the bids were submitted I had spoken to Nigel, who was then in Cannes for a meeting of the board of the Grandmasters' Association, the players' union, of which he was president. He told me that he was heading for the Italian port of Ancona, to catch a ferry to Greece on Monday the 22nd, and that he would be incommunicado for about two days. I told him to ring me when he finally got to his home in Athens, if he wanted to be filled in on developments. He replied that he would do so, but he would expect first to hear from Fidé, who were obliged, under their own rules, to consult both him and Kasparov before awarding the match to any bidder.

On Tuesday, 23 February, less than twenty-four hours after receiving the three bids, the Fidé secretariat in Lucerne announced that 'after the Fidé president consulted the World Champion and Challenger ... and taking into account Fidé criteria such as the views of the players ... he resolved to award the 1993 World Championship Match to the City of Manchester'.

I was astonished. I knew, unless Nigel had changed his plans, that he was unreachable while the bids were being submitted and still out of touch at the time that Campomanes had announced a winner. How could he possibly have been consulted, as Fidé claimed?

I immediately telephoned Raymond Keene, the chess correspondent of *The Times* and of the *Spectator*, who was at that time acting as a kind of unofficial press spokesman for Garri Kasparov. What was Kasparov's position? Keene said that Campomanes had told Kasparov on Monday the 22nd that he was minded to award the match to Manchester, since it appeared to be the highest unconditional bid. Kasparov had replied that he preferred the Channel Four bid, in part because he regarded Manchester as Short's home patch, but that, if necessary, he would agree to play there. Kasparov seemed to be under the impression that Short had already indicated his assent to Manchester. Keene went on to tell me that he was just about to issue a press statement via *The Times* in which Kasparov would publicly, but with regret, accept Campomanes's decision.

I told Keene not to put out the statement, and explained why I believed that Nigel was not aware that the match had been awarded to Manchester and could not have been consulted about the decision. Keene seemed amazed, and he insisted that I telephone Kasparov, who was at that moment supposed to be playing his first-round game in the Linares grandmaster tournament, but was in fact lying in his hotel room with flu.

I was a little reluctant to do this: Kasparov knew that I had been the conduit through which Nigel had three weeks earlier described him variously as 'an animal', 'an arsehole' and 'a baboon'. I didn't think, especially if he was feeling unwell, that the world champion would give me a sympathetic hearing. Keene became even more excited: 'Don't you see? Kasparov has been waiting for something like this to happen ever since 1985.'

For those who have not been following Kasparov that long, it is necessary to explain the reason for Keene's excitement. In February 1985, Florencio Campomanes, then, as now, President of Fidé, unilaterally suspended in mid-play the first world championship match between Karpov and Kasparov. Fidé had controlled the world championship since 1948, but had never intervened in a match once in progress. It was meant to be merely an authorizing authority, leaving the running of events to the national chess federations. Campomanes took his unprecedented action because his friend Anatoly Karpov, the defending champion, was in danger of physical collapse. At one point in the match, which was to go to the first player to win six games, Karpov led 5–0. But as the Russian winter dragged on and the match entered its sixth month, Kasparov pulled the score back to 5–3, having won the forty-seventh and forty-eighth games. It was at that point that Campomanes flew into Moscow to rescue Karpov and declare him still undefeated champion. A year later Kasparov took the title from Karpov in a rematch. But he never forgave Campomanes for, as he saw it, robbing him of possible victory in his first attempt at the world championship. He vowed to avenge himself against Campomanes, but in several subsequent attempts to wrest power in the chess world from Fidé, he had not been able to convince his fellow grandmasters that he was a more desirable despot than Campomanes.

No wonder Keene thought that Kasparov would be very interested indeed if Campomanes could be shown to have behaved improperly in his handling of the bids for the match against Short.

When I called Kasparov he seemed very surprised to hear from me, and, as I suspected, he was not altogether welcoming. He had assumed that Short was in favour of Fidé's decision. I said that it was possible that he was. All I knew was that he had told me that he would be unreachable until the next day, Wednesday the 24th, and that, if that was indeed the case, Campomanes's assertion that Nigel had been consulted was a scandalous untruth. 'It would be typical of him,' Kasparov replied. I ended the conversation by saying to Kasparov that at this stage he should stop Keene from issuing the planned press release accepting Fidé's decision, do nothing publicly and just wait for Nigel to get in touch with him. With a snuffle Kasparov agreed, then put the phone down.

The next morning, at about ten o'clock, Nigel, having finally arrived at his flat in Athens, telephoned me at my home in London. 'I've got some news for you,' I said. 'Are all the bids in?' asked Nigel. 'Yes,' I said, and listed them. 'Uh-huh.' Nigel did not seem very impressed by the prize funds. They were all a long way below the £3 million which Manchester's advisers had discussed with him. 'Now,' I went on, 'here's the most interesting news of all: according to Fidé you were consulted and, following that consultation, Campo has awarded the match to Manchester.' There was silence. 'Hello?' I said. The line from Athens to London seemed to have gone down. 'Hello?'

'You're joking,' Nigel finally replied. I said I wasn't. 'You're joking,' Nigel said again, this time almost shouting. I again said I wasn't, and this unremarkable piece of dialogue was repeated several more times, rather in the style of a Harold Pinter play.

Eventually Nigel accepted that I wasn't teasing him. 'Has Gazza accepted Campo's decision?' I told Nigel that I had rung Kasparov and had, I hoped, prevented him from publicly signalling his acceptance of Fidé's decision. I also told Nigel that Kasparov was expecting to hear from him, and gave him the direct line into Kasparov's hotel suite in Linares.

'They think I'm just a bunny rabbit,' Nigel suddenly said to me. 'They think I'll just do as I'm told. They're making a big mistake.' It was true: Fidé had underestimated Nigel, rather as many of his recent opponents had done. He does look a bit like a bunny rabbit, and a young bunny at that. He did seem to be the sort of frail school swot who can be pushed around by anyone with a talent for bullying. It used to happen, too.

In the 1986 Chess Olympiad, when the twenty-one-year-old Short was already far and away Britain's best player, ranked tenth in the world, he was made to play on the third board for the England team, simply because the selectors, who included the gentlemen playing on boards one and two, believed – correctly – that he would put up and shut up. Nigel had silently brooded on that injustice ever since – it still rankles with him. And for years tournament organizers welcomed Short, not just as the West's outstanding prospect, but also as a self-effacing lad who would not make a big fuss about bad conditions; he would just get on and play.

What the normally shrewd President Campomanes of Fidé failed to see was that Short, for so long the friendly, goofy kid on the tournament circuit, had – through the unforgiving medium of world championship matchplay – become an adult, and an adult, moreover, who was still full of resentment at all the condescensions he had endured on the way to the top of grandmasterdom's greasy pole. Fidé, rather unluckily perhaps, was about to pay a heavy price for one condescension too many. Also, of course, it should not have lied. Perhaps Campomanes assumed that Nigel would simply be delighted to play in his home city of Manchester. Anyone who actually knew Nigel would also know that his sentimental attachment to that part of the world is close to nil.

But what could never have occurred to Fidé was that the same Nigel Short who had only three weeks ago been calling Garri Kasparov 'an arsehole' and 'an animal' would be able, let alone willing, to call on the world champion for support. That, however, is what happened.

Two hours after our conversation, after he had regained his composure, Short called Kasparov in Linares. 'First,' Nigel reported back to me a little later, 'I told Gazza that Fidé's awarding of the match to Manchester had nothing to do with me. He just said, "Huh!" That obviously wasn't going to lead anywhere, since he clearly didn't believe me. So then I said, "Let's play our match outside Fidé." He paused for a few seconds, and then said, "Nigel, I have been waiting eight years for this moment."' Eight, of course, was the number of years which had elapsed since President Campomanes had suspended Kasparov's match with Karpov to save the former champion from possible defeat. It is said that revenge is a dish best eaten cold. This was revenge served up in an ice-bucket and delivered personally by Nigel Short to Kasparov's hotel suite.

I recall the next two days with mixed feelings. I was staying at our favourite hotel, Cliveden, for what was meant to be a short holiday with my wife and our baby. Instead the Cliveden switchboard was jammed with the efforts to liaise between Kasparov in Linares, Raymond Keene in London and Nigel Short in Athens. The objective was to put out an agreed statement by the weekend, which would both announce and justify the players' decision to wrest the world championship from Fidé, having first obtained detailed legal advice about the potential risks of such a decision. The reason for the rush was simple: the greater the delay, the greater the chance of something leaking out and alerting Fidé to the imminent *putsch*. (In particular Andrew Page, Kasparov's British manager, was, initially, very much against the breakaway.)

On the morning of Friday, 26 February, just before the break with Fidé was to be made public, I made one last call to Athens. I quoted to Nigel that most famous piece of strategic advice by the great chess teacher Aron Nimzovitch: 'The threat is stronger than the execution.' In other words, I said, why didn't he and Garri threaten Fidé with a breakaway unless they gave the players greater control over the match and its financing? 'No,' Nigel replied, after a little thought. 'They didn't negotiate with us. Why should we negotiate with them?' Then he laughed. 'And anyway, I don't believe in Nimzovitch as much as I used to.'

At lunchtime the players launched their attack on the Fidé position and in particular its king, Florencio Campomanes:

> This is not the first time that Fidé under Campomanes has shown disregard for its own rules. It is clear that Fidé cannot be trusted to organize the most important professional chess competition in the world. Accordingly both Garri Kasparov and Nigel Short have agreed to play their match outside the jurisdiction of Fidé. The match will be played under the auspices of a new body, the Professional Chess Association. Both players have agreed to donate 10 per cent of the prize fund from this match to establishing this body, which is intended to represent chess professionals worldwide.

(This last gesture was less extravagant than it sounded. One of Nigel's objections to Fidé, which Kasparov shared, was that it took 20 per cent of the players' prize fund, and a further 5 per cent 'tax' on top. In return for this, Fidé provided nothing more than authorization – the organization of world chess championships had always been left to national federations.)

Later the same day, Fidé responded, very much along the lines that we had expected. It announced that 'Fidé has legal title to the World Championship and will take all necessary legal steps to protect those rights.' But Fidé's counsel was able to offer no more than the same advice which we had received earlier in the week: that no one had legal title to the phrase 'world chess championship'. It was up for grabs, and the only thing that counted was what the marketing men called 'credibility'. And as Nigel said to me during the frenetic two days before the breakaway, 'Campomanes can have his Fidé world championship. Everybody knows that the guy who beats Kasparov is the real chess champion of the world.'

At that stage we gave the Short–Kasparov match the provisional title of the 'Professional World Chess Championship' and called on bidders to submit offers for the event by the end of Friday, 19 March. Then, in deliberate contrast to the murky *in camera* nature of Fidé's methods, we announced that the bids would be opened for the first time in public, at a press conference to be held at Simpson's in the Strand – a traditional centre of British chess – on the morning of Monday, 22 March. This was a very risky strategy, which did not altogether appeal to Kasparov and his manager Andrew Page. If, as was quite possible, the bids for an unofficial match failed to match those which had already been received under Fidé's auspices, the players and their advisers would be humiliated in full view of the press and television cameras.

Ray Keene, however, soon managed to persuade his employer, *The Times*, that the event was worth going for, and it soon became clear that News International, which owns *The Times*, was prepared to participate in a bid of about £1.3 million. And Matthew Patten's London Chess Group, which now had backing from the BBC and the London *Evening Standard*, was still very interested.

What we hadn't realized was that the date we set for the public opening of the bids was also the day that the International Olympic Committee was due to visit Manchester to assess the merit of its campaign to stage the 2000 Olympic Games. And the city of Manchester had publicly linked its bid for the world chess championship with its Olympic campaign. It would be an enormous embarrassment if the visit of the IOC to Manchester were to coincide with the city's loss of a sporting event about which it had been boasting only a month earlier.

While Nigel left for the Virginia home of Lubosh Kavalek, Manchester and Fidé joined forces secretly to swing Kasparov back behind their bid. I say secretly only because neither Nigel, nor I, nor indeed Raymond Keene and *The Times*, knew anything of it. On the evening of 16 March, Keene invited Kasparov, Page and Bob Rice, the champion's American lawyer, to a celebratory dinner at Simpson's. They merrily celebrated away, and Keene went home to bed a happy man.

Kasparov, Page and Rice, however, went on at midnight to the Conrad Hotel at Chelsea Harbour to visit a gentleman who had just arrived from the Philippines: Florencio Campomanes. Another late-arriving guest was Tony Ingham, the organizer of the Manchester bid. Ingham informed Kasparov and friends that Manchester was now prepared to bid £1.6 million for the match, provided it remained under the auspices of Fidé. Campomanes and Kasparov then began to haggle over the precise terms, both monetary and political, of such a *démarche*.

I heard of the meeting the next morning and rang Nigel to warn him of the development. For the second time in a month, he was, most uncharacteristically, reduced to something akin to rage, 'I'm fucked! I'll be made to look a complete idiot and Gazza will get all the extra money. I can only think that a lot of money is being offered to him under the table. He has always done this with organizers. It might take only an extra half a million to get Gazza to agree to Manchester. He's not a man of principle, is Gazza. He's forgotten everything we said in our joint press statement.' Nigel paused for breath, then added in a much quieter voice, 'Of course, it's my own fault for doing a deal with one of the most unpleasant people in the chess world.'

The main problem for Kasparov and his manager was, as Nigel pointed out, that the world champion had already appended his name to a document which announced that both players would attend a press conference on 22 March at Simpson's, to open the bids for a match 'outside the jurisdiction of Fidé'. And on 17 March Keene – whose role as Kasparov's spokesman seemed suddenly a distant memory – made it clear to the world champion in a sulphurous telephone call that, if he stuck with Fidé after all, the press conference would not be cancelled, and the world champion's double-dealing would be revealed by his absence.

On the following day I received a fax marked 'urgent' from the general manager of Simpson's, Brian Clivaz, which read, 'Dear Mr Lawson, I have just spoken to Andrew Page in Moscow who tells me that Kasparov and Short spoke last night and agreed that the press conference should be postponed. Is this what was agreed?' A quick call to Nigel confirmed that he had agreed no such thing, and that Kasparov and Page were simply attempting to bounce Nigel into touch while their own negotiations with Manchester and Campomanes were finalized.

I called Clivaz and told him that he had been unaccountably misinformed by Page: Nigel would attend the press conference and open bids for the PCA World Chess Championship. If Kasparov chose not to attend, because he was unavoidably detained elsewhere, that would be a pity, but not a tragedy. The manager of Simpson's, after some hesitation, agreed to go ahead with Short and, if necessary, without Kasparov. He sounded a little confused by the turn of events, which I took to be the sign of a rational man in such circumstances. I had already decided that anyone who was not confused by the way things had developed was either mad or a crook, or both.

In any event, the next day, Friday the 19th, the negotiations between Kasparov and Campomanes broke down – this time, it seemed, beyond rescue by even the most tawdry and lucrative compromise. Kasparov wanted Campomanes to hand all power over future world championship matches to him, as champion. And Kasparov was also insisting that Fidé hand over the $400,000 deposit that the original Los Angeles bidders had paid over and forfeited when their $4 million bid collapsed. 'Let's have it back, Campo,' Kasparov told me he had said to the Fidé President, and, re-enacting the scene, made a gesture as if pulling large wads of money out of a drawer. (At least that was my interpretation of the gesture. I have never pulled a large wad of money out of a drawer, but I somehow imagined that in the world of Kasparov and Campomanes large wads are regularly pulled out of, or indeed stuffed into, drawers.)

But Kasparov had in fact pulled some money out of other people's drawers. *The Times*, via Ray Keene, felt obliged to raise their bid by £300,000 to the level they knew Manchester was now prepared to offer, £1.6 million. Keene was irate, and not just because he felt betrayed by his old 'friend' Kasparov. 'The bastard has cost us £300,000. We were going to have chauffeurs and houses laid on for the players during the match. Not any more. He's wrecked our budget. They'll have to hire their own taxis.' I suggested to Ray that, in exchange for an extra £300,000, I was sure that the players would be content to travel to the match by public transport.

During all of the events of the previous few weeks, in which Kasparov and Short had effected nothing less than the overthrow of the world's second-largest sporting bureaucracy, the two principals had never actually met. Now that the stake had finally been driven into Campomanes's heart, Nigel flew in from America, for the first face-to-face meeting with his hated opponent and deadly ally. It was the night of Sunday, 21 March, the eve of the opening of the bids for the match. Nigel asked me to come along: he knew that Kasparov would have his lawyer present and did not like to be outnumbered, especially in a jet-lagged state.

As usual there was a misunderstanding. Kasparov thought there was an arrangement to meet at Simpson's. Nigel had understood we were to meet next door, at the Savoy. So what actually happened was that the Kasparov delegation met the

Short delegation rather embarrassingly in the middle, with each side accusing the other of waiting in the wrong place, and muttering, 'We were just leaving.' Nigel attempted to improve the atmosphere by a little joke. In place of Fidé's motto, 'Gens una sumus', constantly cited by Campomanes during his presidential election campaigns, why didn't the new Professional Chess Association adopt the counter-slogan 'Mens una sumus'? Kasparov's muddy grey-green eyes turned on Nigel in a dead, unenquiring state. The world champion might understand Latin; but Latin puns? And at a time like this? That was asking too much.

So we silently climbed the three floors to Kasparov's Savoy suite, room 308. Almost before we had sat down – but not before Bob Rice, who looked just like a sharp Manhattan lawyer should, handed me his card ('Milbank, Tweed, Hadley & McCloy') – Kasparov launched into a lengthy description of how the Professional Chess Association would be run. 'The world champion', he pronounced, 'should of course have the dominant role.' Nigel, who had been nodding patiently up till then, interrupted at that point. 'If I have been nodding, Garri,' he said, 'that does not mean I necessarily agree with you. It just means I understand what you say.' Kasparov looked irritated: 'Did you agree with what I just said?' 'No,' said Nigel, 'I didn't.' Kasparov leapt up from his chair. 'Oh! Oh! Now we have crisis! Major crisis!' I suddenly realized – rather late in the day – what a drama queen Kasparov was, and felt sorry for Nigel. It was bad enough to play chess for two months against Kasparov. But to do business with him looked to be, if anything, more unpleasant.

As we left the Savoy together, I commiserated with Nigel over his fate. 'Don't worry,' he replied. 'I always knew that negotiating with Kasparov would be like this. But I'll be all right. If I win the match, things will have to change.' 'And if you lose?' 'If I lose, then unless Kasparov mends his ways I will get the hell out and watch a rampant Gazza bring everything crashing down around him.'

With that Nigel handed me a small parcel. It contained a cassette tape. He explained that it was a recording of what seemed to be a conversation between Kasparov and Rice, as they plotted with Fidé to subvert Nigel's plans for a breakaway match. 'I think this is a present from Campomanes,' said Nigel. Having played it over many times, it is clear to me that the tape has been heavily edited. It sounds as though the voice of a third party has been excised, presumably the party who was taping the conversation. The identity of that person, who presumably also caused the tape to end up in Short's hands, can only be guessed at.

The sending of the tape to Nigel was, I imagine, a last-ditch attempt – on the day before the press conference launching the Professional World Chess Championship – to persuade Short that he would be mad to deal with Kasparov and Rice, and should instead return to Fidé and Manchester. In the taped conversation Kasparov seems to be envisaging a situation on 21 March in which the players discover, the day before the official opening of the bids for the Professional World Chess Championship, that there are no high offers. Then Kasparov would pounce on a disappointed and disoriented Nigel, and drag him back to a deal with Fidé and Manchester. Here is a transcript of the edited tape:

KASPAROV: There are too many rumours circulating. I don't want anything to appear in the press. I'm afraid that this meeting could be very damaging to myself. . . . I'm sure I'll win it [the match, presumably] . . . Nigel Short will be under the impression that there is a great deal of money for this match, but I suspect he will be disappointed by the amount. I think his interest will not extend too much after this world championship match. Even if he continues to be part of the Professional Chess Association or whatever it's called. Because I will insist on changing it. . . . By having Nigel at the table alone being disappointed, being confused, I think there's a chance to bring the match back to Manchester. . . . The only moment to catch him is when he sees the bid figures.

RICE: Yup.

KASPAROV: If the figures are not great he will be disappointed and confused. That's the best moment for me psychologically . . . to tell him another story.

RICE: I spoke to Nigel for some time yesterday and in many

ways he was childish, no, child-like is a better phrase. . . .
Obviously Garri is Garri, and when you two are alone in a room
together, without Ray Keene whispering in his ear, you can say,
'Listen, I am world champion and you are not and we need to
do these things.' Garri holds all of the cards and this will be
made clear to Nigel on Sunday.

KASPAROV: Bob, it's more important that Nigel will be
isolated from some other people who are unfortunately much
closer to his ear. [I took this as a great compliment.]

RICE: Right!

KASPAROV: And that's what we agree for Sunday, to keep
him separately in a closed room some time after the bids are
opened. As long as we can get his signature on the paper we can
have something real. On Sunday I'll do my best to get most
information from the bidders. Then we will have to discuss exact
strategy, because I think I can catch Nigel. In one room. I'm just
a better player [laughs]. I think we have a fair chance.

RICE: Oh, excellent!

KASPAROV: I think we have a very good chance.

RICE: Right!

Of course, by the time this was in Nigel's possession he had
already discovered Kasparov's duplicity: the tape merely confirmed much of what he suspected. In Nigel's position I would
have gained much amusement by letting Kasparov and Rice
know that I had a tape of their plotting. Nigel, characteristically,
found it far more amusing that they did *not* know.

The tape also suggests that Kasparov thought that he could,
in effect, steam open the bidders' envelopes before they were
officially and publicly opened on Monday the 22nd by the
manager of Simpson's in the Strand. Matthew Patten, whose
London Chess Group was generally thought likely to be the
highest bidder, was alert to just such a possibility, especially after
his experiences at the hands of Fidé. He submitted his bid on
the due date of Friday the 19th, but placed it in a steel safe, to
which only he had a key. When Nigel and I met Kasparov on
the night before the bids were to be declared, the world
champion declared himself perplexed by Patten's precautions,
but still felt able to joke about it. As we left his suite at the Savoy

on Sunday night Kasparov gave one of his big crocodile grins: 'You know, if Matthew Patten doesn't turn up with his key tomorrow, we're fucked!'

Matthew Patten did turn up with his key, and his bid, as announced, was indeed the top one of five, at £2 million. *The Times*, in conjunction with a television promotion company called Teleworld, pitched in at £1.7 million. Short had been vindicated. The two bids from the London Chess Group and *The Times* were substantially higher than those Fidé had solicited for the same event. And there would be no 25 per cent rake-off for the organizing body this time.

In effect, Nigel's phone call to Kasparov a month earlier had earned the two players a share in an extra £1 million. For Kasparov, this may not have meant a vast amount. For Nigel, living in a two-bedroom flat and the owner of a 1986 Nissan, it meant a lot. And he had got it by using the same tactics he had been using in his matches against Speelman, Gelfand, Karpov and Timman: channelling aggression and resentment into concentration on a single objective. Those who had interpreted his single-mindedness as simple-mindedness had made what chess-players call a serious strategic error.

Not that Nigel did much to dissuade those who wanted to think he was simple-minded in comparison with the mercurial champion. At the press conference to mark the opening of the bids for the PCA world championship the players were invited to address the 100 or so journalists from around the world who had gathered at Simpson's. Kasparov launched into a fifteen-minute free-form tirade in which, among other things, he associated Campomanes and Fidé with the 'dark forces' attempting to overthrow President Yeltsin. The manager of Simpson's eventually managed to stem the world champion's flow by saying loudly, 'And I now call upon the challenger, Nigel Short, to address you.'

Nigel blinked into the camera lights. A hundred or so pencils hovered over a hundred or so notebooks. The challenger stood up and cleared his throat. 'Thank you all very much for coming,' said Short, and immediately sat down. I heard some titters from the audience, and I knew what they were thinking. Immediately afterwards, as we went up to Kasparov's suite at the Savoy to discuss the bids in detail, I told Nigel he shouldn't have left the field so completely to Kasparov, but he seemed to have a reason.

'I'm quite happy if Gazza wants everyone to think that all this was his idea, and that everybody turned up just to see him. But why were all those people really there? To hear the bids for our match. And where have all the bids for our match come from? England, and nowhere else. So I don't need to say anything: the money is doing the talking, in sterling, and what it is saying is that it wants to see an Englishman play for the world chess championship. Even Kasparov knows that, although he can't admit it.'

He certainly couldn't. As the various bidders came up to his suite to present their offers in detail for what they all termed the 'Short–Kasparov match', Kasparov was clearly becoming increasingly irritated. Finally he came out with it: 'Why do you all keep calling it the "Short–Kasparov match"? I'm the world champion, you know.' Nigel just laughed.

Kasparov's tenseness was understandable. The next day he was to be stripped of his Fidé world title, the title he had fought over 150 mind-sapping games against Karpov to win and to retain. But now he would lose it, and Karpov would be the main beneficiary.

It was obviously playing on Kasparov's mind. After the bidders had made their presentations, he looked worried. Then he began making loud sniffing noises. I asked him what he was doing. 'Some of these bidders smell a bit fishy. I've got a good nose for this sort of thing.' Then he turned to Short. 'Just remember, Nigel, I got Manchester to offer £1.6 million, with Fidé agreeing.'

'I know, Garri,' Nigel replied, 'but we would have looked like arseholes if we'd gone back on our word.'

'Hmnh!' grunted the world chess champion. As Nigel himself had earlier pointed out, but perhaps had temporarily forgotten, Garri Kasparov did not care overmuch whether people thought he was an 'arsehole'.

That was bad luck for Matthew Patten, the co-ordinator of the £2 million London Chess Group bid. Kasparov was deeply suspicious about it. According to the documentation of the bid the BBC was committed to guarantee £1 million, but the head of BBC Enterprises, the only man who could personally authorize the payment, was unavailable and out of touch somewhere in South-east Asia. 'Where is the money man?' Kasparov yelled at a bemused Matthew Patten. 'When can we expect to see the dollar people? Where is the hard cash?'

The other problem was that although Intel, the American microchip manufacturers, had backed Patten's bid to the extent of about £500,000, their European sponsorship agent, Rod Alexander, had surreptitiously let it be known to one or two other bidders that Intel would want to be involved in the match, whichever bid ultimately succeeded. Ray Keene needed no further encouragement: he immediately attempted to detach Intel from the London Chess Group and swing the company into the *Times* consortium.

On 30 March, at a meeting at the offices of Simon Olswang, the legal firm representing the *Times* consortium, Short's and Kasparov's advisers agreed to negotiate with the *Times* group exclusively for fourteen days. It was on the clear understanding that they would be able to get Intel to defect from the London Chess Group, and that the result would be an enhanced bid. There was also a clear understanding that there would be no press statement of any kind.

The next day Short's and Kasparov's advisers were astonished to see *The Times* putting all over its front page that it had won the right to hold the world championship with its existing bid. As one of the parties to the negotiations admitted to me, 'At the time that was complete crap. I think it was an attempt by *The Times* to bounce the players and make Matthew Patten throw in the towel. And there never was an enhanced offer, because Intel wanted its name on the championship and *The Times* wasn't having it. But by the time that became apparent, Matthew Patten had withdrawn his bid.'

When I rang Nigel the day after *The Times* had announced that it had won the right to hold the world championship, he said he was 'shocked', and added, 'I spoke to Gazza about it and he was really upset too. *The Times* have been trying to persuade me to give them a quote to the effect that their front-page story was true. I just told them they had dug themselves into a hole, and they could dig themselves out of it.'

The sad conclusion to be drawn, however, is that while grandmasters like Kasparov and Short are fantastically skilled at outmanoeuvring their opponents over sixty-four squares, they are mere beginners in the world of business, and, on that particular chessboard, no match for the Mr Fixits of Rupert Murdoch's News International.

And by the end of the negotiations both Short and Kasparov were completely exhausted. Nigel was in Monaco, having months earlier committed himself to participate there in a lethally demanding blindfold chess tournament – the first such event in chess history. He played like a zombie. From Monaco he complained to me that he was in 'chronic depression' and that all he wanted was 'to lie in bed for a week and watch TV'. A journalist who visited Kasparov in Helsinki at the same time reported that the world champion seemed almost incoherent with exhaustion.

It was not just that the two men, and Nigel in particular, were unfamiliar with the special strains of business negotiations. They had, in the space of a few weeks, risked more than mere money. Kasparov had relinquished his official Fidé world title, and Nigel had played double or quits not just with the biggest pay-day of his career, but also with his reputation; he knew his name was murkier than mud in his home city – even his own father had reproached him, to his great sadness – and, all over the world, many people he counted as his friends had publicly denounced him over his siding with Kasparov against Fidé. Above all, there was the awful sense of anticlimax, which tends to affect Nigel, as it does many people, after the immediate elation of success.

It was scarcely a consolation to Short that Kasparov, who used to ridicule him, now seemed almost respectful. Talking to the American magazine *Chess Life*, Kasparov said, 'There are now a lot of negative things being said about Nigel Short in the chess world. But I have reconsidered his former attitude towards me. Notwithstanding the shortcomings he has, much like most other people, Nigel has some unique virtues. I would like to point out the determination with which Short made his move . . . thanks in large part to his determination, Nigel is riding high on a wave of enthusiasm sweeping across England which, it seems to me, may envelop the entire civilized world.' I reported these gracious words back to Nigel Short. 'Well, I still think he's a scumbag. But not quite so much of a scumbag.'

The day after Short and Kasparov finally signed the contract for their match, Nigel was surprised to get a phone call from Gazza. He told Nigel that he was leaving London for Moscow the next day and would like to have dinner with him. No agenda – just a way of saying goodbye . . . for now.

Kasparov booked a table at Ken Lo's Memories of China in Ebury Street. At the end of the dinner, when the Russian was paying the bill, the waiter suddenly seemed to recognize Nigel. 'Excuse me,' the Chinese asked Short, 'but aren't you the world chess champion?' 'Kasparov looked amazed,' Nigel told me, giggling with the memory of it. 'So I said to the waiter, "No, I am not the world chess champion. I am the next one."'

CHAPTER FIVE

There is a recurring theme in Western films, usually ones starring Clint Eastwood, in which the hero, having suffered a messy reverse at the wrong end of the barrel of a gun, retires to a cave. There our man staunches his wounds, and practises interminably with his own six-shooter until the day comes when he is fully prepared, and ready to meet his destiny in a final shoot-out.

It is as good a metaphor as any for the predicament and progress of Nigel Short in the four months leading up to his mental shoot-out with the fastest brain in the East. I had never known him to be as depressed, even despairing, as he was in the immediate aftermath of the negotiations with Kasparov and *The Times*.

It was not just that he had been exhausted by the negotiations, at a time when he wanted only to recover from the strains of three years of eliminating matches. A point of particular bitterness was that he had been roundly castigated for his break with Fidé by a number of hitherto friendly British chess grandmasters whom he had counted as friends. They grouped together, under the auspices of the British Chess Federation, to publish their recriminations, with their home telephone numbers attached to a press release. Grandmaster Murray Chandler, the editor of the *British Chess Magazine*, who was a regular guest, with his wife Nemet, at the Shorts' London home, accused him of 'ill-timed opportunism . . . which has caused enormous ill-will'. Julian Hodgson, the current British chess champion, with whom Nigel had played together since childhood, said that 'Short's behaviour has been unbelievable . . . total hypocrisy.' In public, Nigel seemed to laugh off these attacks. In private he was very angry, vengeful even.

When I rang him in Monaco, where he was playing in the blindfold tournament, Nigel had just been reading – and not in Braille – the British Chess Federation's collection of diatribes. 'I never really thought about winning this match against Kasparov,' he said to me. 'Up till now I had thought only of getting this far. But now I really want to win. You know why? Because of all these arseholes who have been criticizing me. I want to say "fuck you" to the lot of them, and winning is the best way to do it. I am the first British chessplayer ever to qualify for a world championship match and the British Chess Federation is the one organization in the country which doesn't support me. Well, fuck them too.'

But anger is not enough. Nor, as Lubosh Kavalek was wont to intone in his sing-song Czech accent, is 'ambition without ammunition'. Nigel finished in last place in the Monaco tournament and, in a dazed voice, at the end wondered aloud whether he had 'lost it'. And by 'it' he did not mean the blindfold tournament, or the world championship to come, but his very ability to play chess. Memories of his adolescent humiliation in 1980, when he had been thrown – by the British Chess Federation, as it happens – into the deep end of grandmaster chess and lost almost every game, were stirring uneasily in his mind. It had taken him two years to recover – if he had ever completely recovered – from that débâcle. Now he had only four months to prepare for a twenty-four-game match against the most awesome and destructive player in the long history of chess.

And Kasparov was particularly awesome and particularly destructive against Short. Nigel had won only one game in fully fledged tournament chess against the world champion, and that was as long ago as 1986, in a messy encounter which Kasparov, with some justice, described as a 'fluke'. Nigel had overlooked the loss of a piece, and it only became clear subsequently that his 'blunder' was an unintentionally brilliant sacrifice. After that a vengeful Kasparov had won eight games in a row against Short, a remarkable record given that on average half the games between grandmasters end in a draw.

This was a psychological stranglehold, and both men knew it. It had little to do with the relative chessboard strength of the two grandmasters, although Kasparov was clearly the stronger player. But the history of chess is littered with examples of great

76

players who simply cannot play well against a particular opponent, for no apparent reason. The ex-world champion Mikhail Tal, for example, invariably lost to the would-be world champion Viktor Korchnoi even though, on paper, the two men were very evenly matched.

The point is that, after one or two defeats, the losing grandmaster becomes convinced that he can never beat the other, and the successful opponent sits down at the board buoyed up by the belief that he has 'cracked' his rival.

The same process can be seen in tennis – according to Boris Spassky, the closest game to chess – where apparently equally gifted players often have very one-sided encounters. It is all in the mind, and the mind is everything. In tennis, this is known, and often written about, as the 'inner game'. But chess is entirely an 'inner game' in which, contrary to popular belief, the rational intellect is usually the slave of the 'irrational' ego.

Kasparov, more even than any of his predecessors as world champion – all of whom had an intuitively shrewd apprehension of this phenomenon – understands and uses the weapon of psychological terror. As he explained, for the benefit of anyone who doubted this process, 'When you win at chess you destroy your opponent's ego. For a time you make him lose confidence in himself as a person. . . . Before you lose at the board, or before you resign, or even before you get a bad position, you have to lose it psychologically. You have to be frightened by the very strong moves of your opponent, or by his very strong character, or just by some other factors. This process has not been studied yet. We don't understand how it happens. But in long matches – and I have played already five world champion-ship matches with Karpov – I feel that if you have weakness inside you, if you show weakness, you are in major trouble. Even if your opponent is not experienced enough to see it, it will be shown in your moves, because your hand will not be as steady as before.'

That was certainly Nigel's apprehension, in both senses of the word, as he began to prepare for the match against Kasparov. We discussed this at my home on his return from Monaco. 'The trouble is', Nigel said, 'that against any other player in the world,

I always felt I stood a good chance – even against Karpov, which is why I had the strength to beat him. But I have a crushing psychological disadvantage against Kasparov. I have become frightened of him – of what he can do to me. If I played a match against him now, I would be utterly crushed. Not a chance. I have to build up inner strength. It's like a muscle. You have to exercise it all the time.'

But while contemplating how to build up his own self-confidence, Nigel was not going to miss any opportunity to destabilize Kasparov's own never entirely balanced mental state. 'I have some ideas about this,' he told me with a mischievous giggle, back in April. 'I noticed, during the European team championships in Debrecen, that Gazza fell completely for a seventeen-year-old chick who was playing for the French ladies' team. He would stand there staring at her with his mouth open. He kept trying to have assignations with her, but she wouldn't see him and he was beside himself. I think I should get her to come to London for the match. Perhaps I could get her to sit in the front row. I call this the French Defence.' The French Defence is, in fact, the name of a real opening, and one which Nigel has played very often. But this was a variation which Garri Kasparov could never have anticipated.

'Did you think this up yourself?' I asked Nigel, not sure exactly how serious he was. He was serious: 'Yes: although, strangely, Michael Stean suggested the same idea to me independently.' (Grandmaster Stean, Nigel's manager, had been Viktor Korchnoi's second in his 1978 world championship match against Karpov in Baguio City. That bitter contest, between a recent Soviet defector and the Brezhnevite Soviet world champion, had become a by-word for off-the-board shenanigans. At one point Korchnoi hired the rather unspecific services of three members of an obscure religious sect, who were jointly and severally wanted for murder. Nigel's suggestion – reminiscent of a French farce rather than a murder mystery – was of a far less scandalous nature than events which Stean had already witnessed at first hand in the paranoid world of world championship chess.) Nigel discussed the idea also with Jon Speelman, whom he was planning to take on as a second during the match. 'It's too risky,' said Speelman, apparently. 'She might fall for him.'

It seems that Speelman's advice was close to the mark. By the end of July, when I spent a week with Nigel and Rea in Athens, it was clear that the 'French Defence' had been refuted – and by Kasparov himself, in the most conclusive manner. 'It won't work,' Nigel informed me, almost casually. 'I have intelligence that Kasparov has been spending time away from his training camp in Croatia, and has been seen on several occasions in Montpelier.' I looked blankly at Nigel, so he patiently explained that Montpelier happened to be the home town of that young member of the French women's chess team whom Kasparov so coveted. 'I think', said Nigel, 'that this is rather too much of a coincidence.'

Indeed; and how maddening it would have been to Nigel, having placed the apparently unattainable temptation in the front row, to have seen her staring adoringly at a grinning Kasparov. It was still very impressive, though, that Nigel had managed to spy so effectively on his opponent's movements. It seems that the source of this intelligence was none other than Josef Dorfman, Kasparov's chief second in three world championship matches, who had left the disintegrating Soviet Union, set up home in the South of France and was now the coach of the French chess team.

'I met Dorfman in Cannes' was all Nigel would concede. But he added that Kasparov's former ideas man 'told me what defence Kasparov would play against me'. According to Nigel, Dorfman claimed Kasparov would be worried that his favourite Sicilian Defence was vulnerable to Nigel's attacking skill, backed up by four months of preparation with Kavalek. Dorfman told Nigel that Kasparov would take 'only one hit against the Sicilian' and then switch to another, much less double-edged opening, one he had never played before. 'Joe told me what that opening is,' said Nigel, with justified pleasure at the recollection of the conversation.

In fact Dorfman had not worked intensively with Kasparov since 1987, and the two had parted on less than good terms; his information on Kasparov's opening repertoire, while fascinating, had probably gone well past its sell-by date. But every little scrap of insight into the way the world champion prepared was immensely valuable for Nigel: he needed to build up as complete as possible a picture of the thought processes of his adversary. The more he could do that, the more he would build up his own confidence that he was properly armed for the combat.

I asked Nigel whether he had considered taking on Dorfman as a second: it would certainly have enraged Kasparov to see his former number-one ideas man in the enemy camp. 'No,' said Nigel. 'Lubosh doesn't care to work with Russians.' Wise man.

The great Chinese military strategist Shen-tzu is famous for remarking that in order to win a battle it is first necessary to understand your enemy. But he also said that it was necessary to understand yourself. Similarly, at the outset of his preparations for battle, it was not enough for Nigel to choose the weapons which he thought would most discomfit Kasparov, both off and on the board. He also needed to understand what he had been doing wrong in the many games he had recently lost against the champion.

Careful re-examination of these defeats – which cannot have been a pleasant exercise – showed that Nigel's play against Kasparov was more and more transparently that of a frightened man. Normally Short, with the White pieces, plays very sharply in the opening, taking calculated risks in search of a big advantage. But, in many of his games against Kasparov, he had attempted, even with the advantage of the first move, simply to attain a position of harmless equality. Such indirect means were simply not suited to Nigel's direct and straightforward chessplaying style, which is, after all, nothing more or less than a reflection of his own personality.

After this discovery the general strategy – if not the exact weapons – to be used against Kasparov was decided. By May Nigel's mind was made up, as he explained to me when we met in London before he flew off to Virginia and intensive preparation with Lubosh Kavalek: 'I have decided how to play the match. My plan must be to challenge head-on. I must go straight for the crisis. In the past I haven't challenged because I've been frightened, and it's been a complete disaster. I've noticed that those players who do well against Kasparov are not necessarily the strongest, but they haven't shrunk from challenging him right out of the opening.'

Playing the devil's advocate, I pointed out to Nigel that this would be taking on Kasparov on his strongest ground. There had never been a player in history who relished a sharp fight more than Kasparov. And, backed in the past by funds from the Communist Party in his home state of Azerbaizhan, and more recently by his own considerable retained foreign-currency earnings, Kasparov had for years enjoyed a retinue of Russian grandmasters – 'lackeys and slaves' Nigel called them – who kept him primed with all the latest twists and turns of modern chess opening theory. For the match against Nigel, Kasparov had taken with him to the Croatian island of Brioni at least three such grandmasters: Zurab Azmaiparashvili, Sergei Makarichev and the former Soviet champion Alexander Beliavsky. This last, very strong, player had the added advantage, for Kasparov, of having a playing style and opening repertoire very similar to Nigel's.

Did Nigel really want to meet this chess machine head-on, I asked? Couldn't he try some off-beat openings, rather than hurtle down the most controversial lines with which at least one of the Russians would be familiar? Apparently not. 'I tried some rather dodgy off-beat lines against Karpov, and those tricks worked because he had become a bit lazy in his old age, and could not be bothered to work out exactly what might be wrong with them. But Kasparov could destroy such openings at the board, and then I'd be fucked. I must play a real man's opening. No quiche. It will be bloody hard work, because Kasparov is fantastically well prepared. But that's exactly where I must contest him. If I can win a game early on, by challenging him in this way, then maybe he'll be a little bit shaken. And then, who knows?'

'By the way,' Nigel added, 'we had some good news today, Kasparov's wife just gave birth to a little girl. Gazza, of course, wanted a boy. He told me so when we were in London.'

Family, however new, was not, I suspected, on Kasparov's mind. Apart from brief forays to Montpelier, he was firmly installed at his Croatian training camp with not only his three tame grandmasters, but also, among other retainers, two dedicated 'fitness coaches' Alexander Kosik and Yevgeny Borisov. Garri Kasparov had created a wife-and-child-free environment completely dedicated to the retaining of his world championship.

Nigel's routine, however, was a clear compromise between his needs as a family man and his needs as a chessplayer. He would divide his time equally between Virginia and Athens, regularly enduring the ten-hours-each-way flights from one to the other. He did try to do some chess work in Athens. But the conditions were far from ideal.

He, Rea and Kyveli shared a small one-bedroom flat without air-conditioning in a 1960s block in crowded Arivou Street. Their narrow, almost corridor-like sitting room was also used by Rea for her own psychotherapy practice during most afternoons.

Nigel, in effect, was homeless for much of the day, which he would spend swimming and sunbathing nude around the collection of coves on the outskirts of Athens known as Vouliagmeni. Yet, having spent a week with Nigel disporting in this fashion, I began to suspect that Rea's psychotherapy extended beyond the clients crowding into her tiny apartment. She was well aware that Nigel's time with Kavalek consisted of little else but study. But he needed to build up more than merely chess strength; and the long days spent semi-submerged in the waves of the Aegean were gradually turning her pale and unfit husband into a much less tense and strung-out individual.

In the evenings the three of us would meet up for dinner. But even over the retsina and souvlaki Rea was never entirely off-duty. At some point during almost every meal she would look at her husband and ask, 'Do you believe that you will win?' And Nigel would always parry by saying with a laugh, 'That's a good question!' I once tried to intercede with the remark that the most important thing was simply for Nigel to play to the very best of his ability. Both husband and wife exclaimed almost simultaneously, 'No!'

'No,' Nigel continued while Rea nodded vigorously. 'Playing

my best is not good enough. Not good enough at all. I could play better than I have ever done, and still lose horribly. To win I have to believe that I will win, and just score as many points as I can, by whatever means. Playing well is another sort of chess, chess for the textbooks. I'm talking about sweat, grind, effort.'

Rea pushed a plate of dolmades towards her husband. 'Yes, my love, and that's why you lose so much weight in these matches. So eat up.'

Lubosh Kavalek grabbed me by my elbow and ushered me out of his house in Reston, Virginia, and across the garden to the front. Then he pointed back at the window which covered almost the full width of his study. It was late at night and an intense light shone out from the book-lined room. 'Look,' said Lubosh. In the window a man sat motionless at a vast chess table. The man seemed simultaneously to be looking at a book and at the pieces on the board. But he never moved the pieces. Occasionally the man picked at the roof of his mouth with his forefinger, in what seemed like a spasm of concentration. We stayed out there for about half an hour, enjoying the warm night air of a Virginian summer. But the man in the window remained motionless – apart from that strange plucking of the mouth – the chesspieces unmoved. This was Nigel Short, attempting, in his own way, to plumb 'the abysmal depths of chess'.

Lubosh turned to me as we walked back through the porch. 'It's strange, isn't it? We know what is going on up there, but people walk past here all the time and see Nigel in the window, and think nothing of it.'

That, in fact, was one of the beauties of working in Reston. It is a model suburban town of a very American type, full of clean-cut American families in clean-cut avenues with clean-cut Japanese cars parked by clean-cut front lawns. The chances of a European chess grandmaster, even the greatest, being recognized or bothered here were about as remote as that of the town appointing a communist mayor.

But in this unlikely setting Lubosh Kavalek had built some sort of chess shrine. Three rooms seemed to be full of nothing but chess books, in English, German, Czech (of course) and Russian. Bound volumes of Soviet chess magazines going back to the early 1950s lined one entire wall. I counted 103 books on one chess opening alone: it was the Sicilian Defence, Garri Kasparov's life-long favourite. I asked Kavalek whether he knew of a bigger collection of chess books. 'Oh, yes,' he replied. 'Not far from here, actually. The Library of Congress.'

But one thing the Library of Congress does not have is 'The Beast'. The Beast was kept under lock and key in the basement. But it never howled. It just hummed. The Beast was Kavalek's computer chess database, and, largely as a result of Nigel's successes, it had become famed and feared throughout the world of grandmasterdom. The machine, manufactured by the Technology Advancement Group, had been specially adapted by Kavalek. Patting it as one would a much loved family pet, Kavalek proudly told me that the machine scanned through its database at the rate of 2000 entire games per second. So it was a matter of moments, for example, to feed in the name of one of Kasparov's seconds and obtain from the Beast a complete breakdown of that player's repertoire against certain specific openings which Nigel liked to play. Such a file would be very relevant, since it would give a neat encapsulation of the sort of advice that Kasparov might be receiving. With another flick of a switch a chessboard would appear on the screen, and games could be viewed at epilepsy-inducing speed, or, much more laboriously, new analysis by Kavalek and Short could be fed into a file called 'Kasparov Match'. Lubosh would never let me look when he typed out the code word to enter the 'Kasparov Match' file. 'This code word is worth about half a million dollars,' he would insist, 'the difference between the winner's and loser's prize for this match.'

Perhaps it is characteristic of a coach to believe that his manual was the difference between winning and losing. But Kavalek had good reason for his suspicions. If Kasparov could get his hands on the file named in his honour, then Nigel might just as well not bother to turn up for the match: the world champion would have the key to his opponent's every plan and trick. And, Lubosh claimed, his voice sinking from its usual

84

bass-baritone to basso profundo, 'When I was in Lucerne in February for the first round of bidding for the match, Campomanes came up to me and told me to be very, very careful. He said that Kasparov's guys will stop at nothing, they will do whatever they can to get information. Even eavesdropping. Kasparov will have KGB guys with him during the match. He always had connections with these guys. He will try any trick to get the maximum advantage.'

It was not clear to me where Campomanes's warning ended and Kavalek's suspicions took over. But neither was quite as farfetched as it might seem to the chess ingénu. During both his 1983 and his 1990 world championship matches against Karpov, seconds working for Garri Kasparov had been approached and offered bribes in return for handing over the secrets of their man's opening preparation. In 1983 Joe Dorfman was offered a measly 50,000 roubles, but by 1990 Zurab Azmaiparashvili was tempted with a promise of $100,000. In both cases, according to Dorfman, the originator of the bribes was not Karpov himself but Russian mafiosi involved in a betting ring which had placed money on the outsider, Karpov, to win.

In the 1987 match with Karpov, Kasparov claimed that one of his seconds, Vladimirov, did actually sell his opening secrets directly to Karpov. Vladimirov was sacked, but Karpov has always ridiculed Kasparov's allegations. Nonetheless, Honi soit qui mal y pense, or as Lubosh Kavalek would more likely put it, these former Soviet grandmasters are all as bad as each other, and you can't be too careful.

Indeed, while I was staying with Nigel and Lubosh in Reston it became clear that some of their most cherished secrets had leaked out, although not necessarily to the enemy. On 5 August, while we were having a lunch consisting of tinned clam-chowder soup on Kavalek's terrace (lunch always consisted of tinned clam-chowder soup: food for thought is about the only sort that chess grandmasters can cook up), the telephone rang. The caller was the US chess champion, Patrick Wolff, a very ambitious young man. He told Nigel he would like to be part of his analytical team for the world championship match. Nigel expressed his appreciation for the kind offer, but said that there was no vacancy. At which point, to Nigel's horror, Wolff named two of the variations that he and Kavalek had been preparing to use against Kasparov, and said, 'I hear you have been having some difficulty with these lines. I'm sure I can help; I know a lot about them.'

Nigel bluffed his way to the end of the conversation, and came back upstairs at more than his usual slow tread. But other than that I was amazed at the calmness of his reaction. In his position I think I would have thrown my soup against the wall and yelled the house down. If it had been Kasparov, Kavalek would probably have been dismissed on the spot. Nigel just continued eating, and then said, with an understatement remarkable even by British standards, 'This is bad.' Lubosh disappeared to make a few telephone calls of his own. Within minutes he had tracked down the source of the leak. He recognized the lines in question as ones that he and Nigel had studied in April with the eminent Slovak theoretician Grandmaster Lubomir Ftacnik. He, it transpired, had roomed with Patrick Wolff during the US Open Championship. A further call back to Wolff confirmed Ftacnik as the source of the leak. There followed a final call to Ftacnik. I don't speak Czech, but the thunderous roaring from Kavalek left little need for translation. The next day Ftacnik faxed a grovelling letter of apology to Nigel. 'It's a pity I don't have any Croat spies to gather leaks from Kasparov's camp,' was Nigel's deadpan comment.

But there were little dribbles, if not leaks, from the other side. Nigel discovered – how, he would not tell me – that Grandmaster Tony Miles, the man he had ousted as the top British chessplayer, had offered his services to Kasparov. Nigel was far from worried: 'Tony really has never forgiven me for eclipsing him. He hasn't beaten me since I was a kid: and now he proposes to tell Gazza how to win against me. It would be wonderful if he took him on: it would improve my chances immeasurably.' Unfortunately, if understandably, Kasparov rejected Miles's offer.

A more useful dribble of information from the other side came via Malcolm Pein, the proprietor of the London Chess Centre. Pein – who for some reason Nigel always referred as 'the weasel' – called to say that a man associated with Kasparov had ordered an obscure and out-of-print monograph on a particular opening variation known as the Poisoned Pawn. It was not altogether a surprise – Kasparov was known to have played this variation – but such little pieces of intelligence are the next best thing to outright leaks, and they all were fed by Kavalek into the ravenous 'Beast' in the basement.

Up in Kavalek's study there was another beast, but this was his fourteen-year-old King Charles spaniel, Pupjo. Pupjo was blind, and had no sense of direction. He would regularly crash into the chess table as the two men analysed, sending the pieces wobbling on their squares. 'Pupjo!' Kavalek would cry out with a mixture of despair and affection every time the dog's calloused head thumped into the foot of the table, and Nigel steadied the pieces.

In fact that was about the only moving of pieces that Nigel seemed to do for the entire time I was with the two grand-masters. While Kasparov loves to whirl and pound the pieces around the board when he analyses, often crying out 'Shach!' to his bewildered seconds, Short seems to find the idea of banging the pieces on the board, or even moving them at all during analysis, ineffably vulgar. Once the key opening position was set up he would analyse it in his head, as if playing an actual game. Then he would eventually break the silence with a remark such as 'Let me show you an interesting variation, based on the unprotected state of White's queen's rook,' and he would slide the pieces silently around the board, until White's queen's rook did indeed find itself caught between another rook and a hard place.

Kavalek beamingly approved of Short's look-no-hands approach to analysis. 'I won't analyse with the US team any more,' said the coach, 'because they don't sit quietly and analyse properly. New chess positions have to be absorbed slowly. And the less you use hands, the closer you are to a real match situation.'

When Kavalek said 'slowly' he meant it. Quite often the same position would stay on the board for a whole day, with neither man able to agree on even the first move to be played.

On one occasion they spent nine days analysing one move in an obscure subvariation of the Queen's Gambit Declined. At lunch on the ninth day Nigel paused slightly while applying himself thoughtfully to yet another bowl of tinned clam-chowder. 'It doesn't work,' he said, and slurped on. When we sat down together to study the position at the chess table it was clear that Nigel was not hallucinating from an overdose of clams. The cherished opening idea was indeed no good. Days wasted? Nigel didn't seem to care, but simply burst into a raucous rendition of 'Another Opening, Another Show' from *Kiss Me Kate*. On the other hand, when the analysis seemed to be working, Nigel would chant, like some football supporter when his team has scored: 'Here we go, here we go, here we go!' This made Lubosh very happy.

Laughter was never far from the surface, even when, at times, great schemes crumbled into dust. For much of the day coach and player enacted an elaborate charade of pretending that Kavalek was some ancient oriental mystic and Nigel his devoted slitty-eyed pupil, called, for some reason, Caterpillar. 'The sky is high,' Kavalek would say in a mock Japanese accent. 'But there is always something higher than the sky, Caterpillar.' Occasionally Kavalek would break out into real Japanese. Wagging his finger at Nigel he would boom, 'Kazutaka! Takafumi!' ('Respect for harmony! Respect for education!').

There did seem to be a strange rapport between the twenty-eight-year-old Englishman and the fifty-year-old Czech, and Nigel, though a much stronger player than Kavalek had been even at his considerable peak, seemed willing to defer to the older man's judgement – or let him think that he was doing so – on many occasions.

When he did want to discard Kavalek's suggestions, it was usually with gentle humour. On one occasion Lubosh came up with a very strange series of manoeuvres which he wanted his man to try against Kasparov. 'After every one of these moves he will need to calculate for fifteen minutes. So you will gain forty-five minutes on the clock. This is good rope-a-dope stuff.' 'Lubosh,' Nigel replied, 'Gazza isn't a dope. If I play *that* against him, my best chance is that the guy will die laughing.'

On the surface Nigel appeared to be content with the way the preparation was going, but one evening when we had dinner alone in Reston he revealed that he was in fact very concerned. 'Lubosh has been a great coach, in many ways. But I'm worried that, of our new opening ideas for the match so far, I've come up with ninety per cent of them. No, make that ninety-five per cent. Lubosh seems almost totally incapable of coming up with any new ideas himself. And the trouble is that Gazza knows the way I think, so any ideas which are purely my own might not surprise him. The other problem is analysis. Lubosh has a deep knowledge of chess, but he's no longer an active player, and he's not as young as he was. We are going to get some adjourned positions which will require enormous analytical effort: it will be sheer mental effort of calculation, and, with all the other things he must do, Lubosh will be far too tired to do that properly.'

In the match against Timman, the eleventh game had been adjourned in an ending which looked hopeless for Nigel. Kavalek's somewhat sketchy analysis seemed to bear this out. Then at midnight, just as we were despairing, a fax came from London. It was from Jon Speelman, the man whose own world championship aspirations Nigel had destroyed in the quarter-finals. The fax went on for page after page, each one covered with the obscure hieroglyphics of international algebraic chess notation. Some of the moves Speelman had come up with were so paradoxical that Nigel was reduced to helpless giggles as he read through the fax, visualizing the positions. But, at the end of it, his former rival had proved the position to be drawn, and Nigel was as near to being overcome with gratitude as I had ever seen him. But afterwards he brooded on the inadequacy of Kavalek's analysis.

Now, in Reston, on 3 August, barely a month before the match, Nigel decided he needed Speelman on a paid and permanent basis. Down the telephone from London, Speelman expressed his doubts. Quite simply, he was frightened by what he saw as the awesome responsibility. The thought of advocating an idea, whether in the opening or the ending, and then seeing it contemptuously refuted by Kasparov, terrified him, and he was not afraid, at least, to admit it. Nigel calmed him down: 'If you make a crap suggestion and I'm stupid enough to play it, then that's my fault.' On that understanding, Speelman signed up for the duration.

But even after this addition to his intellectual resources, Nigel still felt that the team, in some indefinable way, lacked 'bottom'. He regarded himself as lazy and unmethodical, despite all the unaccustomed work he was now putting in. And Speelman, though an endgame analyst of genius – 'He's a brilliant calculator,' Nigel would say, 'I can just give him a position and switch him on like a computer' – was known to be a 'wild man' in his general approach to the game. Ideas of astonishing brilliance tended to alternate with ones which wasted valuable time. Like most lovers of paradox, Speelman's mind often wandered dangerously from the fantastic to the fanciful.

Two weeks earlier, as we flew together from Athens to Dulles, Washington, Kavalek's local airport, I had suggested to Nigel that, if he wanted a real heavyweight on his team, he could do no better than Dr Robert Hübner. Hübner, who became West German champion at the age of eighteen, and twenty-seven years later was still his country's number one, was the most rigorous analyst in the chess world, with the possible exception of Kasparov himself. Dr Hübner's remarkable analytical mind spread itself over much more than sixty-four squares. His main professional pursuit was the decoding of ancient Egyptian papyrus texts, for which he was justifiably renowned. As a hobby he translates and publishes Finnish satirists into German. For good measure, he was also the only European to compete in the Chinese chess world championships, and was a regular visitor to Peking for this annual event.

But it was as a player of vulgar, modern Western chess that Hübner's machete of a mind most excelled. He had reached the semi-final of the world championships in the late 1970s and was still a match for the best. In particular, he had proved a very difficult opponent for the otherwise rampant Kasparov, and was the last player to have defeated the champion in a tournament game. His approach to the game was a complete contrast to Nigel's reliance on fighting spirit and gut instincts. Hübner was simply a thoroughbred logician, whose published analyses of even a single move from one of his games frequently covered many pages of international chess magazines, to the anguish of their less rigorous readers. His main weakness was that his powers of self-criticism were too finely tuned, and he would often resign in less than hopeless positions, depressed by the discovery of some flaw in his calculations. Characteristically, his only autobiographical chess book is a collection of his own blunders, entitled *Fünfundfünfzig feiste Fehler*.

When I suggested Hübner's name to Nigel he was immediately enthusiastic, pointing out what I had forgotten: that he and Rea were friends of Robert; that the German grandmaster had himself used Kavalek as coach during his own campaign for the world chess championship, and that the two men had remained on good terms. This last point was the most important of all. In a world championship match the analytical team's situation is akin to that of prisoners sharing a cell. For two months they are doomed to virtual incarceration in the same set of hotel rooms, and, with violent intellectual disagreement inevitable at some stage, it is vital for team spirit that the members should have mutual respect and, if not fondness, then certainly toleration for each other's mannerisms.

On 13 August Kavalek called Hübner and asked him to climb aboard. 'It is a very interesting idea,' said Dr Hübner. 'Give me two days to think about it.' Two days later, he called back and asked to speak to Short. 'Nigel,' said the German champion, 'the match starts in three weeks. I would have hoped that your preparation had gone better and that you would not need to call me.'

'I'm sorry, Robert, but we couldn't think of any *good* analysts,' Nigel replied, picking up on the undertone of humour of Hübner's comment.

'Had you thought of Garri Kasparov? He is very good.'

'I believe he is otherwise engaged.'

'So am I,' said Hübner, tantalizingly. 'But I am now cancelling all my September and October commitments.' In other words, Robert Hübner was on board. It was only just in time. Within a few days of starting work, the good doctor's mental nutcracker had shattered one of Short's and Kavalek's prepared opening variations. 'Still,' said Nigel with a rueful grin, 'it's better Robert does it now than Gazza at the board.'

Nigel now had the intellectual resources, innate and acquired, with which to fight Kasparov and his team on something approaching equal terms. But the *mens sana* was of little use if it was not inside *corpore sano*. A match for the world chess championship is as much a strain on the body as it is on the mind. To play twenty-four chess games at that level over a period of two months burns up calories at a prodigious rate, partly through the expenditure of pure mental effort, partly through the sheer stress of the experience.

At times Nigel underestimated this phenomenon. During the negotiations in London back in March, I was in Kasparov's hotel suite when the two men had a disagreement over the pacing of their forthcoming match. Kasparov wanted there to be a three-day break in the middle of the match. 'No,' said Nigel. 'Why should we have a holiday?' Kasparov looked amazed. 'Nigel, you have never been involved in a match of this intensity. I can assure you that it is no holiday.'

Kasparov owed his world title in large part to his extraordinary physical robustness. His first match against Karpov, in 1984–5, was subject to a now abandoned system under which the victor was the first to win six games, no matter how long it took. Karpov rushed into a 5–0 lead, and Kasparov's chess obituary was widely published. But then the younger man dug in and the match dragged on for six months, well into the Russian winter. At this point Karpov was a regular outpatient at a Moscow clinic, and began to lose game after game, before his friend Florencio Campomanes 'stepped in to prevent', as the boxing writers put it, 'further punishment'. As Kawabata wrote in his own novelistic account, *Master of Go*, of the no less exhausting struggle for the supreme title in the Japanese equivalent of chess: 'The required concentration cannot be maintained or the tension endured for whole months. It means something akin to a whittling away of the player's physical being.'

'Whittling away' is a very exact description. I was disturbed by Nigel's appearance, even after his final eliminator with

Timman. He admitted that he had lost four kilos during the match and that 'If I lose kilos at the same rate in the match against Kasparov I will shed ten per cent of my body weight.' And it is not as though Nigel was a man carrying much surplus flab in the first place.

Since Rea was unable to persuade her husband to fatten himself up, even with the most tempting dolmades, the only alternative was to make himself as physically fit as possible, and hope to get by on pure stamina. In London, back in March, Nigel had paid a visit to the physiotherapist of the world 100-metre champion, Linford Christie. The medic declared the chess Grandmaster to be disgustingly unfit, but, as Nigel proudly reported to me immediately afterwards, 'He went over my whole body and said that I had an "excellent inner balance".' In other words, there was no reason, other than laziness, why Nigel should not become very fit. So off Kavalek dragged his pupil every day to the Reston Health Club, one of those gyms which resemble a torture chamber, with rows of racks and pulleys.

I went once or twice myself, and joined Nigel on the computerized rowing machines. I started at a great lick, and noticed after a few minutes that, according to my screen, I was about ten lengths ahead of Nigel. I made the mistake of telling him. Suddenly he began to accelerate and all the while he looked from his screen to mine, to see if he could outpace me before the race came to its timed end. As he overtook me, he let out a whoop, and then as he ploughed further into the lead: 'You're gone! Busted! Not a hope!' Nigel Short adores winning.

The trainer at the Reston Health Club, a gimlet-eyed strip of muscle called Craig, was suitably puzzled when Kavalek introduced Nigel and explained the reason for the new member's arrival. 'Chess?' said Craig. 'Are the pieces *sooo* heavy? Har, har!'

A few weeks later, however, Craig thought he had finally worked out the real reason for the Limey's regular visits. 'I got it! You want to be able to beat the guy up if you lose to him!'

Perhaps Nigel secretly harboured similar thoughts. If so, pictures published in the *Sunday Express* soon disabused him of such notions. They showed Kasparov at his training camp in

Croatia, supervised by his 'fitness coaches' Alexander Kosik and Yevgeny Borisov, lifting what appeared to be a weight of 100 kilograms, substantially more than the champion's own body-weight. 'A hundred kilos!' Nigel exclaimed as he flicked through the pictures. 'I'm doing forty! He's like Tarzan beating his chest in the jungle. He's an ape-man.'

The challenger was not too worried, despite his astonish-ment. His own exercises were much more attuned to endurance than to explosive physical strength. As Kavalek told the Reston gym instructor, 'We are training for a marathon, not a sprint.' And Nigel had formed a very definite view about the champion's metabolism, which, he hoped, might work to his advantage in the match.

He recalled vividly the speed chess match they had played in London in 1987. In the six-game match played over three days Kasparov led by four wins to one with one game to go. For the final afternoon's game Nigel was driven in the same car as Kasparov to the venue. 'I was amazed,' Nigel recalled. 'He seemed completely shattered, almost unable to stay awake.' Nigel duly won the last game, via a completely losing position, which Kasparov was too exhausted to exploit.

During their negotiations together in London, Short had a much closer and sustained opportunity to see how Kasparov ticked. 'He is quite extraordinary,' Nigel told me after one such bout of negotiations. 'He became very tired, but he didn't realize it. Then his mood-swings became wild: from being affectionate towards me to screaming at me, all within moments. That's when he's vulnerable. I can imagine him turning on his seconds when things go wrong, which will use up even more of his energy. He doesn't have a stable temperament, so I must exploit that in some way, make him frustrated.'

I pointed out that Kasparov seemed to have more than enough energy to spare for all his needs, particularly over the chessboard. But Nigel insisted that he had found a weakness. 'Kasparov has a particular kind of energy. It's very intense. But it exhausts him. I've seen him fail to win many games he should have, in the fifth and sixth hour of play. That's when he's most vulnerable. You have to absorb this great burst of energy, this weightlifter's energy. Perhaps it might work for me like Muhammed Ali against George Forman. Something like rope-a-dope. But it's not in my hands. I have to wait for Gazza to become frustrated or tired. Then he might begin to become irrational.'

Perhaps it was modest of Nigel to say that it was not in his hands. It seemed that he had worked out a way to provoke such frustration on the part of the champion, if only off the board. Soon after both players had arrived in London for their match in the last week of August, Short gave a press conference at which he ridiculed Kasparov's claims to be a Western-style democrat and reminded the press of the champion's previous support for the communist Gorbachev, which featured in the first edition of Kasparov's autobiography, but was, in old Stalinist style, cut out of the next edition.

Short went on to claim that Kasparov had been 'trained by the KGB to intimidate his opponents'. Kasparov was confronted by these accusations almost as soon as he touched down at Heathrow airport, and duly lost his temper, describing the KGB allegations as 'complete lies'. That evening I rang Nigel and asked him the source of the information about Kasparov's KGB training. It was a Serbian grandmaster renowned for his credulity. 'Are you trying to get Kasparov wired?' I asked. Nigel could hardly stop giggling, as he contemplated his opponent's consternation. 'Well, it certainly can't do me any harm.' This rather unscrupulous tactic served another, more important purpose. It was meant to demonstrate to the champion that the challenger was not afraid.

Not afraid, perhaps, but getting nervous. On Friday, 3 September, the two players were obliged to attend a lunch together at Simpson's in the Strand, at which they would draw lots to decide who should have White in the first game of the match. The night before, I spoke to Nigel and he suddenly seemed very nervous, his voice tight. Was the proximity of the battle suddenly sinking in? 'No,' said Nigel. 'I just don't want to socialize with the guy before the match. I just want to play some chess.'

If Nigel was reluctant to see his opposite number, the same could not be said of Rea. Her opponent was not Kasparov's wife Maria. She had been left behind with the baby in Moscow.

Kasparov's source of domestic security, delegation chief and padded shoulder to cry on was, as ever, his mother Klara. As Klara, wearing a turquoise Chanel suit, walked into Simpson's, Rea's eyes followed her, taking in her every nuance. 'Good,' said Rea, as we stood drinking champagne in the milling crowd. 'Look at Mrs Kasparov. She has dyed her hair blonde. She is wearing clothes that are too young for her.' I asked Rea why that was so wonderful. 'I thought Mrs Kasparov was a very strong woman. But if she is desperately trying to hold on to her youth, then that is a weakness. Maybe she is less strong than she was.'

Meanwhile her husband was drawing lots with Mrs Kasparov's little treasure. Following an excruciating fanfare of trumpets the champion was asked to open one of two Russian matruschka dolls presented to him. One would contain an effigy of Short, the other an effigy of Kasparov. Whichever one emerged would denote the player to perform the second stage of this elaborate operation. Kasparov rattled one of the dolls. 'This one sounds like you, Nigel,' he said and opened the doll. Out rolled Nigel's effigy.

To another fanfare, even more out of tune than the first, two gigantic chess knights, towering over the players and each draped in the thickest red velvet, were wheeled into the dining room. Nigel stared at them for a few silent seconds, and then waved his arm at the shrouded figure on the left. A final fearful fanfare, and the velvet drapes were lifted away to reveal a Black knight. The world champion would have the advantage of the White pieces in the first game.

As Nigel sat down next to me I attempted to console him by pointing out, somewhat fatuously, that he would have the White pieces in the twenty-fourth and last game, upon which the result of the match could depend. He waved the arm which had just chosen Black: 'I couldn't care less what colour I have for the first game. And, anyway, what makes you think I'll let him go the distance?'

I left the opening ceremony in the company of Kavalek and we wandered into the Savoy Theatre; in four days' time it would become the scene of the struggle he had prepared so long for, but now it was empty and quiet. I remarked that everything seemed so calm; it was hard to imagine what was to come. 'At this stage we are now in the eye of the hurricane,' said Lubosh. 'Imagine you are in a house in the exact eye of a hurricane. There is complete calm. But you know you have to go out, and when you go out the winds will hit you.' Lubosh smiled. 'And, until you step out, you have no idea how wild and strong those winds will be, and whether you can survive them.'

CHAPTER SIX

I f one must leave one's house in the middle of a hurricane, it is as well to be attached to something large and heavy. Not just any piece of furniture will do. Perhaps some such thought lay behind Nigel Short's choice of chair for his two months of intimate physical and mental proximity to Garri Kasparov. He selected an imposing high-backed mahogany number, with a thin coating of brass-studded leather the only forgiving element in an otherwise rigid composition.

Great significance attaches to such matters in world championship matches. The contestants will be spending well over 100 hours fixed in one spot, under the most appalling mental stress. Every other world championship contender in recent memory has demanded a low-slung soft leather affair with plenty of give and suspension. That was exactly the sort of chair which the world champion chose for his two months on the stage of the Savoy Theatre, and he commented with some incredulity on the apparent discomfort of his opponent's old-fashioned throne-like construction. During the match however, Kasparov discovered the one tactical advantage of the heavyweight chair: whenever Nigel pushed it back in order to leave the board, it grated deeply and noisily against the floor.

It has become the fashion in such matches – I believe Boris Spassky was the originator – for the players to sit at the board only when it is their turn to move, or when the position has become particularly tense and exciting. At other times, they retire to 'rest rooms' off-stage, where they can view the game on a closed-circuit monitor and reflectively munch a sandwich – or in Kasparov's case build up further energy by incessant consumption of bars of chocolate.

On the last weekend before the match Nigel was given a form to fill in by the match managers, CPMA, asking what he wanted to have provided in his rest room. Under 'special requests' Nigel

98

inscribed in his tiny, neat handwriting, 'Coffee; any sandwiches other than ham; regular massages from Madonna.' On Monday, 5 September, the day before the first game, CPMA responded, 'Mr Short: Massages from Madonna arranged. Coffee proving a bit more of a problem.'

The organizers, however, also seemed to know when Mr Short was not being facetious. He had become concerned at the possibility – one could put it no higher – that he might be bugged. It was a question not just of his own suite at the Savoy, but, more critically, of Kavalek's, a few doors down on the sixth floor, which also contained the office in which the two of them, together with Robert Hübner and Jon Speelman, would throughout the match discuss and analyse the variations designed to confound all of Kasparov's tricks.

It was not that Nigel specifically thought that Kasparov would be trying to hack into his opening secrets – he did not have that low an opinion of the champion, although Kavalek certainly believed that the man was capable of it. The challenger himself was more concerned that some freelancer might think that there was money to be had in the taping and passing on of such material.

On the afternoon before the first matchgame I walked into Nigel's suite to find three men in his bedroom – and only one of them was him. One of the two I didn't know was attaching a strange device to the bedside telephone. The other seemed to be scanning the room with what looked like a particularly vicious ghetto-blaster. These were the debuggers, requested by Nigel and supplied by the organizers. I asked the man with the ghetto-blaster what he was doing. 'Scanning the frequencies,' he said. I nodded sagely. He carried on, 'First we search; then we find.'

'And then you destroy?'

'Yes. Or we can use their device to send back false information.'

Nigel thought this was wonderful: 'That's more like it! That's more like it!'

After about two and a half hours, during which the debuggers said what a pleasant change this made from boardroom battles and high financial skulduggery, they found nothing. They then declared that 'The environment is sterile'.

'But', they lectured us, 'it's up to you to keep it sterile. People coming in with presents, or just leaving things in the room. Or hotel staff who aren't.'

'Don't worry about that,' said Nigel, 'I've got security.'

Indeed he had. The organizers had also provided him with two bodyguards from a firm called Showsec, and, appropriately for a chess grandmaster, one was white and one was black. The white guard, known as Rob, sat outside the bedroom with massive dignity, stirring only to accompany Nigel on his regular walks, most often around St James's Park. Rob's improbable physique was at once a source of admiration and bemusement for Nigel. 'Garri Kasparov claims he can lift one hundred kilograms,' he would say to the guard. 'How much can you lift?'

'Two hundred,' said Rob, without a hint of pride.

'Well, if you see a hairy Russian wandering around here, just do your stuff.' Rob said he would be sure and do his stuff.

The hairy Russian, a.k.a. the world chess champion, in fact had a suite and two other rooms three floors down at the back of the Savoy, but he preferred to stay at a rented house near Regent's Park. There were two advantages to this from Kasparov's point of view: the Savoy could not spare the space for all of his swollen retinue of grandmasters and fitness coaches; and the home from home could be run entirely by his mother according to his wishes.

On a walk with Nigel and his seconds on the morning of the first game, I asked Rob how his colleagues found working for the world champion. 'Oh no,' he replied, 'he said he didn't need any looking after from us, although we was offered by the organizers. He said he had his own people.'

I asked who these people were.

'Well, the talk among the lads – and lots of us have worked in Russia – is that they're people who used to work for a certain organization, but are now self-employed.'

'You mean a certain organization with three initials?' I asked as Rob cleared our path down the Strand like a whale scattering minnows in its wake.

'Yeah,' said the guard, 'and it's not MFI.'

I laughed much more than the joke warranted. Of course, I was nervous. The first game was due to start in about three hours' time and then Nigel's pretensions, claims and ambitions would start to be revealed: perhaps as a humiliating sham, perhaps as a glorious gamble, and perhaps as the simple, unstoppable truth. As we walked the last tourist-tangled few yards down the Strand, Nigel turned to me: 'When I win this match, Kasparov will like me for it.' Hübner, Kavalek and I stared at him. 'Just mark my words. Something odd is going on here. Something very odd. He has a great burden, which he wants me to take on. But he doesn't quite realize it. He just envies me my normal, happy family life. I sense it. And it's something the world chess champion can never have.'

'I think', said Robert Hübner, in his very deliberate accent, stressing every syllable, 'that he will not give you this great burden. You might have to take it from him.'

Rea, at any rate, was leaving nothing to chance. That morning she had gone to Harrods and bought Nigel a special tie which, she told me with a light laugh, was 'very naughty'. When Nigel ceremoniously put it on in front of me in his hotel room, I could see what she meant: it had one of those patterns of black and white zigzagging lines which, if looked at for more than a few seconds, have a strangely hypnotic effect. He was delighted with it: 'Perhaps Gazza will fall asleep, looking at it. There's a chance.' (Robert Hübner was less impressed when I told him later about this sartorial addition to the match preparations: 'Oh, this tie business – it's a very old idea.')

Another idea of Rea's was that Nigel should try to sleep, or at least rest, for an hour before the beginning of every game. She did not altogether care to see her husband work himself up into a frenzy, which he had before some games in the Karpov match. As I left them, Nigel seemed unable to believe the moment had actually arrived.

'I feel nervous,' he said as he gently strummed his guitar, 'but not that much. I felt much worse before the Timman match. My hands were shaking then, but now they're steady. The thing is, I have no idea whether I'll feel right until the moment I touch the pieces, actually feel them in my hands. If I am on form then I won't worry about my brain, because the first move that comes into my head will be the best. I can just play with my hands, quickly, with a good rhythm.' Nigel put down the guitar. 'But if I start to think for a long time, then you can tell that I'm in trouble.'

I went off to Kavalek's room where the coach sat with his good friend and compatriot Milos Forman, the chess-mad film director, who was in London to see the first few games of the match. At twenty past three, ten minutes before the game, Nigel came in, wearing a brand-new suit, which hung on him crease-lessly. We all stood up, as if royalty had entered the room. It was a strange moment.

'Okay,' said Kavalek. 'Now the fun begins.' 'It's showtime,' said Forman, equally unconvincingly. Nigel walked up to each of us, and we slapped hands with him, rather self-consciously, in the black-American style. Nigel liked to do this before a game, but now it seemed a little forced, or perhaps we were all too tense.

Then Nigel disappeared. The Savoy had, at first reluctantly, given him permission to use an old fire-exit route from the hotel to the theatre, which meant that he would never need to walk through the hordes waiting outside for a glimpse of the players. Apart from anything else, on the first day of the match alone, 500 journalists were accredited, many of them photographers. It was with some difficulty that Kavalek and I, travelling economy class, made our way through that mêlée and down into the auditorium.

It was probably just a coincidence that the champion, playing with the White pieces, was wearing a white suit, while the challenger playing Black, was attired in a subfusc number: but it made a good picture for the banks of photographers as the players walked in from opposite sides of the auditorium and shook hands. One of the two match arbiters, the former Soviet champion Yuri Averbakh, started the champion's clock. Each player would have two hours to complete his first forty moves.

The other match arbiter, Carlos Falcón of Spain, had whispered to Nigel as he moved towards the board, 'Mr Short: Mr Kavalek asks me to send you his very best wishes for the game.' This was a ritual from Nigel's match against Karpov, where Mr Falcón was also the arbiter. Kavalek then had arranged for Falcón to say this to Short at the start of every game, and the Czech, a great believer in the power of ritual, wanted the same routine to operate in London.

Unlike Karpov, Kasparov seemed not in the least bothered by this exchange, bared his teeth at Nigel in his best crocodile grin, and played the opening move we had expected, pawn to king four. It was not a foregone conclusion. Unlike most grandmasters Kasparov is equally happy playing kingside and queenside openings. But it was to be the kingside for the first game, at least. The players headed off down the most routine line, until Nigel's seventh move signalled that he was prepared to play the most controversial gambit in all of chess theory, since it was first played seventy-five years ago – the Marshall. The idea is to give up a pawn, perhaps more, in return for an attack whose soundness is questionable but as yet unrefuted. This would be the manly, non-quiche-eating chess that Nigel had sworn he would play against the champion. It was a declaration, barely ten minutes into the match, that he was not afraid.

But was the champion afraid? He smiled ruefully at the move. He could either play the standard reply and be prepared to take on what he knew must be reams of prepared analysis by Short and Kavalek. Or he could sidestep the threatened gambit with a move which would force the contest into serene strategic waters, not thought to be the champion's strong point. After a few minutes' thought, much of them spent staring not at the board, but at Lubosh Kavalek sitting next to me in the front row of the stalls, Kasparov sidestepped, with a rather anaemic line known to chessplayers, logically enough, as the Anti-Marshall.

It was not, of course, pure cowardice. The champion had made the first discovery of the match, that his opponent was prepared to offer a particular gambit. Now, at the board, he had avoided it, but he could go back to his safe-house after the game, and instruct his team to subject the Marshall to intensive analysis.

If they found a hole in it, one could be sure the champion would not duck Short's challenge a second time.

Even having avoided the most critical line, in this first game, Kasparov still managed to build up an imposing position with the simplest of means. But, in chess, nothing is as difficult as simplicity. Kasparov was running short of time. And Nigel was consuming equally prodigious amounts of thought. Only a few hours earlier he had told me that I would know he was in trouble if he was moving very slowly. So I knew, or thought I knew, that he was in trouble. On the other hand, neither grandmaster had played a chess game in anger for at least four months as they honed their armouries for the match. Perhaps Nigel was just a bit rusty. Perhaps they were both rusty.

By move thirty-two, Kasparov had only two minutes to play his last nine moves to the time-control. Nigel had just one minute left. At that point the champion threw the dice. He sacrificed a pawn for what looked like a direct checkmating attack on Nigel's king. In a flurry of hands darting across the board Kasparov thrust and Short parried. The moves, through software implanted in the squares below the players' pieces, were immediately registered on two giant electronic screens at the back of the darkened stage. At the speed the players were now exchanging blows the pieces seemed to be flitting about on the screens like fireflies in the gloaming. And Nigel's seemed all of a sudden to be in the ascendant. He was still a pawn up, and Kasparov's attack had evaporated.

The players had long since given up writing down their moves, or even marking the number on their score sheets with frenzied dashes. The two arbiters, Carlos Falcón and Yuri Averbakh, had stepped to the side of the board, Falcón keeping a count of Kasparov's moves and looking at the champion's side of the clock, Averbakh doing the same for Short. Suddenly Averbakh stepped forward and said something to Short. He seemed to have difficulty in understanding what the arbiter was saying. Then he appeared to grasp it and slumped back in his chair. Silently he mouthed the words to Kavalek in the front row, 'I have lost on time.'

The audience, however, could not read Nigel's lips, and

many of them were shouting out that Kasparov had resigned or possibly had lost on time. The game had clearly come to an end, and neither player looked very happy. And both clock flags appeared to have fallen. In fact, as Nigel told me later, Kasparov's clock flag had fallen only seconds after his own. Finally, Averbakh stepped round to the front of the stage and ended the pandemonium in the audience by announcing, in his heavily accented English, 'Ladies and gentlemen, I have to tell you that the challenger has lost the game by time-default. The champion leads the match by one point to nil.' The groan in the theatre reminded me of nothing so much as Covent Garden when it is announced that the star Italian tenor has a sore throat and his place will be taken by some nonentity.

Nigel finally stood up; Kasparov remained seated and tried to engage his opponent in a discussion of the game, but without much success. A few minutes later I rushed up to Nigel's room, where he was being consoled by Rea and Robert Hübner. Kavalek was nowhere to be found. Nigel did not appear to be taking much in and was leaning against his bathroom door with a puzzled expression on his face. 'I had no idea I had so little time,' he said in a voice even slower than his usual measured cadence. It looked almost as if his lips were not in synch with the words which were coming out. 'I had no idea I had so little time,' he repeated. 'They said my clock fell just as I played my thirty-ninth move, but I had the impression I'd played even fewer moves. I was just concentrating on the position.'

This rang true. Most grandmasters, when short of time, frequently look back and forwards from the clock to the board; this division of concentration often leads to bad moves being made. Nigel, however, has a peculiarly intense concentration, even by the standards of chess grandmasters, and he rarely lets his eyes become distracted from the position on the board. On this occasion, he was immersed in such depths of concentration, as he repulsed Kasparov's attack, that he simply forgot about time altogether.

As he wandered in from the bathroom to the sitting room, Nigel began shaking his head. 'It was very strange. I felt like a zombie throughout the game. I didn't feel nervous at all. It was almost as if I was watching myself from above.' He pulled out a tissue and blew his nose. I knew that he had had a slight cold for days, although characteristically he did not blame anything on that. 'No, I just wasn't calculating well. That's why I was taking so long over my moves.'

Then he smiled. 'You know, the guy offered me a draw, the move before I lost on time.' I think we were all astounded. Nigel – who had not won a game against the champion since 1986 – in the first game of a world championship match, with the Black pieces, with virtually no time left on his clock, and with the final wave of the attack yet to be beaten off, *had turned down Kasparov's offer of a draw*? Robert Hübner broke the silence of our wild surmise. 'Nigel,' he said in his most level voice, 'I think that, with the benefit of hindsight, you should have accepted his offer.'

'But, Robert, you should have seen what happened. The guy tried to swindle me. He played a pawn sacrifice to frighten me in my time-trouble. I play some accurate moves, and finally one which he had missed. So he tries to grovel out, plays a check and says "Draw?" He's been torturing me throughout the entire game, and now I'm a pawn up with a better position, and he thinks he can get a draw whenever he wants. Maybe he realizes now that he can't swindle me and get away with it.'

'Well, I still would have accepted the draw,' said Hübner, 'but then I admit that I am terrified when I have less than ten minutes left on my clock.'

Of course Nigel did not realize he had barely ten seconds left when Kasparov offered him a draw. And his explanation of why he spurned the offer was a much more detailed version of what must have gone through his mind at the time. Film of the game shows that, when Kasparov offered the draw, Short just ignored him and moved instantly. It was the best move in the position, and, in the circumstances, also the worst.

We went downstairs and found Lubosh Kavalek and Milos Forman carousing in the bar. Rea's face was a picture. She was scandalized that her husband's chief second should be having a good time with an old drinking partner rather than attending to the post-game discussion. Kavalek did not notice Rea's thunderous look, however; but he was brought up short when Hübner told him that Nigel had turned down a draw in the time scramble.

'He offered you a *draw?*' Kavalek asked, not once but twice. 'Yes,' said Short. Kavalek fell silent. It was left to Milos Forman to give the advice. 'Nigel,' he exclaimed, 'promise me, promise me, that you will never ever again in this match forget about your clock.' Nigel promised.

The next morning, on the rest day allotted between games one and two, I went over events with Rea. She was still furious at Kavalek's behaviour, and in particular the fact that he was spending more time with his film-director friend than with Nigel. 'On the night before the first game he was boozing with Forman. During the game he is sitting next to Forman. After the game he goes out and has another good drinking session with Forman. Is he Forman's coach or Nigel's? Who is paying him?'

I asked Rea why she hadn't said anything to Kavalek about this. 'I am going to be all sweetness and light, the model of hypocrisy. He will not know what I am thinking. But when the time comes, I will act. And so will Nigel.'

CHAPTER SEVEN

C hess grandmasters are frequently compared to tennis professionals. On that analogy, Nigel Short is very much a serve-and-volley player. When he is receiving – playing with the Black pieces – he will often concede draws, however reluctantly, to relatively weak players. But when he has the White pieces he is universally feared. Pawn to king four is his serve, and it is the inevitable prelude to any one of a number of violent attacking formations, all played with the chessic equivalent of vicious topspin.

Which is all another way of saying that Nigel Short was looking forward to his second match-game against Kasparov. It was not just that Nigel had the White pieces. It was also much easier to prepare for Kasparov when the champion had the Black pieces. Against Nigel's pawn to king four – against *anybody's* pawn to king four – the world champion always played the most challenging and complicated of all defences: the Sicilian. Anatoly Karpov was so shattered by the mauling he received from Kasparov's Sicilian over a number of world championship matches that he had given up playing pawn to king four altogether.

Moreover Kasparov always played the most hair-raising variation of the Sicilian defence, one named after the Argentine Grandmaster Najdorf but actually honed into a deadly weapon by Bobby Fischer. Kasparov played the Najdorf variation, as Fischer did, with immense sharpness and precision. For these two world champions the Sicilian was not a defence at all. It was an attempt, against the logic of the game taught to children down the ages, to prove that Black need never defend, but can fight for the advantage from the first move.

There is one, most critical move against the Najdorf variations which leads into the most vertiginous complications of all. This response by White on the sixth move, moving his king's bishop to attack Black's king's knight, forces the game into some of the most head-spinning mêlées known to chess theory. It is a brutal attempt to bust the Najdorf variation. It is called, simply, the Main Line. But Nigel Short had never played the Main Line against Kasparov. Like almost every other grandmaster, including Karpov, he had never dared to. Instead Nigel had devised another, less direct sixth move, with the same king's bishop. He had played it with such success that it had become taken up by other professionals all over the world and was now known to chess theory as the Short Attack.

Nigel's only full-scale tournament win against Kasparov came through playing the Short Attack against the champion's Najdorf variation. But that was in 1986, and since then the champion had given the Short Attack a fearful mangling whenever its originator had played it against him. Nonetheless, with the world championship at stake, Kasparov would have expected to see Nigel defend the honour of his own variation.

When Nigel pushed his inevitable king's pawn forward two squares to open the second game of the match, Kasparov paused, most unusually, for a full minute. Perhaps, as Nigel explained after the game, it was Kasparov's way of hinting, either truthfully or as a decoy, that he had many other defences prepared, and that the challenger should not count on a Sicilian.

But it was to be a Sicilian, and the first few standard moves flashed up on the illuminated screens behind the players. Then, on move six, Nigel picked up his king's bishop, lifted it clean over the square demanded by the Short Attack, and placed it to attack the champion's knight. This was the Main Line. Kasparov's thick black eyebrows, always a wonderful source of expressiveness, performed a dense little pirouette. Again he turned to look at Kavalek in the hall to try to read the eyes of Nigel's trainer. But Kavalek was way up in the dress circle with Milos Forman, so Kasparov just stared into space, drumming his fingers on the table distractedly.

We had thought that there was no way back for Black in this position, that a head-on collision was inevitable. But Kasparov found a devious way to sidestep even the Main Line, with an obscure sixth move hardly seen since the 1970s. Nigel looked very puzzled. Like Kasparov he tends not to look at the board when he is in such a quandary. But unlike Kasparov he turns away from the audience and towards the demonstration boards. It is all an attempt to hide from the opponent's eyes any uncertainty in one's own.

Nigel seemed to be smiling as he stared at the flickering images to his left. For a second time the champion had chickened out. Again, he had rapidly avoided the main challenge of Short's opening. And, again, it made perfect sense. This was a twenty-four-game match. Kasparov would now subject the Main Line to hours of midnight oil. And at some point, in one of the even-numbered games, he would be ready to plunge into the awesome depths of Main Line chess theory, pitting his team's prepared analyses against Nigel's. But not now, not today, not on Thursday, 9 September.

Nigel spent about half an hour reorienting himself to the new sort of position, avoiding half-forgotten tricks which had caught out grandmasters twenty years before. And, emerging from the unfamiliar opening, he got the sort of position he likes: it pointed in the direction of his opponent's king. Kasparov, however, suddenly began to look very uncomfortable. He loosened his tie and began to wipe his forehead with the back of his hand. He spent an hour over three ugly-looking but defensively essential moves. Then he removed his watch from his wrist, and placed it in front of him, as if to remind himself of the need to move more quickly. Even from several rows back in the auditorium one could see the muscles in his jaws rippling under the skin. The champion was grinding his teeth, as Nigel later confirmed to me.

As the position became less and less palatable, Kasparov's moves seemed almost to dry up. His clock showed that he had seven minutes left to make fifteen moves. Short had thirteen minutes. We were in for another time-scramble, and in this one Nigel had the advantage. But with three moves left to make, and two minutes left on his clock, Nigel let slip the one clear winning opportunity which Kasparov's desperate defence had allowed.

During this game, as in every game in the match, there was a room set aside in Simpson's, two doors down the Strand from the theatre, in which visiting grandmasters analysed the game and prepared a bulletin. It was very interesting to see how they consistently overestimated Kasparov's moves and underestimated Nigel's in this game. Manoeuvres which had Kasparov sweating at the board were roundly and instantly denounced as 'premature' by the grandmaster pundits. It seemed to me that the extraordinary mystique of Kasparov's invincibility and the presence he generates at the board had enough power to sway the judgement of grandmasters 200 yards away.

At the board itself, Nigel could easily sense Kasparov's sheer relief as the position ebbed away towards a draw. It was clear, however, that Kasparov did not want to be the one to offer it this time. Instead he kept glancing up at Nigel in an enquiring fashion. Nigel just looked away and kept on playing. It was not that he was still trying to win, as the game dragged on into a sixth hour. It was just that he needed to savour the struggle for a few moves more. Finally Nigel did not so much offer a draw as force it, with an elegant little sacrifice. Kasparov blew out his cheeks and sank back into his chair. The grandmasters at Simpson's were busy saying how Short was fortunate to have escaped with a draw. Garri Kasparov knew better.

Just after the game, up in his hotel room, I told Nigel how some of the pundits had been writing off his position at various stages. He looked amazed. 'I can tell you, he was frightened. When I doubled my rooks against his king I smelt it.'

'Smelt what?'

'I smelt his fear.'

It wasn't just this olfactory pleasure which had Nigel grinning in that exaggeratedly toothy way of his. He was also pleased at the way he had not faded during the fifth hour of play, as the game moved into its second session. 'I'm sure this is the result of my physical preparation. In the old days I would have been feeling really tired at that stage, but in the fifth hour today I experienced almost no loss of energy. And perhaps he could feel that, which is why he wanted a draw.'

Nigel moved towards the bathroom and then popped his head back round the door: 'And by the way, did you notice how he chickened out in the opening again? I play a *hombre* move, and he runs.'

Downstairs, however, Kavalek was much gloomier about developments. 'Kasparov is being very clever, Nigel. He is finding out everything. He has found out that we intend to play the Marshall. He has found out that we will play the Main Line against the Najdorf. Now he can pick his moment to hit them when he wants.'

Nigel looked immensely irritated. 'What has he found out about the Marshall? He knew before the match that I play this variation. But he's yet to find out what new ideas I have. What has he found out about the Main Line? I've shown nothing yet. And you know very well I have another big hit prepared against the Najdorf which he can't even guess at.'

There was another reason for Nigel's irritation. Kavalek had asked him to come out for dinner that evening with Milos Forman and another of his glittering friends, Peter Ustinov. But after over five hours of brain-to-brain combat with Garri Kasparov, the last thing Nigel wanted was a long viniferous dinner of wit and repartee with such loud and exhausting characters. He left it to Rea to decline the invitation, which she did with great pleasure.

Meanwhile, he told Kavalek to do some specific work on the Anti-Marshall which Kasparov had played in the first game with such success and which was likely to recur in the next game, when Kasparov again had the White pieces. He gave the same work to Hübner and Speelman, which I thought an odd use of resources, but Nigel, as ever, had a reason: 'So far Lubosh has done no work in London at all. If I give him the Anti-Marshall to analyse, it probably won't get done at all. Robert and Speely I can rely on.'

The next afternoon all five of us met up in the analysis room, to discuss collectively the results of the team's separate analyses. It was immediately clear that Nigel's suspicions were well founded. Kavalek produced precisely nothing and looked increasingly ill at ease as first Speelman and then Hübner demonstrated the results of their work. Some of Speelman's characteristically byzantine and spectacular pieces of analysis – often ending with the phrase 'And it's checkmate, arsehole' – visibly delighted Nigel. Sitting next to Hübner he grinned across

112

the table at Speelman: 'That's what I like to see! That's what I like to see!' Kavalek, I noticed, did not even have a place at the table, but lay on a sofa by the side, like a disgruntled pasha.

Nigel himself rarely offered analysis, but merely expressed gut feelings about the positions which were offered to him by his seconds. 'This feels fine,' he would say, or, quite often, 'No more analysis on this line, please, guys. The whole idea smells.' That approach occasionally seemed to puzzle Speelman, who loved to chase every idea down to its final conclusion, like a ferret after a rabbit. But, as with many child prodigies, Short has always been a natural player, one whose instant, intuitive judgement of a position was more penetrating than most players could achieve through many hours of calculation.

The forty-five-year-old Hübner and the thirty-seven-year-old Speelman were also opposites, though in a different way. The only thing they had in common – apart from the dress sense which scandalized the stuffed shirts at the Savoy – was extreme short-sightedness: both peered at the board through spectacles whose lenses appeared triple-glazed. But Hübner was small and blond, turning bald; Speelman tall, with a superfluity of dark curly hair. And in the chess sense they were opposites too: Speelman desperately seeking to find the exception to every rule; Hübner – in common with many of the greatest German players of the past – convinced of the basic truths of certain principles, which he would then apply with steely reductive logic to any given position. When some of Speelman's more outlandish suggestions offended against these dogmas, however, he was more amused than outraged, occasionally collapsing in hysterical laughter, trying helplessly to utter the word 'Impossible!' Nigel was at least getting two completely divergent views of most positions: the Teutonic and the Anarchic. It was up to him to supply the Pragmatic, if neither of the other approaches appealed.

The outsider, if he looked at the moves of the third London match-game between Kasparov and Short, would judge that the Anarchic tendency had prevailed: its climactic moments were of a complexity and ferocity that reduced the spectators in the Savoy Theatre to gasps of astonishment. They were already keyed up. Short's attack on Kasparov in the previous game had raised the hopes of the home supporters, and this, the third game, was on a Saturday: there was something of the football-crowd atmosphere.

When Nigel's name was announced and he stepped out of the shadows towards the board, there was at least two minutes of thunderous applause, punctuated by whoops and the odd, deafening whistle. Nigel looked a little taken aback, and then his face broke into an immense grin. Although he seems an aloof, even cold man, he covets what support he gets from the British public. He himself is an avid supporter of British teams and sportsmen, whatever the event.

Nigel had rung me in a great state of excitement from America, when Linford Christie won the world 100 metres championship, and was almost unable to contain his exhilaration. And likewise he would expect me to call him in America with all the latest England Test scores. His elation when England finally won a Test was something to listen to: 'It's really lifted me for the match,' he exclaimed. 'These things matter to me.' And I recall that his parting words to a good friend, a few days before the match, were 'For Albion!' So I knew that the cheers Short received at the start of the third game would fire him up, make him even more determined to give of his best.

As in the first game Nigel offered to engage Kasparov in the cut and thrust of the Marshall Gambit. Again Kasparov steered the game into the quiet strategic character of the Anti-Marshall. Again, with the White pieces, the champion rapidly established a clear strategic advantage. And again both players consumed excessive amounts of time on the clock as they sought to find the perfect move at every turn.

This, perhaps, was not too uncharacteristic of Kasparov, who was quoted by his most recent biographer Fred Waitzkin (in the outstanding *Mortal Games*) as follows: 'I want the best, best, best. I'm not playing against my opponent. I'm playing against God.' But Nigel was perhaps unused to this form of struggle. He generally prefers to play quite rapidly, relying on the flow of the moves to generate an almost physical momentum. Unfortunately it seemed he was being dragged into the mire of the Russian's more complex thought-processes. Nigel once laughingly told me that the one advantage of playing Kasparov 'is that he works himself up into a terrible state worrying about moves you would never dream of playing'. It seemed that, in London, Nigel was perhaps seeing too many such phantoms himself.

Whatever his thought-processes, by move twenty, only half-way to the first time-control, Nigel's position was strategically lost. There are two things to do in such a situation. One can curl up into a ball and be slowly suffocated, which is what the vast majority of Kasparov's victims do. Or one can say, as Napoleon's general, Marshal Ney, did: 'My flanks are in retreat, my centre is collapsing: I attack!'

Nigel took the Marshal Ney approach, which at least guaranteed value for money for the Saturday matinée audience at the Savoy Theatre. With brutal directness he simply shifted his entire army towards Kasparov's king. That symbol of the world champion's invulnerability was, however, shored up behind a superbly constructed interlocking carapace of pawns and pieces. With five minutes left on his clock, and still fifteen moves to make before the time-control, Nigel unleashed a series of sacrifices which drew shouts of disbelief from the audience. At first it seemed that his pieces were simply being impaled to no purpose on the barbed wire of the champion's defences. But after the sacrifice of a knight, followed by a rook offer, followed by a knight again, Nigel finally revealed the stunning point: a queen sacrifice which, if accepted, would lead to the instant checkmate of the champion's king.

This last, spectacular coup, Kasparov admitted to Nigel after the game, he had missed. But he still played the only good reply instantly. The world champion too was by now very short of time. Indeed, when I look at my score of the move times, it shows that Nigel's five-move cascade of sacrifices and Kasparov's five replies all came within the space of two minutes. Seeing it at the time was like watching two great tennis players, both at the net, playing ten successive volleys at angles and at a speed which the eye can barely follow. Unfortunately, Short's last volley did not come from the centre of his mental racquet.

On move thirty-one, with three minutes left for ten moves,

Nigel missed the final move of a combination which would have justified his attack, one which would have given him excellent chances to draw – and more, if the champion did not continue to find complex defensive manoeuvres at breakneck speed.

It was horrible to watch Nigel commit the fatal error; from ten yards away I could tell that he knew it was somehow not the right move, but he was still haunted by the loss on time in the first game: he was looking at the clock as much as the board, even as he played the losing blunder.

Many people expected Nigel to resign once the time-control had been reached at move forty. But he looked white with anger, and I knew that, in such a mood, he would play on to the bitterest of bitter ends. Finally on the fifty-ninth move, with the world champion's eyebrows indicating a Kasparovian amazement that surrender had not been tendered long ago, Nigel stopped the clocks and said quietly, 'I resign.'

I arrived in Nigel's room back at the hotel before he did. Rea, Kyveli and Michael Stean were also there. The loser, to his evident displeasure, had first to attend a post-game interview with *The Times*. When he came in, he looked desperately depressed. But then he noticed his little daughter and stroked her head distractedly, before getting up to go towards the bathroom. Daddy had had a tough day at the office. His white shirt was almost translucent with sweat. He took it off and, as he stood, the light from the bathroom seemed to be reflected in the moisture on his bare, hairless chest.

'God, that was terrible,' he groaned. 'The guy completely outplayed me. And the worst thing was, I had no idea what he was up to until after he'd done it to me. I thought I was fine, and then suddenly I woke up to find I was completely busted. Just nothing to do at all.' I tried to console Nigel by complimenting him on the ferocity of his counter-attack. 'No, no,' he waved his hand dismissively, 'that was only possible because Gazza missed an obvious move earlier. I should never have been given the chance to get as far as I did. I didn't deserve it.'

Michael Stean, himself a retired grandmaster, chipped in to say that Nigel had clearly been badly prepared in the opening. How else could he have got a terrible position so early on in the game? Again Nigel disagreed. 'No, this was a perfectly decent position right out of the opening. The guy just outplayed me in a simple position. And if I can't play good moves in a simple position, then what can I do?' Rea indicated that it was time for the other men in the room to leave. To be mended, Nigel's mood needed more than the advice of mere men.

The next morning, Sunday the 12th, the team assembled in the analysis room adjoining Kavalek's bedroom to try to find some improved response to Kasparov's Anti-Marshall, which had now scored two wins from two games. Nigel wandered in to find Kavalek still in his bedroom.

'I told you not to play the line you did against the Anti-Marshall' were Kavalek's opening words. Nigel bridled immediately. 'Lubosh, you were here when we all decided this was the line I would play on Saturday. If you didn't agree, why didn't you say so then? You said not one word against it, while we spent hours analysing it.'

'No, no, I told you months ago, in Reston, that you should play the Main Line against the Anti-Marshall, not the stuff you have been playing here.'

At this point Nigel became so angry that he left the room rather than continue the argument. He could recall no such warning. And he knew there was no special preparation in their files on the line that Kavalek was now saying he had suggested.

Nigel went to see Robert Hübner, who said he was amazed at Kavalek's attitude and confirmed that the coach had made absolutely no such objection to the line he and Speelman had prepared for Saturday's game.

The next morning Nigel called me. His voice sounded strained, and even quieter than usual. 'I'm sacking Kavalek,' he said.

'What, now?'

'Now. I want him out on the next plane. Well, he can spend tonight at the Savoy, but that's it.'

When I asked Nigel why he was acting so precipitately, the floodgates opened. 'He is doing no work at all. Sure, he comes with me on my walks. He swims with me every morning at the RAC Club. But no chess work at all. Just a large variety of excuses for not doing any analysis. Now he says he has a cold. Fuck it, I've had a cold for a week, and I'm playing Garri Kasparov. And Kavalek's cold hasn't stopped him having a high old time every night with Milos Forman, I notice. And as if all this wasn't bad enough, he has to come up to me after I lose with these smart-arse comments about how if I had done as he told me then everything would have been okay. Which is complete bullshit, because he had told me nothing of the sort. I understand, he's upset that I lost these games. But who is the most upset, who has the most to lose? Me. And I just don't need depressing influences at the moment. I need people around me who will offer support, not told-you-so criticism.'

There was, at the back of it all, another reason for Nigel's rage. Shortly before the Timman match, Kavalek had refused to continue as Nigel's coach unless he was also guaranteed employment right through to the end of the world championship cycle. And he had driven a very hard bargain. For his twelve weeks of work with Nigel in Reston, and a further eight weeks during the match with Kasparov itself, Kavalek had negotiated a fee of $125,000, with a bonus of a further $125,000 should Nigel beat Kasparov. 'Only a tiny handful of the very top grandmasters make that much money off their own bat in an entire year,' Nigel complained to me when it was all signed up.

In fact, Kavalek's terms were so tough in certain other ways that Nigel had almost decided to switch coaches. But Rea had been convinced that Kavalek was essential to Nigel's success and, after some very heated discussions in Athens, had persuaded Nigel to stick with his trainer. She felt that, if Nigel's motive was money, that was the wrong reason to ditch the man. The trouble was, however, that because Nigel had long felt he was overpaying for Kavalek's services, he had become almost vengeful once the quality of those services declined. Probably as a result of his experiences as a child prodigy, when he was pushed around by older players and tournament organizers, Nigel has an almost pathological sensitivity to exploitation or manipulation by others. That, in essence, was why he reacted so violently when Fidé decided to award the Kasparov–Short match to Manchester without consulting him. Now Lubosh Kavalek was getting the treatment meted out earlier to Florencio Campomanes.

Having told me he was sacking Kavalek, Nigel then asked if he could spend the next few hours at my house. He explained that he didn't want to be in the Savoy while Kavalek was being fired. Rea would do the deed, with Michael Stean on hand, should the situation develop into a legal wrangle.

As soon as Nigel arrived at my flat and slumped down on a sofa, I asked him the obvious question: was he sacking Kavalek because the match was going badly?

'No. He's not a scapegoat. And my losses have absolutely nothing to do with our opening preparation. But I can't have someone around who is doing no work and just blaming me, because that's a constant source of irritation. Then I have no peace of mind. And I must have peace of mind, or I can't play at all.'

Nigel leant forward and made a movement with his hands as if compressing something into a ball. 'Now things are hard, I need to draw people around me, I need to have a close-knit group of people absolutely behind me. I don't want anyone else.'

This was, of course, a pretty fair definition of the bunker mentality. On the other hand, who would not have felt the same way in Short's position? I tried to steer the conversation towards the next day's game, in which Nigel would have the White pieces. Tomorrow, I said, he must concentrate on killing Kasparov.

'Yes. Tomorrow I must kill Kasparov. But today I am killing my father.' I said I didn't quite see it that way.

'I do,' said Nigel. 'I have spent three years of my life with this man. He was my mentor. In the past year I have seen as much of him as I have of my wife. No, in fact I have spent more time with him than I have with Rea.' Nigel got up to go to the lavatory. He went there four times that afternoon. The thought of the discussion his wife would at that moment be having with his surrogate father was making him almost incontinent with anxiety.

On one return trip he suddenly said, 'Don't you feel the

brutality of this moment? It's parricide.' I began to feel like an extra in *Oedipus Rex*. The only difference was that Oedipus killed his father without realizing the identity of his victim. Nigel understood the significance of his actions. It was torturing him. I have been to films with Nigel when the slightest amount of gore sent him rushing to the gents. Away from the chessboard, he has less tolerance for violence than any man I know. Now he felt violent, even vengeful emotions, but their necessary consequence disgusted him, even as he caused it to be carried out.

By late afternoon, Rea, who felt naturally at home in such a Greek drama, arrived at my flat from her encounter with Lubosh Kavalek. She said that Lubosh had taken his sacking remarkably calmly: 'It was almost as if he had been expecting it.' He had tried to explain why he had had such difficulty in getting any analytical work done in London, but without any great conviction. He had rapidly agreed to leave the next day, Tuesday, 14 September, provided that he could have a letter signed by Nigel's lawyers to the effect that he would be paid in respect of his contract. 'I knew it,' said Nigel, as he lay stretched out on a sofa. 'It's just a question of money for him.' If it was just a question of money, I said, then Kavalek could simply sell all of their opening secrets to the Kasparov camp. A lesser man would have had no hesitation in taking such revenge. But Nigel seemed completely unworried by such a possibility. 'No, all he wants is to be paid off by me.'

Maybe, in the end, it was. But Robert Hübner, who saw Kavalek that evening, told me that he thought Lubosh seemed to be in a state of shock. Perhaps the same was true of his former pupil. When I saw Nigel the next morning his first words were 'I'm free at last. Lubosh has gone.' Then he laughed. 'Do you know, he finally did some analysis, last night, after he had been sacked. He left it with Robert this morning. I suppose it was designed to make him feel less ashamed.' But Nigel's cheerful manner was a deception. He looked exhausted, and admitted, rather unwillingly, that he had scarcely slept at all, and indeed had done not much better the previous night. 'Parricide' had murdered sleep.

This promised disaster for the fourth game, scheduled for

later that day, Tuesday the 14th. Everyone needs sleep to function well, but Nigel has always needed large quantities of it, particularly in major tournaments, to restore his energy to a level where he is capable of calculating variations for five hours without a break. Nine hours a night is his desired minimum. He is not a brute of a man, like Kasparov, who can perform remarkable intellectual feats while physically very tired.

During lunch, less than an hour and half before the fourth game, Nigel began to nod off while sitting upright in his chair, but not before telling me that he had lost three kilos in weight during the first three games of the match. At that rate, he said, there would not be very much left of him after the scheduled twenty-four games. I began to regret that this match was not being played under the old Fidé rules which permitted each player, on four occasions, to postpone a game if he was feeling under the weather. Nigel, however, had denounced this when the rules for the *Times* world championship were being drawn up. 'It's absurd,' he would say, 'whoever heard of a tennis professional at Wimbledon postponing a match because he doesn't feel well? It's just tough.' Now it was tough for Nigel.

As Short walked on to the stage at the start of the fourth match-game, the arbiter, Carlos Falcón walked across to him. 'Mr Short,' he said with his customary conspiratorial smile, 'Mr Kavalek asks me to send you his very best wishes for the game.' Nigel gave a wry grin. Mr Kavalek, of course, entertained no such sentiments, but no one had told Mr Falcón of the sudden change of arrangements in the Short camp.

This irony was as nothing to that wrapped up in the game itself. For the first time in the match, Kasparov, admittedly with his eyes wide open, walked headlong into some of the most devastating analyses prepared by Nigel and Kavalek in Reston. But Lubosh was not there to see the fruits of his labour. He was already 35,000 feet up in the air, and nearer to Washington than to the Savoy Theatre.

In the second game, when Short had offered to take the champion on in the Main Line of his favourite Sicilian variation, the Najdorf, Kasparov had ducked the challenge. Now Kasparov had had five days to study the Main Line, and anticipate at leisure what improvements Short and Kavalek had prepared. Kasparov did not duck the challenge this time: he confronted it head on by electing to play the most double-edged response of all. This is the Poisoned Pawn variation. Black grabs a pawn with his queen in a manoeuvre condemned in principle by most textbooks but warmly endorsed in practice by Bobby Fischer, who played the Poisoned Pawn variation at any and every opportunity. But the tactics involved are so hazardous and complicated that no players at the highest level other than Fischer and Kasparov have made it a regular part of their repertoire.

For thirteen moves the fourth game between Short and Kasparov followed the eleventh game of the 1972 Reykjavik match between Spassky and Fischer, the last occasion on which the fiendish ramifications of the Poisoned Pawn variation had been seen in a world championship match. By move twelve Kasparov started to think deeply. He knew that an improvement on Spassky's play in that twenty-one-year-old game was about to be unveiled, but still he could find nothing better than to follow Fischer's path.

Then on move fourteen Nigel unveiled what he likes to describe as 'a biggie'. The grandmasters sitting around chess-boards at Simpson's suddenly began to get very excited. Nothing excites jaded grandmasters more than a theoretical novelty. It lifts them from their seen-it-all-before torpor and reminds them that there is something new to be found in their wrinkled old game after all. In fact Nigel's concept, a stunningly unlikely retreat of a knight, in a position where White is supposed only to advance, was not new. It had been played once before, in an obscure game from a regional Russian championship in 1963, and then promptly forgotten. But Kavalek's musty volumes of thirty-year-old Soviet chess magazines had yielded up this secret. As Nigel said to me at the time, in Reston, 'Researching opening variations is like archaeology: you dig to find the forgotten secrets of the past.'

It was strange – and, in the circumstances, poignant – to see re-created on the board in the Savoy Theatre the very same position which I had watched Nigel and Lubosh poring over with such suppressed excitement in Reston all those months ago. Kasparov thought it was very strange indeed. The secret move, that is. Up till now, the world champion's behaviour at the board during the match had been uncharacteristically exemplary. But now, for the first time, he began to go through his repertoire of mocking faces, starting with the one which almost comically expressed the opinion, 'What sort of rubbish is this?'

I asked Nigel after the game whether he had noticed these expressions. 'Of course, but for once I didn't mind. He's so bloody arrogant, Gazza, he thinks that if he didn't see a move, then it can't be any good. I just sat there and thought, "Okay, matey, let's see whether you can find a good reply. Take your time."' Kasparov did indeed take this time, and began, visibly, to sweat as the venom in Nigel's obscure retreat of the knight became apparent to him. By the time he played his reply to Nigel's fourteenth move, the champion had already used one hour, Short only seven minutes.

At the same time, it was awesome to see Kasparov turn his mind to destroying over the board, under the merciless pressure of the clock, the edifice so laboriously created under laboratory conditions by Short and Kavalek. As his mental machete sliced through all the thickets and thorns of the new variation the world champion's body appeared to be completely still. But, from under the table, there came an incessant, rhythmic squeaking. It was the heel of one of Kasparov's shoes rubbing furiously against the other: the outward manifestation of extreme concentration.

Eventually Kasparov came up with a plan of counter-attack, one which Short and Kavalek had thought the least likely of possible responses. It also permitted Nigel, on the twentieth move, to force a draw. At that point the challenger deliberated for twenty-four minutes. While Nigel was sunk in thought, Kasparov walked to the side of the stage and began looking through the audience with a puzzled expression on his face. I knew he was trying to find Kavalek, to try to read from the coach's expression whether his player was still in prepared analysis or in uncomfortable new territory. Immediately after the game Kasparov said he believed that Short's new move was an unexploded bomb from Kavalek's work as Bobby Fischer's coach in the 1972 match against Spassky. 'This was a secret weapon created twenty-one years ago,' pronounced the world champion. Wrong, as it happens, but how gratified Lubosh would have been to hear the remark.

Short finally moved, spurning a draw offer for the second time in the match. The position was, at that stage, certainly no better for Nigel. But I knew that he would not settle for the draw, and not just because he was already two points down. Nigel had treasured this opening innovation, had carefully honed and polished it for weeks. It was designed to blow a big hole in the champion's favourite defence and thereby wreak psychological havoc. It just could not be tossed away on a measly twenty-move draw. There was another point: Kasparov could never again be thrown off-balance by this move. If Short could not win with it now, when he had the element of surprise in his favour, then it was unlikely he ever could.

So Nigel played on. But two moves later, in a position in which he had only one sensible move to play, he thought for a further thirty-five minutes, completely eroding the time-advantage he had held over the champion from the early stages of the game. I was sitting next to Rea in the audience and she became more and more agitated. 'Move, Nigel, move,' she muttered, rightly worried that her husband would yet again subside in a time-scramble.

Eventually he did move, but during that second long think he had lost the psychological initiative. Whereas before he was moving the pieces emphatically, now he shifted them almost apologetically into position. Kasparov, however, who had earlier looked so perplexed, was now screwing his pieces emphatically on to their squares, like a pianist embellishing a cadenza. In fact, the position was still balanced, but, as so often in chess, perception counted for far more than reality. Kasparov felt at home in the position. Short no longer did.

Inevitably in such a situation, Nigel blundered. It was, at least, an imaginative blunder. He had calculated a beautiful seven-move variation, culminating in a queen sacrifice on move thirty and forced checkmate on move thirty-three. The first move involved sacrificing his most important pawn. But as soon as Kasparov took the pawn, with a dismissive little sweep, Nigel looked shocked. His concept had a gigantic hole in it and, as Lubosh Kavalek liked to say in such situations, 'Kasparov is a good plumber.' What Kasparov had seen here, and what Nigel had seen one move too late, was that Short's intended queen sacrifice would have been comprehensively refuted one move later by a counter-sacrifice of the world champion's own queen.

Nigel began muttering to himself. I had seen him do this once before at the board, in the seventh game of the match against Karpov, when he had blundered away his queen against the former world champion. Now, as then, I wondered whether his Russian opponent was able to make out the curses with which Nigel was undoubtedly chastising himself.

After Short's inevitable resignation the theatre rapidly emptied of the disappointed British supporters. I stayed for a little while in the darkened auditorium, as Kasparov explained to a television reporter how Short should have taken the draw while he had the chance. But what else could I hear? Kavalek's laughter in the dark? I left the theatre hurriedly to see how Nigel was recovering in his hotel room.

He was lying down on his sofa, while Robert Hübner stood at one end. The two of them were not using words, but just talking in chess moves, Nigel in a weak, very quiet voice, with his hand shielding his eyes. Then he looked up and noticed me.

'I just cracked, in a perfectly good position. Suddenly I just felt my energy had gone. There was nothing there.' He didn't mention his lack of sleep; I had never known Nigel to make excuses for bad play, and he did not do so on this occasion either, tempting as it must have been. Then he gave a deep sigh, as he recalled the effort that had gone into preparing the novelty which he had sprung on Kasparov four hours earlier: 'What a terrible waste of a wonderful idea.'

We went off to Nigel and Rea's flat in Hampstead for dinner. This had become increasingly the pattern: that Nigel would spend as much time as possible at home after the games, and return at about midnight to the Savoy, to sleep, or try to. At home, among his family and one or two close friends, Nigel could forget about chess altogether and mend his mood. As the two-year-old Kyveli laughed and played among us, Nigel remarked, 'You know, the wonderful thing about being with Kyveli is that she doesn't care whether I win or lose. It means nothing to her. I love that.'

Later, as we sat around the dinner table, Nigel, wine glass in hand, insisted on drinking a toast: 'I just want to thank all of you for your support.' Robert Hübner, perhaps sensing the danger of too much maudlin sentiment, offered his own robust view of the situation. In Greek, he declaimed the famous words of Agamemnon from the *Iliad*, and then offered us this translation: 'Be men, friends, and remember to defend stormily.'

CHAPTER EIGHT

Nigel Short was officially buried by the bookies after his defeat in the fourth match-game. That night William Hill, who had been making a busy book on the result of the championship, refused to take any more bets on Kasparov retaining his title – at any price.

This announcement was given great prominence in the *Daily Telegraph*, Short's favourite newspaper, and as we read the item over breakfast in the Savoy he flung the paper aside. 'This is awful. I can't even read the newspapers any more. I want to stay in touch with what's going on in the outside world. I don't want to think only about this match. But every time I pick up a paper I can't avoid seeing these terrible pieces about how I'm doomed, or even cracking up.'

On our regular walk around St James's Park, after breakfast, Rob the bodyguard tried to be helpful: 'Tell you what, Nige. I'll to through the papers cutting out everything about the match. Then you can read them with pleasure.' In the end Nigel came up with a different idea. He cancelled his order for the *Telegraph* and *The Times*, and switched to the *Financial Times*. 'There's no chess in the *FT*,' he commented, evidently satisfied that he had found a solution to his problem.

The next morning I saw a copy of the *FT* rammed into the bathroom bin of suite 565, with what looked like sudden violence. I pulled the paper out to have a read. The pink ball sprang open like an umbrella to reveal an article likening Nigel to the Polish player Janowski, who in 1910 lost 8–0 to Emanuel Lasker in the most crushing world championship defeat ever. It looked as though the bodyguard's scissors would have to be pressed into service after all.

It seemed hard – at least I found it hard – to believe that the match had been going for only a week. At the start of the match Nigel had told me that this was his moment of destiny, that Kasparov, for some strange psychological reason, actually wanted to hand over his title. A week later, only an eighth of the way through the match, and Nigel's sense of destiny had been comprehensively ridiculed, by Kasparov, by the press and, worst of all, by his own play in the fourth game.

Kasparov did not know that Nigel, in that game, was suffering from a reaction to the brutal rift with Kavalek, but sensed clearly enough that something, not altogether to do with chess, was amiss. In an interview with *The Times* the champion remarked that 'Short is in big psychological problems,' and added, with chilling detachment, 'I am curious to see how he deals with them.' The Russian, grandly referring to himself in the third person, went on, 'The world champion shows greater resistance than other players. The same techniques do not work against him.' Kasparov recalled that, when he first challenged Anatoly Karpov for the title in 1985, 'It took me thirty-two games before I won one.' Or, in other words, Nigel Short would be doing well to win a single game of the twenty-four scheduled for the shorter London match. It was perhaps just as well that Short had already stopped reading *The Times*.

After another night with little sleep Nigel came up with some way of meeting the psychological challenge thrown down so publicly by Kasparov. 'I'm just starting a new twenty-game match,' he told me on the morning of what was, in fact, the fifth game. 'You know it was going to be a twenty-game match, anyway; Gazza and I were agreed on that. It was only *The Times* who insisted on twenty-four games for some financial reasons of their own.'

Later that morning, as Nigel, Robert Hübner and Jon Speelman were analysing together, I walked in with a copy of the official bulletin on the first game. 'Put that away,' said Nigel. I hesitated. 'Go on, put it away. I want to concentrate on the real match, not the one that has already ended.' At first I thought Nigel was behaving very oddly. But, in fact, how else could he have coped with the situation? It was getting beyond even his powers of self-belief to imagine that he had much chance of winning the match from a position of three games down. And what pleasure could be gained from playing a further seven weeks, just to minimize the scale of his losses? A new match, however, could be won, and the challenge of beating the world champion over twenty games was one that could inspire.

At the same time I couldn't help recalling Nigel's own description of Kasparov's mentality when he had reviewed the champion's autobiography in the *Spectator* in 1987: 'A facet of Kasparov's personality is his ability to manipulate a set of circumstances into a simplistic theory to suit his own emotional needs.' The author of that remark was discovering just how useful such a defence mechanism could be.

Even so, Nigel still seemed in no state to play the first game of the new match, or the fifth of the event Kasparov thought he was playing in. With the departure of Kavalek, there departed also the Kavalek computer and database. Speelman was worried about this, but Nigel was unconcerned, assuring his second, with a disarming smile, that 'I've copied the bits I need.'

Robert Hübner, I suspect, was relieved at the departure of all of Kavalek's high technology. The noted papyrologist was still resolutely true to the methods current when he first became German champion in 1966. He simply wrote every piece of analysis down in long-hand on paper, just like the ancient Greeks he so much admired. While Speelman would anxiously ask Nigel questions such as 'Do you have a Gamma merge-game function on your computer at home?', Hübner would serenely plough on, covering A4 pad after A4 pad with his small, neat handwriting.

But when Hübner and Speelman, in their very different ways, took Nigel through some variations on the morning of the fifth game, their employer seemed to be taking very little in. He was constantly yawning, and pleading 'Move the pieces more slowly, guys. I can't keep up.' I was worried: Nigel had the disadvantage of the Black pieces in the forthcoming game and, if he lost this one, it was hard to see what could prevent complete disintegration, of the sort which was already being widely predicted by the chess commentators, and not just in the binned *Financial Times*.

At least Nigel began the fifth game as if he meant business. None of the first four games had started on time. On every occasion the production company which was transmitting the games live on Channel Four, had kept the players waiting until the advertisements had finished. On one occasion Short and Kasparov had been kept kicking their heels for over ten minutes. At 3.30 p.m. on Thursday, 16 September, the scheduled start of the fifth game, Short finally lost his patience. He brushed aside a frantically waving studio engineer – who mouthed the words, 'You can't do this!' – strode to the board and ordered the arbiter to start the clock for the game. A startled Kasparov rapidly followed Nigel to the centre of the stage, and played his first move.

For the first time in the match that move was not pawn to king four. The world champion, having won two games with the king's pawn, was now going to demonstrate that he could beat Short on the queenside as well as the kingside. He pushed his queen's pawn to the centre of the board, sat back and folded his arms.

On the third move Short flicked out his bishop to attack Kasparov's knight. This is the characteristic move of a defence devised in the 1920s by the Latvian Aron Nimzovitch. It is a defence in name only. Both in style and in content it is a counter-attack. Kasparov looked most surprised. Short had not played the Nimzovitch defence for three years, after a series of Soviet grandmasters had brutally demonstrated to him the inadequacies of the Black set-up.

In particular Kasparov was a killer of the Nimzovitch, and most especially of the line which Short seemed to be preparing to enter. In the grandmaster analysis room, the players, watching the game by closed-circuit television, rushed to their databases. After a few seconds at his computer screen the international master Alec Mortazavi exclaimed, 'Okay! Not only has Kasparov never lost against this line. I can't even find a single draw. Nothing but wins! Wins against Spassky! Wins against Korchnoi! What has Nigel got?'

The answer was, a lot. Of course Nigel knew only too well what Kasparov had been playing to put the Nimzovitch out of commission. He – and Kavalek – had devised an entirely new way of meeting the world champion's patented method. On move ten came the new move, the Black queen pushed out to the far right of the board, precisely the opposite direction to that recommended in all the textbooks on the Nimzovitch defence. In other words, an entirely new concept.

Kasparov looked away from the board and then, very deliberately, put his hands flat over his eyes, fingers pointing upwards. It was as if he was trying to remember in which of his games the move had been played before, and what the correct killing response should be. 'It was a bluff,' Nigel said to me after the game. 'He likes to pretend that he's seen it all before and just needs to use his fantastic memory to drag the right reply from his famous database. But on this occasion I knew he was bluffing, because, as far as I know, my move had never, ever been played before.'

Not played before, perhaps, but, as with many a scientific discovery, others had been working on similar ideas. In particular the great Viktor Korchnoi, twice the official challenger for the world championship, had discovered Nigel's new move independently, in his own chess laboratory. I only know this because Korchnoi was in London on the day this game was played and was sitting next to Michael Stean and myself in the analysis room. When Nigel uncorked his novelty, Korchnoi took a puff of his cigarette and said, in his emphatic Russian-accented English, 'I've looked at this. Unfortunately, it loses.'

Stean, keeping admirable control of his emotions, asked how, and Korchnoi spelt out, in a stage whisper, a long forcing variation. I couldn't follow it, but Stean's grim expression suggested that he both followed and believed it.

Back at the board, however, it was clear that Kasparov, for once, was on completely unfamiliar territory. By the time he replied to the new move, he had already taken three-quarters of an hour, while Nigel had used up only six minutes. In fact Short spent almost no time at the board at all in this game. He played his moves instantly, and then dashed off to his rest room, while Kasparov, surprised at every turn, remained rooted to the table. After every move he played he looked up as the Englishman returned to the board, for all the world like an anxious pupil trying to see from the teacher's expression whether he was doing well or not.

In fact, he was doing very well, even though he had not played the way Korchnoi recommended. Nigel and Lubosh had spent a fortnight on this new variation, and there were a number of intricate traps, which Kasparov had avoided. By move eighteen, the champion had used an hour and a half, to reach a completely equal position. Short had taken just eleven minutes, which simply measured the average of thirty-six seconds that it took him each move to walk to the board, shift some wood and press the clock. After playing his eighteenth move Kasparov offered a draw, which Short, at the same express speed, immediately accepted. He had had the final position of the game on Kavalek's board in Reston four months before, and knew then that it was a dead draw. This was the dénouement that Nigel and Lubosh had dreamed of: to force a draw with the Black pieces against the most well-prepared player in history – by outpreparing him.

'The queen manoeuvre on move ten. Is it new?' Kasparov asked Short, as the players got up from the table. 'I don't know, Garri,' Nigel replied, 'you're the one with the big database.' Afterwards I chided Nigel for being unnecessarily secretive. 'It's not unnecessary at all,' he replied. 'Suppose I said, "Yes, it is new," and Gazza goes to his database and comes across some long-forgotten game in a minor Russian league where this move was played. Then he would know that my database was missing that tournament, and he could start to play some ideas from that event, which he would know I wouldn't have seen.' Simple logic, when you come to think about it. I felt quite ashamed.

After the game Kasparov showed a different brand of churlishness. Asked for his opinion on the state of the match, he observed that he had played five games of chess and Short only four. Nigel snorted when I quoted the champion's assessment: 'He's a fine one to talk. He makes a living out of winning games entirely prepared at home – he's even won brilliancy prizes with such concoctions. Now it's been done to him, and he's just embarrassed.'

However, it was Nigel who was embarrassed when, an hour after the game, Michael Stean came up to his room and reported Korchnoi's opinion that Short's new opening idea had a fatal hole in it. Nigel remained seated on his sofa playing his guitar meditatively. 'Korkie thinks so, does he? What's his idea?' And, while Nigel continued to strum, Stean repeated the long series of moves proposed by the Russian. Suddenly Nigel's hand struck the wood of the guitar. He had visualized Korchnoi's point. 'Oh! I never considered that! Maybe the whole thing is complete crap.'

Such conversations, consisting mostly of nothing more than a series of chess moves, in algebraic jargon, frequently took the place of more normal dialogue in the Short suite at the Savoy. But I never saw a chessboard in those rooms; in fact I don't believe there was one. Nigel was much happier discussing positions from the games 'blindfold', without the unnecessary tedium of actually moving real pieces. And besides, this way his hands were free to play the guitar.

Just after Stean left, Nigel suddenly burst into gales of laughter. It seemed an odd reaction to the discovery that his cherished new idea was fatally flawed. 'No, it's wonderful,' Nigel gasped between giggles. 'Gazza will go home and realize that he missed a win. He'll be absolutely livid. Maybe he'll think that I bluffed him, which is even more infuriating. And, anyway, I think we should be able to find an improvement to deal with Korchnoi's idea.'

The mystery which remained for me was why, with only eleven minutes on his clock, compared with an hour and a half on Kasparov's, Nigel did not play on for a few more moves, to test the champion, even in that dead drawn position. And why did Nigel move at such stunning speed, when a slower pace might not have alerted Kasparov to be so careful? Nigel seemed very unwilling to answer these questions, until finally he muttered, 'Well, if you must know, I was suddenly hit by a migraine half an hour before the game started. I took some Solpadeine, but it doesn't really help.'

Suddenly everything was clear: that was why Nigel was yawning before the game and unable to follow Speelman's and Hübner's analysis. That was why he made all his moves instantly, and then rushed off to his rest room. And that was why he instantly accepted Kasparov's – perfectly correct – offer of a draw. But how well Nigel hid the bleak feelings he must have had at the start of the game, three points behind, and about to take on the strongest chessplayer of all time, with a thumping migraine.

I don't know whether the sudden migraine attack was a further reaction to the traumatic split with Kavalek, but the sacking of the coach had also produced a headache of a more practical sort. Both Speelman and Hübner were committed to playing in the European club championships at exactly the time that Nigel would be preparing for, and then playing, the sixth match-game against Kasparov. The game was scheduled for Saturday, 18 September, at which time Hübner would be in Paris playing for Bayern Munich, while Speelman would be representing the Dutch team Volmac.

And Nigel did have a problem with his opening for the next game. His shiny new move against Kasparov's Najdorf variation had been badly dented in the fourth game, and it needed urgent repairs, of the sort that required the mental pliers of chessboard mechanics Hübner and Speelman. But they were otherwise engaged, and Nigel did not want to use up all his time and energy before the sixth game in a possibly fruitless attempt to do all the repair work himself.

On the morning of the game, a lovely crisp London autumn day, we went for a walk in Green Park and, among the falling leaves and conkers, Nigel deliberated on what new line to play against the champion's Najdorf variation. 'I'm going to play the Sozin Attack,' he said, as we approached the din of Hyde Park Corner. The noise of the traffic drowned out my exclamation of surprise. The Sozin Attack was Kasparov's own favourite set-up whenever a player had the temerity to play the Najdorf variation against *him*. Kasparov knew the moods and character of the Sozin Attack with an intimacy normally associated with the relationship between lovers. And Nigel had never, in his entire career, even caressed the Sozin.

It was a deep, psychological gamble, as Short explained to me while we walked back through the park to the Savoy. 'The

Sozin, yes, it's Kasparov's own favourite against the Najdorf, and he knows it better than I could ever dream of. But that's the whole point. When I play it, he'll be frightened of all the things he knows it can do. He'll be frightened of moves which will never have occurred to me. I will be using his own knowledge against him.'

'But isn't it a bluff? Does he need to assume that you know all the wrinkles?'

'This is where the fifth game comes in useful. That showed him that I am capable of brilliant preparation, of predicting his every move, and playing an entire game without leaving my secret database. So I am in a position to bluff him. He can't be sure I won't know everything he knows about the Sozin. It's like poker. To bluff successfully you must not be seen as a bluffer, or you'll be called.'

'It's a very risky strategy.'

'Of course it's a very risky strategy. Now let's have some lunch.'

In the basement bar of Simpson's-in-the-Strand, where the grandmaster pundits met to discuss, analyse and, if possible, refute the moves of Short and Kasparov, the dominant figure was the reigning American champion Patrick Wolff. His high-pitched New York accent tended to soar over the more muffled murmurings of the European masters present.

This was the same Patrick Wolff who had so desperately wanted to be one of Short's seconds in the match. Whether through disappointment, or just intellectual disagreement, he seemed to find fault with most of Short's ideas, which he would castigate colourfully and colloquially, to the amusement of onlookers.

When, on move six of the sixth game, Short played his king's bishop to the centre of the board, in the characteristic first move of the Sozin Attack, Wolff fell off his chair. That is not a metaphor. I watched the American Grandmaster reel back in his chair with such force that it, and he with it, tumbled backwards on to the floor. After he was pulled to his feet by a couple of

acolytes, the American champion gave verbal vent to the astonishment which he had already demonstrated in the style of a
silent movie.

'Nigel must be maaaad to play this against Kasparov,' Wolff
almost wailed. 'If I hadda been working for Nigel I wouldda
shaken him by the lapels and begged him, *begged him*, not to
play it. This is Kasparov's turf, not Nigel's.'

'It shows an enormous amount of courage,' said one English
player, patriotically.

'It shows an enormous amount of foolishness,' Wolff
snapped back.

At the board, Kasparov did not fall off his chair with
astonishment. He just stared at Nigel, and then rapidly played
the normal response. He did not look like a man likely to be
bluffed.

Unlike the last game, Nigel did not dash off to his rest room
between moves. From the opening he too stayed rooted to the
board, with his head bent right over the pieces. This was not
because he was on unfamiliar territory: he had prepared the
Sozin Attack thoroughly, whatever his remarks about bluffing.
But he had told me before the game that he was 'going to crowd
Gazza today'. What that meant was that Short wanted to impose
his presence almost physically on the champion. By staying at
the board throughout, almost leaning over it, he hoped to add
an additional potent ingredient to the psychological cocktail.

But Kasparov's twelfth move, played after half an hour's
thought, forced Nigel into a genuine spasm of concentration,
rather than a mimed one. It was a new idea, and one that left
Short with a horribly large choice of replies, each one of which
had almost incalculable consequences. Nigel tried to calculate
them. On this one move he thought for over fifty minutes, a
record not just for this match, but, so far as anyone present
could recall, for any world championship match. Watching Nigel
sink into apparent coma was Rea. 'Only six games, and I'm
already getting an ulcer. Why doesn't Nigel bloody move?'

For fifty minutes the watching grandmasters attempted to
guess what Short would play. When he did, eventually, it was a
move which not one of them had predicted. Kasparov himself

described the move afterwards as 'incredible', although he might have meant incredibly bad. Nigel had gratuitously wrecked his entire queenside pawn structure in return for a temporary initiative. If that intangible initiative did not bring an immediate dividend then he would be utterly lost.

In fact, Nigel told me after the game, there was a response which Kasparov could have made which would have led to an immediate draw by a perpetual checking motion. But the world champion was convinced that Short's plan was as bad as it looked, and played his next few moves with flourishes. 'He had this look on his face,' said Nigel, 'which meant, "Now I'm really storming."'

Suddenly, on the twenty-first move, when all the watching masters were forecasting a smooth annihilation of Short's wrecked queenside, the world champion began to look less confident. At the board, the challenger could smell that something funny was going on. It was one of the most fascinating moments of psychological interplay between the players in the whole match. The next day, over lunch at my home, Nigel explained the strange process of thought transference which took place while Kasparov pondered his twenty-first move.

'I actually did not know what my plan should be at that stage. I knew that Gazza thought he was better, and I couldn't see exactly how I should proceed. But then he made some facial twitch, which somehow suggested he had suddenly seen something unpleasant. And at that exact moment, that instant, I immediately saw what it was he was afraid of, and I knew what to play.'

I asked Nigel if he was saying that Kasparov's thoughts, in terms of precise moves and variations, had somehow transmitted themselves, across a distance of about two feet, into his opponent's brain. It had always seemed to me, when I watched players like Short and Kasparov hunched toe-to-toe over a chessboard in mind-wrenching concentration, each trying desperately to read the other's mind, that it would be surprising if some element of thought transference did not take place.

'I don't think it's quite as simple as that, although who knows?' said Nigel. 'But it's clear that you have to attack this guy. Because then he begins to panic about possibilities which you haven't yet seen. And when he begins to panic, then you pick up on it, and you start to see some of the same possibilities.'

It was an ingenious way for Nigel to find some way of challenging a player whom he knew saw far more at the board than he did, and even of turning that greater calculating ability against its originator.

In the past it has often been the stronger player who has avoided defeat by such methods. In his only chess book, *My Sixty Memorable Games*, Bobby Fischer describes his game against the Yugoslav Grandmaster Trifunovich: 'I was considering the blunder, Bishop to Knight Five, but Trifunovich seemed too quiet all of a sudden, and I suspected he had tuned in on my brain waves.' At that instant, Fischer wrote, he saw how Trifunovich would have won if he had played the move he was considering.

In Fischer's case, his opponent had sensed the possibility of a blunder, and the American, in turn, had felt his adversary's suppressed excitement and thus avoided disaster. In Short's case, Kasparov's slight facial twitch had instantly transformed the Englishman's view of the position, and thus, equally instantly, informed him of the right way to proceed.

The result was that when Kasparov, after much thought, actually played his twenty-first move, Nigel replied immediately with the one move that the champion had feared. There was nothing subtle about the move: it was the crudest possible attempt to deliver checkmate. 'Coffee-house chess!' one of the watching masters at Simpson's exclaimed derisively. But, as his colleagues began to study the position, they found it increasingly difficult to see a defence for the champion; and, as Short swung his rook and queen round to form a single-file battering ram against Kasparov's king, many of them rushed into the theatre itself in the hope of witnessing in the flesh, rather than on closed-circuit television, the checkmating of a champion. There they joined about 1,000 spectators: it was a Saturday sell-out at the Savoy Theatre.

What happened next showed that when it came to bluff, and psychological tricks, the world champion was more than a match for his challenger. After playing his twenty-fifth move Kasparov had only eight minutes remaining on his clock to play the fifteen moves left to the time-control. But then he sat back in his chair with a relaxed expression on his face, put his watch back on his wrist and walked off the stage. At that precise moment Nigel had available a sacrificial combination which, after some uncomfortable moments for Kasparov, would achieve nothing more than a draw by perpetual check. He also had another and much more subtle continuation which, Kasparov instantly demonstrated to Short after the game, would have won.

But by his demeanour and body language Kasparov was attempting to suggest to Nigel that he was satisfied with his position, even with so little time left: in other words that the draw by perpetual check was inevitable. And Nigel fell for it. He sacrificed bishop and rook spectacularly. It thrilled the noisy audience, who watched the champion's king scuttle across the board. But, after Nigel's final coup, Kasparov smiled, pushed his king one more square, pressed his clock and offered a draw. Short instantly agreed: his queen and the champion's king were locked in a *pas de deux* which neither could leave without fatal consequences: perpetual check it was.

The audience burst into thunderous applause, which lasted for some minutes. It was indeed a spectacular, even beautiful, finish to the game. And the second draw in a row for the Englishman was heartening for the home crowd. But, when I rushed upstairs to congratulate Nigel on the game, I found Rea alone in the sitting room. 'Nigel's in the bedroom,' said Rea. 'And that's one disappointed guy in there.' When Nigel emerged, in jeans and a sweater, he did look as though he had just lost a game.

'Gazza said I had a win by force on move twenty-six, and that he knew he was losing,' Nigel told us. 'But it's very strange. At precisely the moment he thought he was on the verge of losing, he went icy calm. Icy. There was nothing there at all.'

I said that I'd noticed how the champion had sat back and then walked away from the board at that stage of the game.

'That's it! It now transpires that he believed he was losing, but at that moment he was behaving as if everything was under control. He was icy calm. Icy!' Nigel repeated.

Perhaps, then, a draw was a just result, not necessarily of the moves played on the board, but of the psychological battle of the sixth match-game. First Short managed to find the right move to start his attack, only because he somehow tuned into the thought processes of his opponent. And then Kasparov was able to achieve a draw by deliberately transmitting entirely deceptive thoughts to Short. It was almost as if the champion knew that his earlier difficulties had been caused by a leak of his secret thoughts across the board, and that the only way to recover the situation was to use the same weapon of thought transference against his opponent.

That might seem far-fetched. But these were two men who were in the middle of an extraordinarily intimate struggle. For eight weeks they would be so close that each would come to smell every body odour, see every facial twitch, hear every digestive movement that the other's metabolism had to offer. And for several months beforehand each would have worked and plotted to understand every nuance, strength or weakness of the other's thought processes and habits.

Before the match began, Michael Stean, who was Viktor Korchnoi's second in his two world championship matches against Anatoly Karpov, told me that the game at grandmaster level was about thirty per cent psychology and seventy per cent skill, but that 'at the world championship, it is ninety per cent psychology.' I pooh-poohed Michael's formula at the time. Now I was beginning to believe him.

CHAPTER NINE

When a man is in trouble he begins to find out who his true friends and supporters are. When a man is on top of the world, others want to be close to him, in the hope that their names, too, become associated with success.

Not long after Nigel Short won his semi-final match against the former world champion Anatoly Karpov, he was invited to appear on a public platform with John Major. It was the time of the 1992 general election, and the Conservative leader needed all the success by association that he could find – or rather, that his advisers could find for him.

The Prime Minister's office had indicated at one stage that Mr Major would like to come to see Nigel playing against Kasparov: after all, Short was the first Englishman ever to contest such an event, and it was taking place less than a mile from 10 Downing Street. But, as Kasparov began piling up his lead, official enthusiasm began to wane. Indeed, despite a number of requests from the organizers, not a single representative of the British state or government was willing to offer support by visiting the event.

Not so the official representative of the Russian state, the then Ambassador, Mr Boris Pankin. He lost no opportunity to put in appearances at the Savoy Theatre. His boy, of course, was winning. Perhaps this difference of approach was also symbolic of the divergent attitudes of the Russian and British political systems to chess: the one had always given its chessplayers every possible financial and official support, the other regarded the game as a matter of no interest or importance whatsoever.

Nigel Short, however, was not prepared to see the matter in merely symbolic terms. 'If I had been winning at this stage,' he said to me with more than a hint of irritation, 'I'm sure the politicians would have been queuing up to get a look-in.'

One British public figure, however, seemed willing to risk association with a loser: the Princess of Wales. Though her only

141

previous experience of chess had been watching her eldest son Prince William play, the Princess had become thoroughly engrossed in Nigel Short's struggle at the Savoy Theatre. After his titanic effort to win the sixth game, the Princess asked my wife Rosa, a friend of hers, what she could do to give Nigel some encouragement and support. Rosa suggested that she come to the next game and, perhaps, meet Nigel beforehand.

The Princess's arrival in the royal box at the Savoy caused consternation among the horde of photographers taking their statutory shots of Short and Kasparov at the chessboard. After a few minutes the most observant of their number glimpsed that familiar face staring down at the game and, hastily attaching a zoom lens to his camera, began rapid fire in the opposite direction to his colleagues. In seconds, as if responding to some primordial mating call, they were all swivelling round and firing round after round into the gloomy recess of the theatre where sat their most reliable meal-ticket.

Kasparov's face, as he was suddenly confronted with the bottoms of twenty photographers, rather than the usual smiling, ingratiating faces, was a picture in itself. He had no idea what it could be that was so much more important than himself, and he would have needed his own zoom lens to discern the answer. Nigel, however, seemed completely unsurprised by the tumult and carried on staring at the board. He had the advantage, for once, over his opponent: immediately before the game he and Rea had spent half an hour with the Princess, who had visited them in the drawing room of Nigel's suite at the Savoy Hotel.

In fact the Princess, Rea, Rosa and I were waiting in the drawing room for several minutes before Nigel suddenly burst in. He liked to sleep until half an hour before the game; on this occasion he had overslept and had been feverishly putting on his smartest suit while his guests waited in the adjoining room.

'I've never been so embarrassed in all my life,' said Nigel to no one in particular, when he finally made an appearance, and then, addressing himself to the Princess, observed with a giggle, 'If Kasparov takes me as much by surprise in the game, as you have done here, then I am in big trouble.'

The good news was that in the seventh match-game

Kasparov did not take Nigel as much by surprise as the Princess of Wales had done: yet again the champion played the Anti-Marshall. The bad news was that, for the third time, Nigel lost against this supposedly innocuous opening variation. The end of this game was particularly horrible to watch. After thirty-three moves Nigel had seven minutes left on his clock for the remaining seven moves before the time-control. Then, on move thirty-four, Kasparov played a move with his knight that set up an unstoppable barrage of threats against Short's king. As if to emphasize this, Kasparov played the move with a physical emphasis unusual even for him: he positively screwed the knight into the fatal square with a brutal, clockwise twist of his wrist.

It was pitiful to see Nigel's time ebb away as he searched desperately for a defence which did not, could not, exist. After six of his remaining seven minutes had expired, the red flag on his clock began its inexorable rise to ninety degrees, at which point it would fall, and this game, like the first of the match, would be lost by time forfeit. With his slow, ponderous steps the senior arbiter, Yuri Averbakh, approached the board to stare at the clock, and keep count of the moves. With thirty seconds to go Nigel began glancing at the clock, then at the board, then at the clock again. This is the worst moment for a chess grandmaster: he has no moves and can't quite believe it; he must move rapidly, but is paralysed by the immobility of his own pieces. With about fifteen seconds left for seven moves, Nigel finally bashed out a reply, which he knew was as bad as any other. Two moves later, faced with inevitable checkmate, he extended his hand in resignation. Precisely as he did so, his clock flag fell. The only thing in Short's favour was that you can't lose the same game twice. After an intense debate between the two arbiters, who care about such morbid details, it was announced to the audience that Short had resigned before his time had run out.

Not that Nigel cared very much exactly how his demise would be categorized for the records. He had simply lost and, what was worse, he didn't seem to know where he had gone wrong. In the hallway of his suite, as Robert Hübner and I stood by, trying but failing to come up with some consoling words of support, Nigel lifted up his arms and then let them fall limply at his sides.

'What to do?' He sighed heavily. 'I got a perfectly good position out of the opening, and he just outplayed me. I'm not even sure where I went wrong. It's just so depressing to play your best, and still lose.'

Hübner immediately pointed out Nigel's two decisive strategic errors: the German Grandmaster was vastly more experienced than Nigel at defending such positions – he had been doing so for well over twenty years. 'You should have blocked him from playing pawn to rook five,' said Hübner in his precise, almost clipped English, 'but when he played it there, then you had to take it.'

'I was going to take it,' Nigel replied. 'But then I chickened out. I thought my position was still perfectly all right. I mean this Anti-Marshall he plays is nothing. I got a fine position out of the opening.'

'Fine,' said Hübner, 'and, objectively, there is nothing at all wrong with the positions you are getting against his Anti-Marshall. But you don't seem altogether at home in them. So there may be subjective reasons why you might want to switch openings. Do you want to?'

'No. I want to stick with it,' said Nigel, with a slight edge in his voice, which suggested that the subjective Short mind was not altogether happy with the idea.

'Okay,' said the always objective Dr Hübner. 'I agree with your decision. We must just work harder on this system.'

'But not now.' A woman's voice broke into the conversation. Rea had come into the suite. 'Come on, guys. Let's go home and have some dinner, and listen to some music.' It was the best move by a Short all day.

'I think I'm famous, Dominic,' Nigel said to me the following evening, as if he had made a surprising discovery. That day he had taken his first break away from work since the match began, and had travelled with Rea and Kyveli to Windsor Great Park. Nigel could scarcely move without being pestered for his autograph or, at the very least, being pointed out and stared at.

I told him he should make the most of it while it lasted.

'Yes, but it's very strange, because it's nothing really to do with chess, and I always thought that it was my skill at chess which, in some way, defined me as a person.'

What had happened, I attempted to explain to Nigel, was that he had become that strange modern phenomenon, a 'celebrity', and when people become celebrities the original reason for their becoming celebrated is forgotten. They are simply famous, and that's all.

Nigel was equally bemused by the financial aspects of celebrity. 'I've done this chess video, and it was nothing; it took me less than a day in the studio. But I'm told it should make me up to £100,000. I did this advertisement for Heineken beer, and I won't even tell you how much I was paid. But the thing is, I've always felt that my income should in some way be a direct reflection of my success and results in chess tournaments. It's been like that ever since I was a teenager.'

Perhaps Nigel was puzzled by the fact that, at exactly the same time as he was losing game after game to Kasparov, he was making the sort of money he had never made in the past as a winner. This dislocation between results and rewards was troubling Nigel, who has an almost puritanical concept of just deserts. Just as he had earlier felt that, as a winner of matches against Karpov and Timman, he was being short-changed by Fidé, he was now slightly uneasy with a cascade of endorsement income unchecked by chessboard defeats.

But when I thought of Nigel, under appalling pressure of clock and position, twisting and squirming under Kasparov's confident glare across the board in the seventh game, all this in front of his wife, his friends and almost a thousand other spectators who desperately wanted him to win – when I thought of that moment, I could not bring myself to share Nigel's sense that he was in some way a beneficiary of unearned income. No pain, no gain, the Americans say. Nigel was discovering the truth of that, the hard way.

*

Discomfort and embarrassment, if not exactly pain, was also being experienced by the analytical team of Hübner and Speelman as they worked on improving Nigel's opening from the sixth game. For the next game, the eighth, Nigel would again have the White pieces, and Kasparov would clearly stick to his cherished Najdorf variation. But the more Hübner and Speelman looked at the sixth game, the more they became convinced that any improvements to be found would come only from the Black side. While it was very gratifying for Nigel to be told that his play in the sixth game had been perfect, it was less so to discover that the whole line, which he and Kavalek had honed over many weeks as a fearsome 'hit' for Short's White games, was in fact good for no more than a perilous equality.

The Times, the sponsors of the event, were also becoming extremely edgy. They had belatedly learned of the departure of Lubosh Kavalek and had convinced themselves that the growing one-sidedness of the match – which was endangering their flow of revenues from ticket sales and television rights – was due to the absence of the coach and the sudden gap in Nigel's analytical team. Staff from the newspaper privately told Short that they would pay for any grandmaster in the world to be flown to London to help him recover from his four-game deficit. What Kasparov would have thought, let alone said, had he discovered that the organizers of the match were prepared financially to back one of the participants against the other – him – defies exact prediction. It would certainly have been a spectacular Azerbaizhani outburst.

But Kasparov never found out, partly because Nigel dismissed the *Times* offer out of hand. Or almost out of hand. On the same day that the offer was made, the pop singer Madonna was also staying at the Savoy Hotel. Nigel recalled that he had earlier, somewhat facetiously, asked the organizers of the event to hire Madonna to give him massages in his rest room during the game. Now he instructed his business manager Michael Stean to thank *The Times* for its kind offer, and reiterate, in writing if necessary, his request for back-up services from the American pop singer. I didn't imagine that the *Times'* nerves

146

were steadied by this truculent response to their most earnest offer.

On the morning of the eighth game Robert Hübner wandered down the corridor from his room on the sixth floor and knocked on Nigel's door. The German Grandmaster had finally hit on a new idea which might breathe life into the Sozin attack which Nigel so badly wanted to play again against Kasparov. To ditch the variation after only one game would not just have alerted Kasparov to the fact that he had disarmed one of Short's heavy guns. It would also have meant an enormous amount of work for Short's team in getting up to speed on a new and different way of handling the White pieces.

Nigel joined Hübner and Speelman in the analysis room which adjoined the German's bedroom. He began rapidly checking all of the myriad variations. The pieces flew around the board as the two seconds each demonstrated the point of the new White attack. The idea led to immensely complicated positions in which White accepted a horrible structural weakness in exchange for chances for a blitzkrieg attack on the king. 'It looks like all or nothing,' said Nigel, 'but I like it.'

Speelman still had some doubts. Knocking pieces over in all directions – as he tends to do when very excited – he attempted to show an extraordinary way in which Kasparov could counter the attack by advancing all of his kingside pawns. Hübner waved his hand dismissively. 'We really don't have time to go into all that now. We must concentrate on much more likely responses.' Nigel agreed. 'Yes, that looks like complete crap, Jon. Gazza won't play that.' Speelman mumbled dissent, but to no avail.

At 3.40 p.m. that afternoon, ten minutes into the eighth game, Nigel picked up his queen to play his twelfth move. This was the innovation prepared by Robert Hübner. Kasparov went into a huddle, as Nigel strolled away from the board. But the Russian did not seem altogether amazed. It was clear from his expression that he too had analysed this new move, if not that very morning. After only eight minutes thought he lashed out with his king's rook's pawn, immediately attacking the queen on its new square.

In the circumstances, I thought that Nigel did very well to keep a completely bland expression and make his reply within one minute. For Kasparov had played exactly the response that Speelman had feared and which Short and Hübner had dismissed as improbable. And with his next two moves Kasparov continued to follow Speelman's apparently absurd idea.

Meanwhile Jon Speelman himself was commenting live on the game on Channel Four. Like Nigel, he kept a poker face, although I thought I detected a hint of a smile playing around his mouth as he affected to be seeing these moves for the very first time.

After Kasparov's fourteenth move Speelman's co-commentator, Grandmaster Daniel King, was so impressed with the Russian's concept that he pronounced the champion's position to be 'winning'. Nigel meanwhile locked his feet around the outside of the chess table in his most characteristic posture of extreme concentration.

In the analysis room the American Grandmaster John Tisdall rushed up to me. 'You shouldda seen Nigel after Garri played his last move. He kinda slumped, like he'd been hit by a bullet. Whadda move!' I suppose Tisdall, the Reuters chess correspondent, wanted my reaction as a member of the Short camp. But even if I had told him that Nigel had had this position on his board a few hours before, but had dismissed it as irrelevant, I am sure that the American Grandmaster would not have believed me.

What followed, none of the assembled grandmasters could believe. After half an hour's thought Short came up with a plan that involved, almost in successive moves, the sacrifice of a bishop, a knight, a rook and then another rook, all to rip away the protective pawn formation in front of the champion's kingside. At the end of the sequence Short would be left with virtually no pieces, but those that remained would be within strangling distance of Kasparov's king. The American Grandmaster Robert Byrne, writing in the *New York Times*, described these sacrifices as coming 'from Nigel Short's sinister laboratory'. Evidently the Grandmaster simply could not believe that these remarkable moves were over-the-board inspiration, rather than the result of midnight oil.

The complications were incalculable. Essentially Nigel was trusting in his intuition that the champion's position at the end of this improbably violent sequence of moves would be indefensible. These are the bravest and most difficult decisions for a chessplayer to take. It is easy to sacrifice any amount of material when a clear win can be forced. That requires imagination and calculation, but no more. But sacrifices of material without a clear end in view require a leap of faith, and the willingness to risk universal derision should that judgement be proved faulty.

In fact Short was being universally derided in live commentaries on both BBC2 and Channel Four, as the first move of the sequence appeared on their electronic monitors. None of the pundits, grandmasters almost to a man, could fathom what Short was up to, other than blundering away all of his pieces.

Kasparov, too, seemed unimpressed, playing his first four replies in five minutes. But then on move twenty came the first of the rook sacrifices, and the world champion looked, to quote John Tisdall's words, 'as if he had been hit by a bullet'. His body became – most unusually for him – completely inert. His feet, which normally vibrate incessantly throughout the game, suddenly stopped their perpetual motion and lay flat upon the floor.

Then he turned to glare into the audience, and I followed his gaze. It was directed at his mother Klara, sitting in the third row. She put her hands to her mouth, as if something shocking had suddenly happened. Which, in a way, it had. Her son, for once, had completely lost control of the position. Short's body language was equally transparent. While earlier, as he calculated the variations, he had bent low over the board, shielding his eyes with his hands, now he sat inscrutable, calm, upright in his chair, like some pale, lean Buddha.

By move thirty-one Nigel was still way behind on material, but he was enjoying himself. He could take a draw by a perpetual checking motion whenever he wanted, or he could regain all his material losses with a series of captures which would neatly mirror the series of sacrifices at the beginning of the attack, seventeen moves earlier.

I was sitting in the front row of the stalls at the time. Nigel suddenly turned away from the board and gave me a roguish grin. Then he checked Kasparov's king, deliberately repeating an earlier position. Kasparov looked less concerned. Perhaps this would be a draw by threefold repetition of the position? But then Nigel deviated at the last moment. He shot me another roguish grin and went through the same charade again, repeating the position twice, but not the fateful third time, which would allow the champion to claim a draw.

After the game Nigel explained what he had found so amusing. He said that it had always been a favourite ploy of Soviet players, when they had complete control of the position, to repeat it once and then twice, partly to demonstrate that they were toying with their opponent and partly to tantalize him with the hope of a draw. 'They did this sadistic trick to me on a number of occasions,' he recalled, 'and I just thought I would enjoy doing to one of them what they have always done to others. And besides, I was short of time, and this brought me a couple of moves closer to the time-control.'

Not close enough, unfortunately. The inexorable ticking of the double-headed chess clock was once again Short's implacable opponent, as much as any of the moves of the champion. Nigel had barely a minute left for three moves when the one clear winning opportunity presented itself to him. He had to move his remaining bishop to the square queen four, to set up an unstoppable battery of checks. Looking nervously at his clock, Nigel picked up the bishop, and hastily put it down . . . on the square king five. The move threatened exactly the same demolition of Kasparov's king. But it left uncontrolled one square on the board, on which, several moves later, Kasparov's queen could land to deliver a perpetual check. Which it duly did, and Nigel's hand reluctantly crossed the board to meet Kasparov's in the traditional acknowledgement of a draw.

Almost shouting above the applause of the packed theatre, which was giving both players a standing ovation, Kasparov asked Nigel excitedly, 'Did you see all that? Did you see the second rook sacrifice when you started the combination?'

'Yes, Garri,' said Nigel. Kasparov looked unconvinced. He found it hard, if not impossible, to imagine that any man could see more than he, the world champion, acknowledged as the most profound calculator in the history of the game. But then, grudgingly, he conceded to Nigel, 'Well, if you did see it all, then it was a great attack.'

I couldn't hear these words above the din of the spectators, but Nigel reported them to me, with some asperity, as we drove back to his flat in Hampstead. 'Of course I saw everything when I played the first sacrifice,' he said. 'I almost played like a fucking genius.' Almost, unfortunately, was right. The final twist to the attack, no fewer than twenty-three synapse-sapping moves after the initial sacrifice, had slipped through his hands. 'I saw the right move, bishop to queen four, and I was just about to play it. But I had no time to calculate everything and at the last second I played the wrong move on general principles. It just looked safer. What a waste.'

It was not just the miss of his first win in the match, and his first in a serious game against Kasparov for seven years, which so exasperated Short. There was also the purely aesthetic element. A chess grandmaster regards his most elegantly played games as a painter treasures his finest canvases: they are works of art to be looked at again and again with pride and pleasure. To miss the concluding point in such a glittering attack, especially against the world champion, is like making a final false brush-stroke on a flawless canvas. 'It would have been a historic game, one for the anthologies,' Nigel sighed, as the car drew up outside his home.

As H. G. Wells wrote, 'There is no remorse like the remorse of chess. It annihilates a man.'

Like most sportsmen, chessplayers are firm believers in ritual, and prey to superstition. Anatoly Karpov, the former world champion, would never wash his hair in a tournament, until he lost a game. ('Unfortunately,' as Short once laughingly remarked, 'he was one of the most successful tournament players of all time.') Nigel himself had less eccentric rituals, but he firmly believed – at least before a game – that the wearing of a certain tie or a particular suit might bring him luck.

For the ninth match-game Nigel turned to an old favourite:

his *Blue Peter* Gold Badge. He was proud of this children's television equivalent of the OBE, and always kept it scrupulously polished. Now, as he prepared to leave his suite, and the company of his wife and seconds, for the less pleasant embrace of Garri Kasparov, he pinned the *Blue Peter* badge to his jacket. For this game Nigel had the Black pieces, with which he had scored only half a point out of four games: desperate situations called for desperate remedies.

Then we performed the normal ritual, unchanged since the first game, and which always seemed slightly ridiculous: Nigel would slap hands 'high fives' style with Robert Hübner and me in turn. Then he would turn and leave with Rea for the theatre, accompanied by the bodyguard, who would mutter his movements into a concealed walkie-talkie.

At the board Kasparov's eyes briefly rested on Short's badge and turned blankly away. *Blue Peter* is not big in Azerbaizhan. And besides, the world champion had other things on his mind. In particular he had come to the board determined to avenge the only humiliation he had experienced in the match so far: the fifth game, in which Short, armed with a brilliant new concept in the Nimzovitch defence, had achieved a draw using only twelve minutes for the entire game, while Kasparov had sweated at the board for one and a half hours.

We knew that Kasparov and his three grandmaster assistants, Beliavsky, Makarichev and Azmaiparashvili, would have been subjecting Nigel's new idea – which was immensely sharp and complicated – to detailed forensic analysis in the week since it had first been played. We guessed that Kasparov would also have fed the position into his chess computer program, known as 'Fritz', which was particularly good at solving concrete tactical problems of the sort which Nigel's new move generated.

But Nigel had great faith in his new opening variation. Indeed he felt a proprietorial pride in it: it was his own invention and he cared about its reputation far more than he did about those ideas he had simply adapted from the practice of other grandmasters. So I knew that, if Kasparov decided to take Nigel on in this variation, he would rise to the intellectual challenge, rather than duck it and play something less controversial.

For the first ten moves, the two players followed Short's triumphant analysis of the fifth match-game. As they repeated those moves, like boxers before a fight trying not to blink against each other's stare, Kasparov's eyes constantly flicked up to look at Short, to see if there was any suspicion or doubt. But he got only a dreamy gaze through his opponent's John Lennon-style spectacles. When on the tenth move Nigel played the new idea which had so stunned the champion in the fifth game, Kasparov gave a broad grin and instantly replied with a move which, I knew, Nigel had scarcely considered. He had scarcely considered it because it looked crazy. After only five minutes Nigel responded with the obvious counter, which appeared to demonstrate the craziness of Kasparov's last move. But then, and again instantly, the world champion played another move which seemed incredibly risky. This one Kasparov played with a stabbing movement so violent that his cuffs shot out from underneath his jacket.

Then he stood up, turned on his shiny leather heels, and walked off the stage. It was still only move twelve. The grandmasters watching in the analysis room at Simpson's assumed that we were still in Short's analysis, and that he was just checking his prepared response. But then Jon Speelman walked in and disarmingly confessed, to general consternation, 'We hadn't analysed this.' Then to me, he muttered, 'This looks like Big Al's work.' 'Who's Big Al?' I muttered back. 'Alexander Beliavsky,' he said. 'He's got the sort of mind that could come up with this amazing idea. It's either him or Fritz.' Then he began to slope off, whispering moves to himself, agitatedly. There is no worse moment for a second, when his boss is confronted by a move which ought to have been anticipated but has been missed. The finger of blame is immediately pointed at the analytical team, who are generally described as having 'let down their man'.

As Jon departed in search of a chessboard and a wet towel, the chess journalist Cathy Forbes called after him, 'So, Jon, what has gone wrong?' 'Go forth and copulate, Cathy, preferably with a mongoose,' replied Speelman, without bothering to look back at the harpie over his shoulder.

However bad Jon Speelman was feeling, it must have been

even more uncomfortable at the board. Nigel thought for forty-one minutes over his reply. It was the clearest possible sign to Kasparov that his team had out-analysed Short's. And it was a sweet revenge, with the clock times a complete reversal of the world champion's humiliation in the fifth game. After sixteen moves of this, the ninth game, Short had used up an hour and a half, Kasparov only twenty-eight minutes. In fact the revenge was even sweeter than that: by move sixteen Kasparov also had a strategically winning position, as Robert Hübner, who was watching the game on teletext in his room at the Savoy, gloomily informed me when I asked him if things were as bad as they looked. 'Worse,' said Robert, in his most Eeyorish manner.

From then on the game should have been a stroll for Kasparov. Just after the four-hour time-control was reached Kasparov simplified the game into an ending in which he had a rook, king's pawn and queen's rook pawn against Nigel's lone rook. This is an absolutely standard position which is known to be completely winning for the player with the two extra pawns. It is the sort of ending which Kasparov would have been demolishing as homework when he was a short-trousered kid at Mikhail Botvinnik's chess school. The commentators were mystified as to why Nigel was playing on. The mixture of boredom and irritation on Kasparov's face was comment enough.

Nigel, I assumed, just wanted to postpone for as long as possible the moment when he would go five-nil down in the match. Or perhaps he knew that, by playing on well into the fifth hour, he was guaranteeing that Kasparov's post-victory comments to the press would come too late to make the following day's newspapers.

Unfortunately, as Short wearily churned out his last few moves, the one thing he was not considering was the position in front of him. If he had been, the newspapers would really have had something to rush into a late edition. For on move forty-six, Kasparov, moving quickly, committed a colossal blunder, which permitted Short, by a simple manoeuvre, to win one of the champion's pawns and achieve a dead drawn position. Jon Speelman, who was watching the game, immediately spotted how Short could chop off Kasparov's pawn and could barely contain himself when, with scarcely any thought, Nigel replied with the wrong move. Five minutes later he resigned, and rapidly disappeared from the stage.

Kasparov then bounced into the Channel Four studio, immediately behind the stage, animatedly telling everyone about the great triumph of his prepared analysis, how it had taken him and his team of analysts ten hours to find the key move which appeared to refute Short's new opening line. He was in irrepressible mood. Then Jon Speelman interrupted and told Kasparov he had blundered horribly in the ending. 'No, I didn't,' Kasparov replied angrily. Speelman then gave Kasparov the relevant position, spelling it out in international algebraic notation. 'That position never occurred in the game,' snapped the world champion. But Jon Speelman is a stubborn man. He then directed Kasparov's attention to the computer which recorded all the moves of the game, and which, too, had instantly recognized that Kasparov had blundered and that Short could have drawn. Kasparov looked, appalled, at the computer screen. He spent the next four minutes staring distractedly into space, and then left the studio without a word.

While this little drama was taking place Nigel was in his hotel bedroom. I had never seen him so depressed. He was standing, naked from the waist up, staring at himself in the mirror that covered the wardrobe – not moving, not saying anything, just staring at himself. Fortunately he did not know that he had missed a certain draw from a dead lost position. All he knew was that his favourite opening variation had been answered by a move he had never seen after weeks of his home preparation, and that he was now five points down after only nine games.

I tried to console him by saying that this was just one game, and one loss. Wordlessly Nigel lifted up his right hand, its palm facing outwards, and spread out his fingers. This was not high fives. It was five losses.

There was a knock at the door. It was Nigel's mother Jean, who had sensed Nigel's desperation as he left the stage and knew that she was needed. She took him in her arms. He towered over her as they embraced. Then Jean whispered something to her son and he wandered over to the corner of the room, picked up his guitar and began to play. And, as he played, he began to smile.

Later that night, Nigel's telephone rang. It was the indefatigable Speelman, to inform his boss that he had missed a certain draw five minutes before he resigned. 'Give me the position,' said Nigel. Speelman, as ever, obliged. The official challenger for the world chess championship paused, and then passed his verdict. 'Fuck a duck,' he said.

CHAPTER TEN

C hess grandmasters are not just masters of chess. They are
also masters of the excuse for playing chess badly. Garri
Kasparov in particular finds it so difficult to accept his
rare blunders that he will always find a reason other than pure
human error for his fall from chess grace. The world champion's
need for such rationalization is understandable. According to his
wife Masha he is 'inconsolable' after he has made a bad error, let
alone lost a game.

By the morning after the ninth game, Kasparov had already
come up with his excuse. He told friends that Short should have
resigned long before the mutual blunders took place. In other
words, the game was already over, won. What happened after
that point was irrelevant, not worth talking about.

Nigel Short had his own rationalization, not for Kasparov's
monumental error, but for his own in not spotting it. He
explained to me that he had already mentally resigned the game;
but had Kasparov noticed his own blunder at the board, after
making it, then the waves of panic would have alerted him to
what had happened, and he would have woken up and played
the correct reply.

This did not convince Rea, who was enraged by her husband's carelessness. 'If Nigel is just sitting there playing on for
bloody pride, then it's a complete waste of time. He should
either play proper moves or resign.'

Despite her anger Rea was deeply concerned about Nigel's
state of mind after the ninth match-game: 'I am worried that he
is beginning to lose his belief in himself. This was my biggest
worry when the match was first thought of: that Nigel would
somehow feel he had no right to be up on that stage with
Kasparov, and that this would make it impossible for him to
play.'

It was true that Nigel had become so embarrassed by the
state of the match that he no longer wanted to be seen in public.

It was bad enough to have the chess columnists explain, as they loved to do, how Nigel ought to be playing against Kasparov and how much better he would be doing if only he took their brilliant advice. This Nigel could – and did – ignore by the simple expedient of cancelling his newspaper order. But when people came up to him in the street and offered their own advice on how to beat Garri Kasparov: this was too much to bear. In particular, there was a group of builders just outside the Savoy who would put down their hods when Nigel emerged and shout out to the Grandmaster, 'Pull your socks up! We've got money on you!' or variations on that theme. Sometimes, when we left the Savoy together, Nigel would cross over to the other side of the road and ask me to walk between him and the builders so that they could not see him.

On the day after the blunder-ridden ninth game, Nigel went down with a streaming cold. A doctor would probably say that this explained his play the day before: it's just before a cold emerges that one begins to feel terrible (and Nigel did complain to me immediately after the game that he had suddenly experienced great difficulty in calculating variations). A psychologist would probably say that the heavy cold was an outward sign of inner misery. Whatever the diagnosis, Nigel felt too ill to do the normal amount of preparation before the tenth game and gave Robert Hübner and Jon Speelman the next day – a Sunday – off, their first break in the four weeks since the match began.

By Tuesday, the day of the game, Nigel was still pumping himself full of anti-flu remedies, and over lunch just before play began he complained to me that he did not feel any of the surge of energy that normally washes over him at the outset of a big game. An hour later, and he was sitting down at the board with Kasparov, who could not help but notice that his opponent was coughing heavily and staunching his nose with a rather tired-looking handkerchief.

I fancy that almost any other player in the world, 5–0 down, and feeling fluey, would head for a quick draw against a killer like Kasparov. Short had the White pieces and could easily have used that slight initiative to steer the game into quiet and peaceful channels. Instead he immediately plunged into the same ultra-aggressive variation that he had chosen for his two previous games with White.

But this time it brought him no advantage, and on the thirteenth move, in a position where nothing much seemed to be going on, Nigel suddenly sank into deep, almost comatose thought. While the champion wandered on and off the stage, occasionally looking at his opponent as if to check that he was awake, Short sat and thought, with what appeared to be a look of complete perplexity on his face. Fifty-two minutes passed – almost half the time Short was allotted for all of his first forty moves. And when he finally did make his thirteenth move, to ironic cheers from the more ribald inhabitants of the grand-master analysis room, it was one which had been almost universally predicted at least half an hour before.

The man leading the sarcastic comments in Simpson's on Short's play was, not surprisingly, Grandmaster Tony Miles. This was the man – a former junior world champion – who seemed unable to get over the fact that he had been conclusively evicted by Short as the British number-one chessplayer and had at one point emigrated to the United States, and played for that country, rather than represent Britain on any board other than the top one. Indeed in the 1986 Dubai Chess Olympiad, when his international ranking was already far below Short's, Miles used his position as a selector of the English chess team to ensure that he remained on top board. Short has never forgiven Miles for that, even though Miles's subsequent defection ended the argument once and for all in the younger man's favour.

But now Tony Miles was back in England and could get some satisfaction by turning up at Simpson's for every game and ridiculing Short's play in the grandmaster analysis room with remarks such as 'This is a normal Short position – losing!' It was difficult for the other British players around the table to challenge Miles's barrage of chessic abuse. He was still, for all the decline in his powers, a much stronger player than any of them. And, although gone somewhat to fat, he remained a brutish physical specimen.

'Short's position is totally lifeless,' declared Miles, as his *bête noire* played the interminably delayed thirteenth move. And, to be fair to Miles, everyone else, commenting both in Simpson's and on television, concurred with that view. On move fourteen, Nigel sacrificed his king's pawn, in what appeared to be a suicidal manoeuvre. Kasparov, moving rapidly and confidently, played the moves which Miles had predicted would destroy Short's position. As Nigel thought about his fifteenth move, Miles reached for a sandwich from the tray provided by Simpson's for the grandmasters and announced, 'It's all over, it is just winning for Kasparov.' At that instant Short sacrificed his queen.

In the audience at the Savoy Theatre one spectator was unable to restrain his amazement. 'Jesus!' he exclaimed, before being shushed down by those on either side of him. Kasparov looked scarcely less surprised than the man in the audience, and grabbed Short's queen. It was only after a further three or four moves that the truth became apparent, even to the grandmasters in Simpson's: Short's queen sacrifice was not just unexpected, it was also incredibly strong. Kasparov's position, apparently crushing only a few moves earlier, was suddenly on the verge of collapse. His extra queen was useless: all the squares on the board seemed to be controlled by Short's liberated minor pieces.

It now became clear what Short had been thinking about for those fifty-two minutes, as he reflected on his thirteenth move. Or was it? After the game was over Nigel told me that he had calculated and prepared the queen sacrifice during the fourteen minutes that he had spent on his previous move, the twelfth. The reason why he had spent almost an hour on his thirteenth move was because he suddenly saw that Kasparov could easily have avoided the queen sacrifice, and he was frantically seeking some way to change plans at the last minute. Unfortunately for Nigel, he had no alternative. Fortunately for Nigel, Kasparov's thought processes at the time were on no higher a level than those of the sandwich-guzzling commentator, Tony Miles; he walked right into the queen sacrifice, like a boxer winning on points walking into a desperate haymaker from a suffering opponent.

That, in essence, was the explanation Nigel offered me after the game: 'I could see by the look on Gazza's face that he thought I had gone, that I had cracked. If he hadn't been so cocksure he would have stopped to think what I was up to.'

It was only at move twenty that 'Gazza' finally stopped blitzing out his moves and began to think. By then it was too late. Nigel had a gigantic 'passed' pawn rammed into the innards of Kasparov's position. There seemed to be no way in which the champion could stop the pawn hitting his back rank, becoming a queen and giving Short a colossal material advantage.

On move twenty-two, Nigel pushed the pawn to the seventh rank, one away from the queening square. As if to demonstrate that Kasparov could do nothing to stop its promotion he reached across to the pile of pieces that the Russian had captured and grabbed the white queen. Then he put it, the same piece of wood he had sacrificed only eight moves earlier, comfortingly close to his right hand, ready for its coronation. Grandmaster Raymond Keene, commenting live on Channel Four, noticed Nigel's deft little movement and began singing 'God save our gracious Queen' in punning celebration of the imminent British victory.

But the queen was not there for comfort alone, still less to remind Kasparov of his folly in capturing it in the first place. Nigel, as a result of his fifty-two-minute reverie on the thirteenth move, was cripplingly short of time, much shorter of time than he was at a similar stage in the first game, which he had ultimately lost by clock forfeit. By move thirty-five his position was totally winning: in fact, which was part of his problem, he had about five different ways to win. But he had less than a minute to complete his six moves before the time-control.

Kasparov, naturally, had noticed that Short's clock flag was poised, quivering, at the perpendicular. In a lost position he had nothing to lose by playing, not the best moves, but those which most randomized the position. This he proceeded to do, and at lightning speed. The point was that if he moved instantly then Short would have no extra time in which to analyse the position.

As Kasparov thrashed about like a crocodile caught by the tail, I was forcibly reminded of the comment of the Indian

Grandmaster Anand, the world-ranked number three who has both won and lost several ferocious tussles with the world champion: 'In desperate positions Kasparov fights hand to hand, and kicks savagely. But if you chop off his arms and legs, he defends himself with his teeth.'

The world champion's ankle-gnawing tactics worked, aided by Short's desperate time trouble. Nigel missed simple forced wins on moves thirty-six, thirty-seven, thirty-eight and finally, on move forty, the last move before the time-control. It was later recorded that Short's clock flag fell four seconds after completing his fortieth move. That was way beyond any margin for error. The mechanical chess clock has no second-hand for the players to measure out their final minutes. With seconds to go, it is just guesswork as to whether the flag will fall or stay, tremulously, upright. Nigel afterwards told me that he thought he was probably going to lose the game on time, and that was certainly the view of the commentators at the Savoy, who were scrutinizing the players' clock through binoculars.

After the time-control was reached Nigel, shaking his head and muttering to himself, repeated the position twice and offered Kasparov a draw. The champion's eyebrows shot skywards as he eagerly extended his hand towards Short's. 'You are still winning in this position,' he said, tactfully. Nigel waved his hand dismissively. 'Who knows?' he said, and got up from the board. At its side stood the White queen, a totemic reminder, not just of the stroke of genius which led to its sacrifice, but more painfully, of the panic which prevented it from being triumphantly reincarnated.

A few minutes later, as Robert Hübner and I knocked on the door of Nigel's suite, Rob the bodyguard, who was as usual keeping guard outside, shot us a warning. 'I'd watch out,' said the 200-kilogram-lifting minder, '"E's been effing and blinding like nobody's business.' But the bodyguard had evidently taken the brunt of Nigel's rage. By now he had calmed down and was almost anxious to discuss the débâcle which had just occurred.

'Kasparov is a slippery bastard. Of course, he completely missed the queen sacrifice, although afterwards he pretended that he hadn't. But what good is it if I see much more than the world champion, but still can't beat him?'

I reported to Nigel how not just Kasparov but all the watching grandmasters had missed the sacrifice, and how Tony Miles had declared Kasparov to be winning almost at the very moment that Short played the devastating queen offer. This seemed to cheer Nigel up. 'Poor old Tony,' he laughed. 'Not only does he fail to anticipate my best moves; he doesn't even understand them when they are actually played on the board.'

Then Nigel let slip that Kasparov, in the relief of grabbing a draw from a situation in which many players would have resigned, had told him that the final position was still winning for Short. 'I don't think it was winning for me. Absolutely not. But I felt I'd fucked it up so much anyway, I didn't want to play on. I'd had it, actually. I could have lost if we'd continued playing. I just had nothing left, no energy. I was gone. At the end I could hardly move the pieces – I had such terrible cramp in my right hand.'

Perhaps this was just the result of playing high-tension chess against Kasparov for four hours with a heavy cold. But it was fortunate that Nigel did not make these remarks at the post-game press conference. The amateur psychologists among the reporters, exasperated by his failure to exploit his many opportunities, were already writing that Short had some strange psychological blockage that was preventing him from winning against a player he had not beaten for seven years.

Such a psychological blockage, physically manifested by a crippling cramp in the playing hand at the crucial moment, is not unknown among grandmasters. In the 1960s the leading Romanian Grandmaster, Florin Gheorgiu, was a match for anyone. But he had an appalling record against the top Danish Grandmaster and world championship semi-finalist, Bent Larsen. Finally, in the 1970 Siegen Chess Olympiad, Gheorgiu achieved a completely winning position against the great Dane, with two moves to make before the time-control.

Then the following happened, as described in the tournament book of the Siegen Olympiad:

Eye witnesses present at the closing stages of this amazing encounter reported that Gheorgiu reached out his right hand to administer the lethal blow, Knight to Bishop Six, but at this precise moment the said hand was seized with a convulsive tremble which rendered the Rumanian Grandmaster incapable of transferring the piece to the required square. In the act of summoning up sufficient reserves of will-power to overcome this unfortunate and paralytic state of affairs, Gheorgiu overstepped the time limit.

The night before the first game of the match, at dinner at Nigel and Rea's flat, Robert Hübner, who is a fund of amusing and bizarre stories about the chess world, recounted this episode. Nigel, who knew both Gheorgiu and Larsen well, collapsed in hysterical giggles, while gasping out the suggestion that Gheorgiu should have made the killing move with his left hand. Twenty-four hours later, when Nigel had himself lost in time in a winning position in his first match-game against Kasparov, Gheorgiu's fate did not seem so amusing. And now, four weeks later, in game ten, Nigel seemed almost to have been struck with the curse of Gheorgiu in its full form: psychosomatic convulsive cramp in the playing hand, at the very moment of victory.

Almost, but not quite as bad. Although Kasparov claimed immediately after the game that Nigel was still winning when the draw was agreed, the world champion, once he had calmed down, confirmed to Nigel that the final position was indeed drawn, and that Short could well have lost the game if he had continued to press for a win.

But all of this was irrelevant to Robert Hübner, who had taken over the mantle of chief coach from Lubosh Kavalek. On the whole Robert was very gentle with Nigel, and, unlike Kavalek, was not inclined to tell his player how he should play the game or how he should organize his life. But, as we met in Nigel's rooms immediately after the traumatic conclusion of the tenth game, Hübner decided the time had finally come to give his boss a lecture.

'If you make your fortieth move with only four seconds to spare, then you have lost control,' the doctor began. 'If you leave

yourself with a minute to make several moves in such a complicated position, then you have no time to analyse. You can even
lose a winning position. You must organize your thinking more.
Of course there comes a stage in a game when you must think
for a long time over one move, perhaps half an hour, at the
most. But to think for almost an hour over one move in the
opening – that is unnecessary, and bound to cause trouble with
the clock later.'

Rea was nodding furiously as Robert spoke. A few days
earlier she had tried to persuade Nigel to 'treat your clock more
gently' but he had rather brusquely told her that he was thinking
for no longer than was necessary. She was right, of course, but
as Nigel said to me at the time, 'It's not very easy to take advice
on a technical chess matter from your wife, who doesn't even
play the game.'

But advice from the vastly experienced Robert Hübner was
quite another matter, although Nigel, rather plaintively, tried to
justify his mammoth thinks and subsequent scrambles to reach
the time-control. 'People keep saying to me, "Why can't you
move more quickly?" Robert, I'd like to move more quickly but
these are not simple games we are playing. They are incredibly
complicated. And Kasparov is getting very short of time too, in
a number of games.'

'Yes, some of them,' replied Hübner. 'But we are getting
more and more games where he has much more time than you
in very complicated positions, just before the time-control, and
that is very, very unpleasant. I know this from my own experiences. You must, if you can, avoid this happening again in the
match.'

Nigel fell completely silent, for about a minute. He is an
implacably stubborn man who hates to alter his chosen approach
to any problem, especially when he is told to do so. He was
never going to say outright there and then, in his oak-panelled
Savoy drawing room, in front of Rea and me, not to mention
Kyveli, that Robert was right. We would just have to wait for
the next game to find out if Nigel would adopt Hübner's
strategy or stick to his own.

The proper balance between the quest for the perfect move

and the pressure of time is one that has dogged grandmaster chess ever since the mechanical chess clock was introduced in the middle of the nineteenth century. Before then it was simply a question of being a gentleman and not irking the opponent by too prolonged a pause between moves. A famous, probably apocryphal, story concerns a game between the interminably slow nineteenth-century German player, Louis Paulsen, and Paul Morphy, possibly the greatest player in chess history, and certainly the quickest. During one of their games Paulsen had been thinking for over an hour. At that point Morphy, who normally never let his eyes stray from the board, broke with the etiquette of the time and glanced quizzically at his immobile opponent. 'Oh,' said Paulsen, 'is it my move?'

More recently, the game at the highest level has tended to divide into two schools of thought: those players who like to play reasonable moves at an even pace, and those who, particularly when forming their plan for the middle game, will spend any amount of time to find the perfect strategy and be prepared to be left with only a few minutes, if necessary, over their last twenty or so moves.

Anatoly Karpov, Kasparov's predecessor as world champion, was very much an exponent of the pragmatic approach: he regarded the quest for the perfect plan or the perfect move as quixotic. 'There is no such thing as the perfect game,' he once said. 'We are only humans, after all.' In his successful defences of his title in 1978 against Viktor Korchnoi – a notorious 'deep thinker' – Karpov won, not by playing the better chess, but simply by playing sensible moves rapidly and waiting for Korchnoi to self-destruct in his scramble to reach the time-control.

But when Karpov played Kasparov, in no less than five matches between 1984 and 1990, he found it very difficult to move at a fluent, even pace and became increasingly enmeshed in horrific time-scrambles. The reason, of course, was that even Karpov's razor-sharp brain found the chessboard problems created by Kasparov's style of play impossible to slice through at anything like the speed with which it could deal with lesser players' ideas.

Nigel, too, had always been a notably rapid player, and was

166

much more in the Karpov mould. But, as he pointed out to Robert Hübner, the complications that Kasparov was able to create, even in apparently simple positions, were simply too hazardous to allow of a superficial approach. An additional problem was that their match was being played at a quicker time-control than any of the Fidé world championships. Under the Fidé rules, the players were allotted two and a half hours each for forty moves. Short and Kasparov had allowed themselves only two hours for the same number of moves. This is, in fact, the standard time-control for ordinary grandmaster tournaments, so both players would be used to it. On the other hand, the world championship is no ordinary grandmaster tournament. The psychological and sporting pressures are of a different order of magnitude. And it was these, as much as the objective strength of Kasparov's chessboard moves, which had been weighing on Nigel's mind and preventing it from solving problems with its usual brisk decisiveness.

As Kasparov opened the eleventh match-game with the White pieces, it was almost as if he *had* succeeded in bugging Nigel's suite at the Savoy. If Short were to adopt a new strategy of moving rapidly in the opening, the best way of countering that would be either to play an opening new to the match or to play a novelty in an expected variation.

Somehow Kasparov managed to do both. For the first time in the match he played the Scotch Game, an antiquated opening much more commonly seen in the nineteenth century than the twentieth. Kasparov had twice brought out this blunderbuss from his private museum of chess armoury to pepper Karpov in their world championship match in 1990. So Short was not entirely surprised by this blast from the past. But in this game, as early as the eighth move, Kasparov introduced an entirely novel form of development, involving an unexpected leap of his queen's knight to the extremity of the board, against all the established principles of opening play.

Short had a lot to think about. After the game he remarked to me that he could have thought for an hour at this stage and still not have known whether he had found the right reply. But he was self-consciously determined never again to allow Kasparov to blitz him in a time-scramble. After only a quarter of an hour's thought Short settled on a simple plan of development, which did not attempt to mount a fundamental challenge to Kasparov's novelty, but merely sought to establish a playable position.

In fact it was by no means the best response to the world champion's paradoxical novelty, and Nigel very soon found himself forced into a horribly cramped middlegame which Tony Miles – naturally – described as 'strategically lost for Short'. However, Short's unusually rapid play in a position which ought to have given him cause for deep concern clearly disconcerted Kasparov. While pondering his own moves, the Russian's eyes kept flicking up into Short's, trying somehow to divine the reason why his opponent felt so comfortable in such an apparently prospectless situation.

By move twenty-five, Kasparov had fallen twenty minutes behind on the clock in a position which, arising as it did out of his own novelty, should have been far more familiar to him than to Short. But it was now Kasparov who was on the edge of a time scramble, while Nigel wandered away from the board, looking confident – even if, objectively, his position on the chessboard gave no reason for great pride.

And it turned out that, when short of time against an opponent with plenty, Kasparov was vulnerable. In his headlong rush to the time-control he blundered away first one, then another pawn. Nigel, meanwhile, had no fewer than twenty minutes left on his clock when he completed his fortieth move. Fortunately for the world champion, his position had been so good that it could easily withstand the loss of two pawns, and Short's extra twenty minutes for the second session were redundant: the position was not one he could win, with any amount of time in hand.

Even so, Nigel was distinctly taken aback when, two pawns down, Kasparov offered him a draw. It was in fact dead drawn, stone cold dead. But as Nigel said to me later that evening, while he savoured only the second draw he had attained with the Black pieces in the match, 'Gazza ought to know that the etiquette in such positions is that the player with the material advantage has the right to offer the draw. It makes no difference that he's the world champion, although he obviously thinks it does.'

The world champion would certainly have noticed Nigel's irritation at the time. As Kasparov extended his hand in the drawing gesture, Short shook his head, played another move himself, said, 'I offer *you* a draw,' and only then met Kasparov's lonely outstretched hand with his own. Rubbing in the point as they got up from the board, Nigel remarked to the world champion, 'You've done very well, drawing against such a strong player, two pawns down.' Kasparov was not very amused.

Even when he is in a high-spirited mood, Garri Kasparov is not a man who takes kindly to being teased. But his mood was anything but high-spirited. After the game Robert Hübner came up to Nigel in the foyer of the Savoy and – for the first time in the match – gave him the accolade of a pat on the back. It was, I think, meant as an acknowledgement of the patient's carrying out the doctor's orders of moving more rapidly and avoiding blunders in a time-scramble. But Nigel was far more interested in talking about the change which he thought had come over Kasparov.

'He wasn't the same in this game. There was something missing. Normally when I play Gazza I feel these great waves of energy, trying to push me off the board. But I didn't feel it nearly so much today, and I don't think it's my imagination. He looked knackered, and after the game he seemed like a complete zombie.' I suggested that perhaps Kasparov had caught the virus from which Nigel had been suffering a few days earlier: they had certainly been as close as two men can get without committing an indecent act. 'In that case, I wish I had had bubonic plague,' said Nigel, as ever the very soul of charity as far as Kasparov's well-being was concerned.

For the twelfth match-game Nigel had his usual two opponents. Over the board there was the looming presence of Garri Kasparov. In the grandmaster analysis room there was Tony

Miles, still apparently determined to ridicule Short's moves, even – or rather especially – the good ones.

By move thirteen, Miles claimed, to his appreciative audience of kibitzers, patzers and the odd master, that Short, with the advantage of the White pieces, had played 'garbage' and that he was 'stone cold dead out of the opening'. After Nigel played his fifteenth move, which happened to be the best available, Miles screeched, 'He'll get murdered!', and when Short played his sixteenth move, again clearly the best, his old rival was so overwhelmed with derision that he started to cackle. At this point, finally, he was gently admonished to 'calm down' by the visiting American Grandmaster Joel Benjamin, who was doing his best to concentrate on the position.

What was true was that Short seemed to have run into the very thing he had been trying to avoid throughout the match: a new variation prepared by Kasparov, or his sous-chefs Azmaiparashvili, Makarichev and Beliavsky, with which he would necessarily be completely unfamiliar. Throughout the opening, Kasparov bashed out his moves instantly, while Short played as if each move of his opponent came as an immense surprise.

In fact the variation – a fiendishly difficult one involving hair-trigger calculation for both sides – was neither entirely new nor entirely unfamiliar to Nigel. Kasparov's kitchen had unearthed from an old Soviet chess magazine some long-forgotten analysis by the Grandmaster Leonid Shamkovitch, and had discovered an improvement on move seventeen. After the game Nigel told me that when Kasparov sprang his prepared line, 'I suddenly saw in my mind's eye this old article by Shamkovitch. But then I began to panic because I couldn't remember exactly how the analysis went, and even whether it was winning for Black.' Yet Nigel, working it out as he went along, faithfully repeated all the moves for White recommended in that furry old Soviet chess magazine, only to be hit by Kasparov's spiky new improvement which picked up where the old analysis ended.

In response Nigel produced a manoeuvre with his king which Kasparov, even as he spent days on the line with his three grandmaster assistants, had failed to see. It was a simple idea, really: giving up a pawn in order to establish better lines of communication between his pieces. But it was the turning-point of the game. Kasparov was clearly angry with himself that he had missed Nigel's idea when studying the position at home under a microscope. The world champion, who had played his first nineteen moves *a tempo*, thought for over half an hour on his reply to Nigel's improvised improvement on the Russians' special homebrew, and then produced a move which sent the position straight into an endgame in which winning chances, if they existed at all, were with Short.

Naturally all the watching grandmasters took the opposite view, some stating that Kasparov was winning, others – the English optimists – that Nigel had some drawing chances. The players on the stage knew better, which, I suppose, explains why they were sharing a purse of £1.7 million, and the lesser grandmasters in the analysis room were being paid pin-money for puerile punditry.

Grandmaster Miles, who in 1986 had lost a non-title match to Kasparov by the humiliating margin of 5½–½, saw the matter differently. Baffled by the course the game was taking, he informed his colleagues after Kasparov's thirty-first move that 'They don't understand anything,' and pronounced Short's excellent thirty-fifth move 'a total blunder . . . elementary stupidity', without, however, suggesting an alternative.

The man obliged to reply to Short's moves over the board, rather than to sneer at them from a safe distance, found things rather less elementary: as soon as the time-control was reached Garri Kasparov instantly accepted Short's offer of a draw, and the first half of the match was over, with the score 8½–3½ in the champion's favour.

In the negotiations over the playing schedule for the match Kasparov had wanted to have a three-day break at this juncture. He had been amazed at Nigel's insouciant insistence that 'We don't need any holidays,' but in the end had agreed to the idea of playing all twenty-four games at an unyielding pace of three a week.

In all his five matches with Karpov, played under Fidé rules, Kasparov and his opponent had also been allowed four 'time-outs' each. Under this regulation, each player could, on four occasions in the match, request a postponement of the next game, at only a few hours' notice. But under the terms insisted on by Channel Four, the television company filming the match, there would be no time-outs in Kasparov vs. Short.

Perhaps it was this unaccustomed pace which was putting a strain on the world champion. Perhaps it was the fact that, unlike almost all previous world championship matches, every game had been fought, as Kasparov himself put it, 'to the last pawn': there had not been a single occasion when, as so often happens in grandmaster chess, both players had tacitly agreed not to fight. Or perhaps it was just that the attention of the politically ambitious Kasparov was painfully divided between the chessboard struggle in London and the power struggle in Moscow, which that week was being decided by Boris Yeltsin in brutal fashion. Whatever the reason, the world champion's less than usually exuberant manner and slightly sallow appearance were giving his opponent fresh hope in an otherwise hopeless situation.

After the twelfth game, as after the eleventh, Nigel remarked to me with bleak satisfaction that Kasparov's energy levels seemed uncharacteristically low. Before the match Nigel had been very concerned that his own energy would be sapped long before Kasparov's. The thirteenth world champion was certainly fitter than any of his twelve predecessors, and even by the more rigorous standards of present-day players he was a byword for stamina and endurance. It was now a matter of chess legend how Kasparov had outlasted the steely Karpov in a match of six months' duration, not breaking even though he failed to win a single game in the first thirty-one played in that timeless series of 1984–5. Eventually Karpov cracked physically and mentally, and the match had to be stopped to save the older man from complete breakdown.

That was, however, eight years ago. Now aged thirty himself, Kasparov was hardly an old man, even by the standards of modern chess, which seems to have become as dominated by precocious teenagers as any of the physical sports. On the other hand the world champion, greying and with a bald patch beginning to defeat the best efforts of his coiffeurs, looked much older than his thirty years. He had borrowed very heavily at the bank of human energy: some day, one felt, if not here and now in London, there would be a very large debt to be paid, and with interest.

If Nigel was surprised by Kasparov's sudden lassitude in the middle of their marathon, I was surprised by Nigel's apparent buoyancy. He had taken a hammering in the early games, both on the chess board, and off it, with the parricidal conflict with Kavalek. After the first four games Nigel had lost over three kilos in weight, a rate of depletion which his coat-hanger frame could simply not tolerate for more than a few more games. Since then he had managed to stabilize his weight, and at the halfway stage was a kilo heavier than at the time of Kavalek's departure.

Short monitored his weight – and his sleeping patterns – with just as much care as he checked on his chess opening preparations. He knew that, if he experienced rapid weight loss or less than a solid nine hours' sleep a night, his chess would disintegrate. He could name and date a number of crucial games which he had lost over the years when he had failed to make proper allowance for his physical and mental condition. In this match he had made this mistake once, when in the fourth game, short of sleep on the day of Kavalek's departure, he had turned down a draw by repetition. The result was a near physical collapse at the board, his worst defeat of the match, and the only one – so far – with the White pieces.

Nigel was determined not to overstretch his physical resources again: and he would often quote to me the rueful words of his friend Boris Spassky after the Russian's first, unsuccessful twenty-four-game match for the world championship in 1966. 'I trained as if for a sprint', he had lamented after his defeat at the hands of the durable Armenian, Tigran Petrosian, 'but I found out that this event is a marathon.'

Short was very proud of the way in which he, and his team, had managed to maintain their high spirits and morale for a month, even when five points behind, and without the fillip of a single win. He was all the more astounded to read in the *Sunday*

Times, on the day after he had drawn game twelve, a completely spurious account of how he was 'near to collapse', that he was in such a bad psychological state that 'the championship could end his career' and which compared him with Eddie 'The Eagle' Edwards, 'Britain's skiing no-hoper'. One of the sources of the *Sunday Times*'s uncharacteristically speculative hatchet-job was, of course, Tony Miles.

Nigel had become used to chess correspondents uncovering his mistakes and gleefully pointing out better moves, which they, of course, would have played, and thus beaten the world champion where Short had failed. He had grown to recognize this as just wishful thinking on the part of weaker players whose fragile egos were in regular need of such restoratives. The *Sunday Times* piece, however, was written not by a known or respected chess correspondent but by a hack who knew nothing whatever about the game, and was prepared to be used as a conduit for the envious ravings of Short's most unbalanced enemies.

The day after the article appeared Nigel called me. He was as angry as he ever gets, which reveals itself in a cold deliberateness rather than any more spectacular effusion. 'Not only is the story a pack of lies, it is appearing in a paper which claims it wants me to write a regular chess column after the match.' (This was true: part of the *quid pro quo* for *The Times*'s sponsorship of the match – or maybe part of the *quo* for *The Times*'s 1.7 million quid – was that Nigel would have to become the *Sunday Times*'s chess correspondent for a year after the match.) 'I'm not going to work for such people,' Nigel went on. 'How could I trust them to look after my interests after this?'

Later that day Short's manager sent by fax the following pertinent comment to the Managing Director of the *Sunday Times*, Anthony Bambridge:

> The hostile tone and content of this article, which is defamatory and possibly actionable, is clearly inconsistent with Nigel putting himself under your editorial control as a chess correspondent after the match. I assume that the *Sunday Times* would not wish to be associated with an incompetent no-hoper and, therefore, that you have no objection to Nigel

cancelling the agreement of 22 April 1993 without further obligations on either side.

As Nigel commented to me at the time, he had expected any dirty tactics to be employed by his opponent, and not by the organization, News International, which was sponsoring the event. Perhaps the *Sunday Times*'s attack could be put down to internal rivalries within News International. The newspaper behind the event was *The Times*, which has always enjoyed, if that is the word, a bitter rivalry with its Sunday sibling. The latter, in particular, has long resented the way in which it has been required to subsidize the losses of *The Times*. It would be quite in character for the *Sunday Times* to mock a *Times* event which had sucked out yet more funds from the organization – even at the risk of fouling its own nest.

As for the absence of underhand tactics from Short's opponent, that was a little harder to explain. But there had been a marked change from his previous encounters with Kasparov, when, as Nigel put it, 'Gazza used to stamp up and down in my line of vision, deliberately, when it was my turn to move.'

The world champion could no longer do this, even if he had wanted to. The London match organizers had made it an absolute rule that the players could not pace up and down the stage; they must either sit at the board, or retire to their private rooms.

I think there was another reason for the improvement in Kasparov's behaviour, which was far more of a reflection of the world champion's own, changed, feelings. In the past he had always regarded the English Grandmaster as an ineffectual character, who merited the occasional sneer – or worse. But Short's decision in February to contact Kasparov, and mount a break-away movment from Fidé, had transformed the champion's view of his rival. Away from the chessboard he now saw Short almost as a comrade in arms, and the two men continued to see eye to eye over the running of their Professional Chess Association.

During the games in London, however, the world champion was still, according to Nigel, 'constantly giving me funny looks, and staring at me, particularly in the opening stages of the game', but somehow this no longer bothered him, as it had in the past: 'I just think "What a silly trick", and get on with the chess.'

Such looks as Kasparov had been giving his opponent were more ones of mild derision, when an unexpected or questionable move had been made. There were rarely the long glares of outright hostility which he had given Short in some of their previous encounters. Nigel's own explanation for this change in Kasparov's behaviour – it was something about which he had ruminated throughout the match – was that this event was being played in Britain in front of a crowd solidly behind the home player, and a television audience similarly prejudiced.

Kasparov, who revels in public adulation, had, said Nigel, obviously worked out that if he tried such overt intimidation against the home player he would achieve nothing by way of result except a very bad press. In this way Kasparov had managed to evade the hostile attentions of the British press, which, in the absence of an obvious 'bad guy', had decided instead to attack his opponent.

Nigel, however, seemed baffled by the fact that he continued to get a daily shoal of letters of encouragement and admiration from members of the general public – I could see them every day, piled up on his drawing-room table – long after the press had either written him off or, in the case of the *Sunday Times*, descended into abuse – or was it self-abuse?

He was discovering what anyone who has represented England at international sport could have told him, through similar bitter experience. The great British sporting public is uniquely supportive of its heroes, so long as they are seen to try their utmost. But the great British sporting press can never forgive any sort of national failure: particularly if its financial interests have been heavily invested in success.

CHAPTER ELEVEN

It is said that boxers who have entered a contest hating each other, sometimes finish it with mutual respect. Kasparov might – as Nigel Short believed – have been behaving better simply because he was worried about antagonizing the home crowd. But Short himself seemed to have become gradually less inclined to rain insults on the world champion. And immediately after the games he would usually stay a few minutes at the board with Kasparov, discussing the most interesting moments. This was something that, before the match, the challenger had vowed not to do.

'We're prisoners in the same cell,' Nigel said, when I asked him what lay behind his cessation of hostility. I don't suppose that the Savoy Hotel has been compared with a prison before, but after two months even the best hotel room can seem like a cell. Perhaps Nigel was in any case referring not to the players' accommodation but to their fate: to sit facing each other for four hours or more every other day, like prisoners linked together in a chain gang, smashing chess variations instead of rocks.

At the beginning of the second half of the match, as it entered its fifth week, Kasparov had evidently decided the time had come for a jail-break, and he did not intend to take his fellow prisoner with him. On the morning of the thirteenth game I received a telephone call from the Reuters chess correspondent, Grandmaster John Tisdall. 'There's something you should tell Nigel,' said Tisdall. 'I have been talking to the Kasparov camp and they say Garri is going to put Nigel away this week. They say their man is over this mid-match blues, and he has the White pieces twice this week. And you know what number today's game is.'

I said I knew it was game number thirteen.

'Exactly,' said Tisdall. 'Garri always says thirteen is his lucky number. He is the thirteenth world chess champion, he was born on 13 April, he achieved his grandmaster title on 13 April – you know how he goes on about it.'

I did. Kasparov, like most chess grandmasters, and all Russian ones, is very superstitious, and it was true that, for all the reasons given by Tisdall, the champion would feel that with the advantage of the White pieces in the magical thirteenth game, he must win.

But I didn't pass on Tisdall's information. While the American Grandmaster was undoubtedly well disposed towards Nigel, I couldn't help but feel that this was a message that the Kasparov camp very much wanted Nigel to receive. Even if it was true that Kasparov was feeling on top of the world and intended to splatter his opponent in the next three games, what good would it do Short's morale to hear this? And in any case Nigel knew very well that, with two Black games coming up in the next six days, this would be a week of enormous pressure, with survival the objective.

Kasparov did not, however, look in good shape when he marched on to the stage of the Savoy Theatre for the start of the thirteenth game. For the first time in the match he was late, and his clock had already been started by the arbiter. In his matches against Karpov, Kasparov had regularly arrived late for the game, often up to five minutes after his clock had been started. That had been a deliberate act of gamesmanship, to ensure that his hated opponent had to stand up in order to shake his hand when he finally came to the board.

On this occasion it looked as though Kasparov had simply got up late. If so, he had good reason: he had been awake much of the night watching CNN's coverage of Yeltsin's storming of the Russian parliament building. On the other hand, Kasparov should have felt inspired: he was very much a Yeltsin man and wholly endorsed the Russian leader's assault with tanks, which he described as 'the only move in the position, and a very strong one'. By the time he sat down to play the thirteenth game, he knew that he was already on the winning side – in Moscow.

The game in London was to be peculiarly Russian also, even in the absence of any tanks. Short played the Slav Defence against Kasparov's Queen's Gambit. To say that this provoked consternation among the live commentators both on television and at the Savoy Theatre would be understating it. Short had never, ever played the Slav, which, as early as move two, introduces a morass of possibilities for both sides.

Nigel's manager, Michael Stean, normally did not interfere with discussions about opening strategy, although as a grandmaster and a former second of Viktor Korchnoi his advice was always based on deep knowledge of both the strategic and psychological aspects of world championship chess. But when Stean discovered that Nigel was going to play the Slav, he became very agitated. 'The Slav defence is in these Russians' blood,' he argued. 'They were bred and brought up on it. You simply can't challenge them on their home turf and expect not to get mauled.' Nigel's somewhat facetious retort that Kasparov was from Azerbaizhan and therefore not a Slav at all did not seem to impress Stean.

But I knew the line of the Slav that Nigel intended to play: I had seen him and Kavalek spend a week's work on it back in Reston, Virginia. It was the variation Kavalek had described as 'good rope-a-dope stuff'. Far from challenging Kasparov with the sharpest and latest line in the opening, Nigel was relying on a move which had once been played by the ex-world champion Vassily Smyslov in 1953. Smyslov, the most extraordinary example of longevity at the top levels of grandmasterdom, then gave the move a rest for forty years, only to play it again this year in an obscure tournament in Rostov-on-Don. I remember Nigel's excitement as Kavalek's computer – the Beast in his basement – spewed out the Rostov-on-Don game by the Rip Van Winkle of world championship chess: 'If Vassily Smyslov thinks that the move is still good after forty years' thought, then it's good enough for me.'

Kasparov seemed stunned enough by Short's second move of the game, indicating the Briton's willingness to play the Slav Defence. On the third move of the game the world champion thought for ten minutes. He had had this position in countless games, but usually against random Russians: never against Short. Then, on move eleven, Short played the Smyslov move. I imagine that the grand old man of Russian chess, world champion in the late 1950s, would have experienced some momentary frisson of pride, or perhaps just amusement, as he picked up his newspaper in Moscow a few days later and saw what Short had played.

Kasparov's reaction was to push his chair back and lean so far down and forward over the board that his eyes seemed to be staring at Short through, rather than over, the pieces. Then, after a quarter of an hour's thought, he played the most brutal and direct response.

As I sat next to Rea in the grandmaster analysis room I must have made some involuntary facial spasm. 'Is that move a problem?' she asked. It had been difficult to answer Rea's questions during many of the games. On too many occasions the most truthful answer was hardly guaranteed to raise her spirits, and yet there was little point in being evasive: Rea knew enough about chess, and certainly enough about human nature, to spot false cheerfulness.

But for once I was able to give Rea a genuinely cheerful response. I remembered seeing this position on Kavalek's board in Reston: he and Nigel had roared with laughter at the very strategy which Kasparov had now adopted over the board which mattered. Kasparov's response was not just brutal and direct. It was also crude and unsophisticated: an attempt to wipe Black from the board without a single pause for preparation or regrouping.

Perhaps Kasparov had been inspired by Yeltsin's brutal assault with tanks on the White House, and wanted to batter Short with the same tactics that the Russian leader had employed against his challengers. But, had the world champion realized that the move played by Short was not one of the Englishman's own ideas but was lifted from the praxis of the great Vassily Smyslov, he would surely have been more circumspect. For Smyslov is a byword for solidity: he would simply not employ a move which could be refuted out of hand, not in 1953, still less in 1993.

With a few deft manoeuvres Short neutralized Kasparov's breathtakingly blunt attack. The players could honourably have agreed a draw by move twenty, so successfully had Nigel taken the wind from the champion's sails. But Kasparov, who could have been driven to play on only by his belief that the number thirteen would again prove lucky for him, tacked away, desperately trying to find some gust, some breath of air, in the position. On the thirty-second move the world champion thought for half an hour, to the near panic of the live commentators, who could see that the position was utterly lifeless and were at a loss to know how to fill the airtime.

From the greater closeness of the front row of the stalls I could hear Kasparov muttering to himself. He was, if only by his own very high standards, experiencing a humiliation. Short, playing Black, had achieved an effortless equality playing for the first time an opening which the Russians, as Michael Stean pointed out, regard as home territory. When the draw was finally agreed, at Kasparov's proposal, the world champion's hand touched Short's for the merest instant, the bare minimum to satisfy etiquette.

At the players' joint press conference afterwards, Kasparov, in a tone almost of complaint, remarked that 'Short is playing in this match all sorts of openings which he has never played before.' Nigel made no comment at the time, but he was bitingly sarcastic about Kasparov's comments that night at dinner. 'Poor Garri! It's so unfair of me to try new openings, rather than the ones he'd prepared for. How mean of me to try something a bit different, when he's five points ahead!'

When playing White, however, Nigel was implacably consistent. While Kasparov oscillated between kingside and queenside openings, Nigel remained rigorously faithful to his opening move 1. P–K4. Even Bobby Fischer, perhaps the most persuasive advocate of the king's pawn opening in chess history, and who described the move as 'best by test', did not consistently play it when he challenged Spassky for the world title.

It was not just Short who was implacably consistent. Kasparov was equally faithful to his Sicilian Defence, and in particular the Najdorf variation. This is an attempt to prove, against all the tenets of classical chess theory, that Black does not need to try to equalize in the opening, but can strive for the advantage from the very beginning. Kasparov had been playing this same variation since the age of twelve, when he was already defending the honour of his favourite Sicilian – and successfully – against Soviet grandmasters baffled by the precocity of the child's opening play.

Some years ago Viktor Korchnoi said that 'The man who beats Garri Kasparov in a world championship match will be the man who beats his Sicilian Defence.' Nigel used to quote Korchnoi's remark to me frequently, though with the self-mocking rider, 'I don't think Korkie had me in mind when he made that remark.'

Karpov, the world champion from 1975 until 1985, when he lost the title to Kasparov, was so frightened of his rival's deadly Sicilian that he gave up opening with the king's pawn altogether. But Nigel was doing more than challenge Kasparov's Sicilian: he was even playing, on move six, the variation which the world champion employs himself, on the rare occasions that an opponent has the nerve to try his own weapon against him. This variation, known to Russians as the Sozin variation, and to Americans, naturally, as the Fischer variation, had already occurred in games six, eight, ten and twelve. In at least three of these games – depending on which of the two players you believe – Short had established winning positions. It was not just a battle for the world championship. It was a battle of principle, over two fundamentally opposed schools of chess thought. Kasparov was claiming that Black need not defend, but could attack from move one. Short, a firm believer in classical chess theory, was insisting that this was too risky an approach, which demanded to be met with condign punishment.

This battle of chess philosophy was resumed in the four-teenth match-game. Again Short opened with the king's pawn, again Kasparov played the Sicilian Najdorf variation, and again Short played the Sozin attack. The familiarity of the two players with the positions reached had become apparent by the speed of their play. After sixteen moves by both sides, Short had taken only four minutes, Kasparov five minutes. The game resembled ping-pong more than chess.

Then Short played what he thought was a new idea, introduced by White's eighteenth move, which he, Robert Hübner and Jon Speelman had developed in the week since the last game in which Short had the White pieces. As he played the move, Jon Speelman, commenting live on Channel Four, announced, with the merest hint of pride, 'This is an innovation.' About five minutes later Eric Schiller, a friend of Kasparov and the editor of the official bulletin of the event, came marching into the grandmaster analysis room. 'Jon Speelman doesn't know what he's talking about. All this has been played before. Our database shows that the players are still following the game Christiansen–Spassov, Indonesia 1982.'

It wasn't clear whether Kasparov knew this game between an American and a Bulgarian, but Short certainly didn't. After Kasparov played his nineteenth move, Nigel looked perplexed, thought for forty-seven minutes . . . and then played exactly the move that Larry Christiansen had played against Luben Spassov in the twenty-first round of the Bali international grandmaster tournament, those eleven years ago.

A number of the masters watching the game, who knew I was part of the Short camp, came up to me during the latter part of Nigel's deep think over his twentieth move, all asking the same questions: 'What is Nigel thinking about? Where is his preparation? Doesn't his database have Christiansen–Spassov?' The real answer, if any of them had stopped to think, was that Christiansen–Spassov, along with hundreds of thousands of other games, was in Kavalek's database, now humming quietly at home in Reston, Virginia, and unavailable to Nigel Short.

Even so, to think for forty-seven minutes in such a position was very odd. No matter that Nigel did not know that this exact position had occurred before, it was one which arose immediately and naturally out of his prepared variation. He had a very thorough understanding of the sort of moves and stratagems which arose in this intensively studied branch of chess theory. In such circumstances, to think for almost fifty minutes is not a sign that something is wrong with the position; it is a sign that something is wrong with the player.

How wrong only became apparent as the game reached its crisis. Yet again Nigel appeared to have built up, by the simplest and most direct means, a winning position against Kasparov's Sicilian. It was six moves before the time-control, but this time, thanks in part to the stern admonitions of Dr Hübner, Nigel had left himself with a quarter of an hour on his clock, even after his big think in the opening.

Meanwhile, despite the apparently perilous nature of his position, Kasparov had played his previous move, his thirty-third, instantly, and had walked off to his rest room with the air of a man firmly in control. Nigel had one move in reply which was the logical consequence of his entire strategy: to advance into the very heart of Kasparov's position. The move would create almost unfathomable complications, but Short could well be winning at the end of them. Yet after only three minutes' thought, Nigel, like the Grand old Duke of York, marched his men all the way back down the hill he had made them climb, and Kasparov's frozen pieces suddenly swarmed back into action.

Immediately after the game was over Kasparov said that he would have been utterly lost if Short had played the correct reply to his thirty-third move. His confident mien, and strut off the stage, was, as usual, a bluff.

Nigel protested to me that he had not been bluffed, but, which was possibly even worse, had simply given up the effort of calculating the consequent continuation and had played what he thought was a 'safe' move, in a position where, for either player, safety was not only irrelevant but actually impossible.

Yet in the end it was Kasparov, and not Short, who succumbed to fear and funk. With one move to go before the time-control, it appeared to every watching commentator that the world champion had established a stranglehold over the entire board. While Short's resignation – for only the second time in the match with the White pieces – was not thought to be imminent, not a single voice could be found to argue that the challenger's position was defensible.

A few of the watching masters – the ghouls – walked the fifty yards from Simpson's to the Savoy Theatre in order to watch the final breaths of life being squeezed out of Short's position. Suddenly the players shook hands, in an extraordinarily rapid movement, which for once justified Channel Four's habit of replaying parts of the games in slow motion. The naked eye could hardly have captured the flitting movement of the two hands, as they touched and withdrew. 'A slightly premature resignation,' announced one of the grandmaster ghouls. 'Short could have played on for a few moves. But he was probably too demoralized.'

The audience in the theatre sat in complete silence, with all the appearance of collective shock. Kasparov, meanwhile, had a very embarrassed expression on his face. Then he turned away from the audience and stared at the back of the stage. Surely, I thought, he could not be feeling sorry for Short. That would be the ultimate indignity.

Then the arbiter, Carlos Falcón, walked up to the front of the stage and with his usual bland expression announced, 'Ladies and gentlemen, the fourteenth game of the match has been agreed a draw. The score now is —' But the rest of poor Carlos's little speech was never heard, drowned in a thunderous, if not incredulous, round of applause from the home crowd.

The world champion looked even more embarrassed. Nigel's own face, I suddenly noticed, carried a very sheepish expression, which it retained throughout the post-game press conference. Under the rules of the event, only the winner was required to attend the press conference, but in the event of a draw, both men had to attend. This was one occasion when both players looked as though they would rather not be called upon to explain themselves.

Kasparov at first seemed quite unable to give a reason for offering a draw. Some grandmasters offer draws in advantageous positions because they are afraid of their opponent, but surely, asked one brave reporter, the world champion was not afraid to play on against Nigel Short?

This, as it was intended to do, provoked Kasparov. 'Enough is enough!' he burst out. 'I had suffered enough in this game. It was very unpleasant for me. I was losing at one point. A draw is not a bad result.'

'Were you tired, Mr Kasparov?' taunted the same questioner. 'Yes,' muttered the world champion. 'Maybe also I was a bit tired.'

Tired was not the word an exuberant Nigel Short used to describe the world champion, as we drove back to Hampstead and dinner with Rea and Kyveli. 'Stark, raving bonkers! He must have been stark, raving bonkers to offer a draw in that position! You saw how I accepted it! In a micro-second! I didn't want to think about it in case he changed his mind.'

It usually took about half an hour to drive to and from the Savoy to Nigel and Rea's West Hampstead flat after each game – Nigel's routine was always to have dinner at home, and then leave punctually by 11.30 p.m., to return to bed alone at the Savoy at midnight. By the time I had dropped him back at the Savoy that particular midnight, Nigel's elation at the bizarre draw he had been offered had given way to pensiveness and a certain wonder.

'Perhaps we are no longer fighting each other, but ourselves . . . something inside our own heads. Why do I think for fifty minutes in a position which I ought to know very well, and just go round and round in circles in my analysis? Normally I would never do that, never. That can't just be to do with playing Kasparov. There must be something in me that's doing that to myself. And why should Gazza offer me a draw in a position which is almost winning for him? There must be something very strange happening in his head, which I don't understand, which maybe even he doesn't understand. Some inner struggle, which got the better of him today.'

It interested me that Nigel that night refused to allow Kasparov his simple excuse: that he was just exhausted, not only from the struggle not to lose the fourteenth game, but from the effort he had expended in building up a five-game lead against the world's second-strongest match-player. And it had not yet occurred to Nigel that these 'inner conflicts' he spoke of were the product of physical and mental exhaustion, the chess equivalent of the shell-shock experienced by the soldier who has been fighting for too long without rest.

But the very next day Nigel seemed suddenly to understand only too well. Our unfailing routine, on the day between games, was to have lunch together at Joe Allen's, the showbizzy restaurant which was only two minutes' walk from the Savoy

186

Hotel. The day after the fourteenth game Nigel walked in, as if in some kind of daze. He sat down and buried his head in his arms. 'It's gone,' he murmured. 'My energy has just disappeared. I can barely stay awake.' And, as if to prove a point, he let out a series of juddering yawns.

To return to the analogy with professional boxing, Nigel was now in a fight which had gone more rounds than any he had previously been involved in. His final eliminator against Jan Timman had ended after thirteen games, and even after that Nigel had been completely drained, losing ten kilos in weight and acquiring the appearance of an anorexic wraith. It was true that he had trained physically for the match with Kasparov, something he had never bothered to do before, but nothing could have prepared him for the traumatic nature of some of the games, with losses on time, and winning positions turning into dust. Nor could anything have prepared him for the traumatic nature of the off-the-board conflict: the split with Kavalek, his surrogate father. It had, as they say, all suddenly caught up with him.

'Now I understand why I was going round and round in my analysis, getting nowhere yesterday. I was just too tired to calculate properly. Perhaps the same thing is happening to Gazza. I don't know. But I do know I'm in terminal trouble if I lose confidence in my ability to calculate.'

Confidence in calculation is the key to success in grandmaster chess. It is at the heart of the inner game, and of the defining properties of self-belief and intuitive self-assurance. Kasparov's confidence in his calculating abilities is so great that, according to Robert Hübner, he calculates all variations once only, before playing his move. This enables him to calculate many more variations in the time available, and to look much more deeply into the position without the normal fear that he must go back to check.

It is not so different from the in-form tennis professional's confidence that when he swings his racquet he will send the ball exactly to the spot where his mind wants it to go, just an inch inside the baseline. If the ball hurtles an inch the wrong side of the baseline, it might not be that the shot has been badly executed; but the player feels suddenly a little more insecure, because his confidence that the ball will obey his orders has been shaken.

The chess grandmaster's confidence in his calculations is often similarly intuitive and finely balanced. If suddenly he becomes aware of one small error in his analysis, he becomes worried that all his analysis might be at risk of error. His play begins to slow down, and he refrains from playing the most critical and complex moves, even if they are the ones which have the most potential for victory.

If Nigel's sudden sense of exhaustion was causing him to doubt his own powers of calculation, he was in enormous danger of chessboard collapse: all the more so because he had deliberately chosen a very sharp opening repertoire for the match, leading to positions which demanded hair-trigger calculations. Had he prepared less challenging openings, there was at least a chance that he could steer the game into positions where long and complex calculations were unlikely to be required. This, after all, was how Anatoly Karpov chose to play in five matches against Kasparov – 'sucking all the energy out of the position', as Kasparov himself ruefully described it.

Back in Joe Allen's, Nigel jokingly suggested to me that what he needed was a shot of anabolic steroids, or perhaps testosterone. 'You know that Kasparov used to have injections from his mother,' said Nigel. 'Maybe that's what put all those hairs on his chest.'

This gave me an idea. I knew that my own doctor had recommended to some of his patients an injection known as 'B–12'. It is nothing more than a collection of vitamins, causing no side-effects. But the intravenous propulsion of vitamins into the system has a galvanizing effect, far more potent than the steady munching of vitamin C pills in which Nigel had been indulging at various stages during the match when under the weather.

Later that day the doctor came round to Short's suite at the Savoy and a brief consultation followed. The patient was a little nervous at the last minute – Nigel is a very squeamish man – but down went the Grandmaster's trousers, and in went the needle.

'The injection will take about eight hours to have its effect,' said the doctor as he shut his case, 'after that you should feel about one hundred and twenty per cent.'

I left with the doctor and didn't see the patient again until the next day, a few hours before the fifteenth match-game. 'How do you feel?' I asked, as Nigel opened the door of his suite. By way of an answer he leapt up in the air kicking his legs, and then began punching his fists in a ferocious shadow-box. Evidently the vitamins had entered the system.

Unfortunately a sudden lack of physical energy was not the only problem affecting Nigel Short. He was also in the middle of a crisis over his choice of openings for the next two games. Generally Nigel, together with Hübner and Speelman, aimed to be at least two games ahead with their theoretical preparation: that is, they liked to feel that Short had at least one new and original idea prepared for each colour, Black and White. But Speelman and Hübner had been investigating the line in the Slav defence which Short and Kavalek had prepared and which Nigel had played to such good effect in game thirteen. And they thought it stank. Robert Hübner in particular warned against Nigel's repeating it in the fifteenth game, and the variations he demonstrated to prove his point made Nigel very gloomy. The challenger had badly wanted to cock a snook at Kasparov by playing the Slav again, especially as the world champion had already put out of commission Short's main queenside defence, the Nimzovitch, by destroying it in the ninth match-game.

'Okay, chaps,' Short finally said to his analysts, after the three of them had spent a total of nine grandmaster hours trying to patch up the Slav defence, 'it looks like I'll have to play the Queen's Gambit Declined.' The two seconds murmured their approval.

The Orthodox Defence in the Queen's Gambit Declined, to give its full name, had been Nigel's favourite reply to the Queen's Gambit for many years. Its basic theory is simple, but in practice it is very difficult: to answer White's pawn to queen four with a blocking pawn on Black's queen four, and then to hold a pawn on that blocking square for the rest of the game. The idea is that, with Black's strongpoint in the centre of the board, he will be able to repulse all attacks, and, when White has dashed his brains against the defensive carapace, might even begin to counter-punch in the late middle-game. In practice Black's game is very much harder to play than White's, which is why Short is one of the few modern grandmasters to play the Orthodox Defence. Most of his colleagues regard it as old-fashioned – its heyday was in the 1920s – and even outmoded.

But Nigel had a sentimental attachment, a devotion almost, to this relic: he had employed it in some of the most critical games of his career, on those occasions when he did not need to win, but absolutely could not afford to lose. He played it in the final game of his world championship quarter-final match against the then world-ranked number three, Boris Gelfand. If Gelfand had won the game, he would have levelled the scores and forced the match into extra time. But the Orthodox Defence prevailed: even though Nigel at one point had a lost position, Gelfand could not crack his rock-ribbed defence. Then in the final game of Short's encounter with Timman, when a draw would win the match and the right to challenge Garri Kasparov, Nigel again employed the Orthodox Defence, and again his carapace proved impenetrable.

This most dour of defences exactly suited Nigel's mood before the fifteenth match-game, as he explained to me over his usual gigantic salad on the day. He had drawn the last five games, and it had begun to occur to him that an even longer series of draws would sap Kasparov's dwindling supply of energy more than his own. Above all he wanted to deny Kasparov a sixth win.

The significance of the sixth win is something not lost on students of the world championship. For many of the great world championship matches, those between Capablanca and Lasker, Capablanca and Alekhine, Karpov and Korchnoi, the winner was the first man to gain six wins. Draws did not count; the overall points score was irrelevant.

Most famously of all, the six-win rule was in force when Kasparov first challenged Karpov for the world title in September 1984. After only nine games Karpov had notched up four wins to Kasparov's nil. There then followed seventeen draws, before Karpov won a fifth game. Only at the thirty-second attempt did Kasparov win his first game. Another fourteen draws followed. Then – it was now February 1985 – Kasparov won games forty-seven and forty-eight. At this point the match was stopped by the Fidé President, with the exhausted Karpov still tantalizingly one game short of victory.

Over lunch at Joe Allen's Nigel laughingly said that his plan for the rest of the match was to fight back with three wins to Kasparov's five, and then persuade the Commissioner of the Professional Chess Association, Kasparov's lawyer Bob Rice, to stop the contest, 'to save Kasparov from further exhaustion'. Although Nigel was joking, he was also serious. He had convinced himself that if Kasparov could not beat him a sixth time, then he would have done what Kasparov himself had achieved in *his* first world championship match. Of course the rules in London were different: the match was simply the best of twenty-four games, the absolute number of wins being as irrelevant as the number of draws under the old system. But Nigel had constantly to set himself targets to retain the highest levels of self-motivation.

Those commentators – most of them – who found it hard to see what was keeping Short so determined, and even buoyant, in such a grim match situation did not appreciate the way in which he was unfailingly able to set himself new targets, new benchmarks, new ways of believing that he had vital motivation. This was Nigel Short's inner match, the one only he was playing, the one only he could understand, the one only he could win.

It was in this mood that Nigel set about his self-imposed task of heroic resistance in the fifteenth match-game: to hold the Orthodox Defence strongpoint against all of Kasparov's prepared attacks – and there could be no doubt that Kasparov would have prepared much against this old standby of Short's.

Just how well prepared, and how well versed, Kasparov was became apparent only during the game. While giving the appearance of deep thought in the opening, Kasparov in fact followed – for fourteen moves – a speed chess game he had played six years before in Moscow against his chief second,

Alexander Beliavsky. Short, needless to say, knew nothing of this game. It might not even have appeared on Kavalek's absent database. But it was certainly in Kasparov's database, and in particular the one lodged between his ears.

After his twentieth move Short seemed to have established the kind of fortress beloved of the few remaining practitioners of the Orthodox Defence. He had his famous pawn strongpoint on the queen four square, defended by another pawn, a bishop, a rook and, for good measure, the queen. Then Kasparov made a remarkable move, playing a knight to a square where it could be exchanged for one of Short's knights. It was a move which seemed to counter one of the most established rules of chess theory, that the side on the attack should seek to avoid exchanges. I noticed that Nigel, normally very adept at disguising his feelings at the board, started visibly when Kasparov played his twenty-first move.

But Nigel could not have known the most extraordinary thing about the concept: that Kasparov had played exactly the same manoeuvre at exactly the same stage of the game – move twenty-one – in his win against Alexander Beliavsky in 1987. Nigel had frequently said to me that one of his main tasks in the match against the world champion would be to lead the games into positions which were 'not part of Kasparov's strategic vocabulary'.

On this occasion Nigel had walked right into it. But he could be forgiven for not realizing the fact: Kasparov was taking an inordinate amount of time for his far from improvised manoeuvres. By move twenty-eight he had used all but six minutes of his time allowance for the first forty. In other words he would need to play at a rate of not more than thirty seconds a move for the next twelve if he were not to lose on time.

As Nigel told me immediately after the game, he suddenly decided at this point to switch plans. Rather than hold the queen four square strongpoint, he would try to plunge the game into a tactical mêlée and hope that in his panic to reach the time-control Kasparov would lose control of the position. Short had salvaged a draw from a dubious position in the eleventh game using similar tactics, and he still recalled bitterly how such an approach by Kasparov had caused him to lose the first game on time.

The drawback to Short's new plan was that the first move of a complex sequence designed to confuse the champion involved an immediate surrender of his coveted Orthodox Defence strongpoint. With that gone, he was strategically lost, and only tactics could save him. And at this point Garri Kasparov showed, more clearly than at any other time in the match, the awesome speed and power of his calculations. He played his next eleven moves in under three minutes, avoiding all of Short's snares and tricks, while at the same time landing several crushing tactical blows of his own. Short's position, in the words of the watching American Grandmaster Joel Benjamin, 'crumbled grotesquely'. Kasparov did not even need to get to the time-control. On move thirty-nine Short, appalled by the slaughter, resigned.

For the first time in the match, Rea took part in the post-mortem in her husband's hotel room. Normally she never involved herself in such technical discussions; but it was almost as if she had decided that Nigel now could do with advice even from her on his opening strategy. 'Was it right to play that defence against the Queen's Gambit?' she asked her husband. Nigel took the question on its merits. 'How can it be wrong to play it? It's the defence that took me to the verge of the world championship. I wouldn't be here without it.' At that bleak moment, it was not obvious that this was a point in favour of the Orthodox Defence to the Queen's Gambit.

After his victory in the fifteenth matchgame, Kasparov celebrated by having his hair cut. One of the world champion's superstitions is that it is bad luck to have a trim during a tournament. But now he felt invulnerable, even to the malign influences of the Delilahs of the West End.

CHAPTER TWELVE

The old man struggled to his feet from the park bench where he was sitting. He looked like some retired soldier, so immaculately shiny were his shoes, so carefully trimmed his grey moustache. 'Well done, Mr Short!' he shouted out in a hoarse voice at Nigel as we walked past. 'You're still fighting that Russian! You're putting up a great show!' Nigel turned round, smiled at his ancient admirer and continued his Sunday afternoon trudge across Hyde Park. But the old man continued calling after us, his words carrying halfway across the Serpentine: 'We're proud of you. You're a real fighter! You aren't going to throw in the towel!' Eventually, out of the corner of my eye, I could see the old man's embarrassed companion tug at his sleeve, and he sat down.

'It's odd,' said Nigel eventually. 'There are so many people like him – my rooms are full of letters saying much the same thing. Yet to read the newspapers you would think I had no support at all, that I have let down the whole nation.' I tried, again, to explain to Nigel how the British public's attitude to sporting heroes differed fundamentally from that of the pundits. The latter judged everything by results – hadn't Nigel noticed that, long before he became a world championship challenger, the newspapers reported only his tournament successes, hardly ever mentioning those he failed to win? But the British public admired something other than victory: they admired guts, never-say-die fighting spirit, heroic failure and, still as always, the underdog.

That is why, while the press consistently ridiculed Frank Bruno, the London boxer still retained enormous public affection and support, far greater than more successful fighters who seemed to have less spirit. That is why a footballer like Paul Gascoigne excites mass popular admiration, long after the pundits have labelled him a disappointment. The British – and perhaps only the British – are not so much interested in technique, or even in winning or losing: what they admire in their sportsmen is heart.

It is an attitude not confined to the sporting arena. British popular history has not so much to say about our national victories. But it lavishes its attention on heroic defeats or setbacks. The evacuation of Dunkirk, the sufferings of the Blitz, are far more vivid in the popular imagination than any of our victories in the last war.

It goes back a long way, this British admiration for heroic defeat. It is hard to imagine any other country celebrating such a farcical military exercise as the Charge of the Light Brigade. Yet perhaps, I suggested to Nigel, there was some slight parallel between that event and his encounter with Garri Kasparov. English chess masters in the guise of journalists had criticized him for the way in which he had hurled himself into the attack against Kasparov in almost every game, choosing often to enter the openings in which the world champion was most heavily armed – the Russian cannons. Although none of these English player–pundits had ever encountered Kasparov across a chessboard, let alone beaten him, they repeatedly argued with remarkable self-assurance that the way to play against Kasparov was to potter about and wait for the Russian to overreach himself.

It is doubtful whether that method would have achieved a better score. And it is certain that such an approach would have aroused far less excitement and support from the chess-playing public. Nigel Short's remark that 'Modern chess is too much concerned with things like pawn structure. Forget it – checkmate ends the game,' shocked the purists, but delighted the mass of chess enthusiasts, who have always admired the attacking player, the king-hunter. That, perhaps, is why, during the match with Kasparov, attendance at British chess clubs quintupled. It is hard to imagine that a dour, defensive style on the part of the challenger would have aroused similar enthusiasm.

As we left Hyde Park Nigel began reciting parts of Tennyson's 'Charge of the Light Brigade', particularly the bit about 'cannons to the right of them, cannons to the left of them', which he seemed to know well. But at the end he added, bathetically, 'I, on the other hand, would rather not be remembered for being completely decimated. I need a victory.'

This particular need was gnawing away at Nigel so badly that the hurt was beginning to show on his face. With Kasparov now only two points away from overall victory in the match, Short had become an overwhelming favourite at the bookmakers to become the first man since Emmanuel Lasker in 1921 to play a world championship match without winning a game. Lasker, who had held the title for twenty-seven years, resigned his match against José Capablanca prematurely, after four defeats and ten draws.

Short was never going to give up, as Lasker had done: he would have been prepared to play on for months if that was what it took to win a game. But there was nothing in the rules of the London match against a whitewash, and that now seemed imminent. This might have mattered less to Nigel if he had had a good record against Kasparov. But it had been abysmal; his current match-score of nine draws and six losses was actually much better, statistically, than his record against Kasparov before the match. And he had not won a game against Kasparov in fully fledged tournament play since 1986. He was now twenty-eight, and he had not beaten Kasparov since he was twenty-one – a quarter of a lifetime ago. For a man whose life has been dedicated to victory in chess, that is an unimaginable frustration, almost a denial of his most basic, and most primitive, need.

On that Sunday, the day after the sixth defeat, I still believed that Nigel would be able to satisfy this aching need before the match's end. But on the Monday, the day before the sixteenth match-game, I was alarmed by what seemed a sudden deterioration in his mental and physical condition. Nigel's face was white, bringing into sharp relief the fact that he had not shaved since the last game. As soon as he spoke, it was clear that he was under assault from some virus, either real or imaginary. 'My head hurts. My stomach aches. Everything feels terrible. I know these symptoms are psychosomatic. I've read enough Freud to know that. But knowing it doesn't make me feel any the less terrible.'

Just then I noticed a brand-new book in Russian on Nigel's table. I could read enough Cyrillic to see that it was by Rudolf Zagainov. He had been Anatoly Karpov's parapsychologist during the ex-world champion's match against Short. Zagainov's job, in part, had been to find out Short's psychological weaknesses, and then help Karpov exploit them. Zagainov, apparently, did not manage to find any worth exploiting – the book's title was 'Defeat' – and Karpov had dispensed with his services shortly afterwards.

'It's about my match with Karpov,' Nigel explained as I picked up the book. It had a handwritten dedication in English inside the front cover. 'Dear Mr N. Short!' it read, 'Believe yourself like I believe you!' And, underneath his signature, Dr Zagainov had helpfully left his Moscow telephone number.

But the only doctor Nigel was consulting was living four doors down the same corridor at the Savoy Hotel. And Dr Robert Hübner was not able to give a very encouraging prognosis for the next game. On the previous day Nigel had told Hübner that he wanted, for the first time in the match, to play the Short Attack against Kasparov's Sicilian. Originally Nigel had not prepared the opening variation that carried his name, in large part because he knew that Kasparov would be expecting it. Nigel had developed the attack, which was a characteristically straightforward attempt to checkmate the opponent's king, as a way to get out of heavily analysed older variations. Now, it seemed, even the Short Attack had been analysed to death by other players.

'It's simple, guys. I just want to rape and mate him,' were Nigel's words to Dr Hübner and Jon Speelman as the three of them sat down in their analysis room to discuss the opening strategy for the sixteenth game.

'Well, I don't think it's so simple as that,' said Hübner, flopping down next to the chessboard a pile of what looked like at least twenty pages of closely written algebraic chess notation. The German had rapidly compiled nothing less than a small book on Short's own opening – but it did not have a happy ending. 'I don't think this idea is good *at all*,' Hübner added, by way of summary, while Nigel flicked through the pages.

For the next several hours, as the daylight outside turned into darkness, Short and Speelman began shaking and rattling all of Hübner's variations, like children trying to find some way of breaking an infuriating new toy. But, at the end of the process, Nigel, who looked even paler and, by definition, more unshaven than when they began, admitted defeat.

'Okay, Robert, so I can't rape and mate him with the Short Attack,' Nigel sighed. And then to no one in particular, or possibly to all of us, he said, 'It's madness anyway. I had six months to prepare for this match, and now I want to get up a new opening in a day. I must be crazy.'

But it was understandable that Nigel should have tried, in what was possibly the last game in the match in which he would have the advantage of the White pieces, to resuscitate the Short Attack. It was, after all, the opening he had used in his one and only tournament victory against Kasparov, a quarter of a lifetime before.

By the day of the game itself, Nigel's psychosomatic cold seemed to have developed into psychosomatic flu, and his feelings of foreboding about the game had become similarly acute. For the first time, as White, he and his team of analysts could come up with nothing new to test Kasparov's Sicilian Defence. Of course, there had been many games in which Kasparov had deftly sidestepped the vicious opening traps prepared by the men Nigel called 'Robert and the Speelwolf'. But that wasn't the point. It gave Nigel a very good feeling to go into a game knowing that he had a concealed bomb which might blow up his opponent. To start the game without even the possibility of mounting an act of terror was at once dreary and depressing.

Even as Nigel prepared to leave his room ten minutes before the game he was feverishly going through some last-minute ideas with Hübner, none of which seemed to work. 'What happens if he plays . . . oh fuck it!' Nigel concluded with a dismissive wave of his hand, and walked off into his bedroom. He came back with two ties. As always slightly superstitious,

Nigel believed that the right article of clothing could somehow influence the result of the game.

'Okay, Dominic, we might as well do some useful opening preparation. The dark tie or the light one?' I pointed to the dark tie. 'That's the one Rea recommended,' said Nigel, looping the silk round his neck. Then he sneezed several times, and rummaged in his pockets for a soggy handkerchief. 'Uuurgh,' said the forlorn challenger, and slid limply out of the room.

A chess killer like Kasparov can smell an opponent's lack of confidence, even if it is well disguised. When he is six points ahead in the match, has just won a game and is confronted by an opponent who is clearly suffering physically, then Kasparov's resemblance to a shark smelling blood is complete.

But it didn't take a Kasparov to smell the situation at the board. Grandmaster Raymond Keene, commenting live on television, was appalled at Short's appearance, while the challenger pushed his pieces around the board as if every piece was inexpressibly heavy. 'He looks as if he's collapsed,' said Keene, determined to prepare the watching masses for the worst.

Short's moves, too, were insipid. In every previous game with the White pieces he had gone straight for the sharpest, most aggressive continuations. But now he was playing with exaggerated caution, ducking every challenge that Kasparov was setting. You can do this as White. But the result tends to be a sterile, tedious equality: which is what Short achieved.

As if trying to gauge whether his opponent was completely devoid of any further ambition in the game Kasparov played a move which invited an exchange of queens, and with it the end of any lingering tension in the position. And, as if to demonstrate his pacific tendencies, Nigel not only left his queen where it could be exchanged but even played a move which seemed to compel Kasparov to hoover the pieces from the board.

Then it would be the deadest of dead draws. And then – or at least at the press conference afterwards – Short would be unmercifully criticized for his insipid play, in what had been billed as his last realistic chance to win a game. If Kasparov drew he would be only one point away from retaining his title, for which he required twelve points, half the twenty-four available.

But the world champion was at that moment making a different and characteristically more ambitious calculation. If he did not draw but actually managed to win the current game, he would have 11½ points. In the next game he would then have White and, having already destroyed any vestige of Short's morale, would very probably win again, giving him the winning score of 12½ points. The match would immediately be over after only seventeen games; Kasparov would have won by eight wins to nil, and his reputation for invincibility would be confirmed.

This at least would explain the champion's twenty-fifth move, which he made after ten minutes' thought. It was a very ambitious idea, based on a five-move sequence, at the end of which Black would indeed have exchanged queens, but under vastly more favourable circumstances.

Over his reply Nigel pondered for sixteen minutes, his longest reflection in a game in which he had seemed too unwell to summon up his usual effort of profound cogitation. And only towards the end of that quarter-hour did he see the hole in Kasparov's calculations. It was six moves deep, simple, and devastating. I could see Nigel's body, which had been limp throughout the earlier vegetative manoeuvring, stiffen slightly in his chair. Kasparov, meanwhile, had suddenly returned to the table, even though it was not yet his turn to move. Watching the game on the closed-circuit television in his rest room, he too had suddenly seen the gaping hole in his analysis. Now if Short played the best move, Kasparov would have to abandon his planned sequence and move his queen instead to a terrible square, where it was a sitting target for Short's lurking minor pieces.

Short duly played the best move. With wonderful sang-froid Kasparov replied instantly, and placed his queen on its new, vulnerable square with a flourish, screwing the piece into position with the wrist-revolving gesture which he normally reserved for his strongest moves. If there was a world championship for over-acting, this would have won. Unfortunately for Kasparov, even a groggy Nigel Short is far too strong a chessplayer to be fooled into thinking that a move is good just because it is played with a confident flourish.

In any case Kasparov's brave front collapsed after Short's next six, very precise moves, as a result of which the world champion's pawn structure looked as though it had contracted dry rot. Perhaps recalling games eight and ten, when he had salvaged hopeless positions by lunging wildly in the direction of Short's king, Kasparov now staggered forward into the attack, leaving his own king to its fate.

When he writes down his moves on his score sheet Nigel Short laboriously notes not just the co-ordinates of the square to which a piece is travelling, but also the co-ordinates of the square being vacated. But my copy of Nigel's score sheet for this game shows that Kasparov's thirty-fourth move is written out in short-hand: only the square of arrival is noted, in a furious scribble. Afterwards Nigel explained to me this lapse in his normally painstakingly complete notation: 'As soon as he played his thirty-fourth move I knew he'd gone.' In fact Kasparov lasted until move thirty-eight, seven away from an inevitable checkmate.

Garri Kasparov does not lose many games of chess, even by the standards of world champions. This would be the first time he had lost, against all-comers, for over eighteen months, one of the longest undefeated sequences in the recent history of the game. Perhaps it was for that reason that the last three moves of the sixteenth match-game seemed to me like the felling of a mighty oak. Or perhaps it was because of the manner of the execution, as Short just sawed the position in half, with the champion's queenside, kingside and centre falling in three successive, brutal moves: one to the left, one to the right and the last straight through the heart.

After that one Kasparov silently reached out his hand to stop the ticking chess clock. 'Yes,' he said, and then without another word rushed from the stage. Even on the six occasions Short had lost, the challenger had remained on stage to discuss the game with Kasparov. Such self-control – or plain good manners – was apparently beyond the world champion. But his unseemly dash from the theatre was quite understandable. At the moment he resigned the audience of about a thousand burst into cheers, whistles, shouts; some even began stamping in the manner of

Last Night promenaders. The din – which went on for several minutes – was far too great for Kasparov and Short to hear each other speak, even had the world champion wanted to discuss the game. And Kasparov *was* distressed. For the first time in the match he refused to sign any autographs as he left the theatre. And for the first time in the match he did not attend the post-game press conference.

In the world champion's absence Short twisted the knife, pointing out, with a deadpan expression, that it had taken Kasparov thirty-two attempts before he won a game in his first world championship match, 'so I have been twice as quick as him'.

But Nigel was anything but deadpan immediately afterwards as we gathered in his room at the Savoy. Channel Four were just starting their programme of recorded highlights of the day's game. I suggested we tune in, and for the first time in the match Nigel agreed. At last he could watch himself winning. As the programme showed in 'real time' the last few minutes of the game, Nigel jumped up from his chair and began shouting at the television set, or rather at the image of Nigel Short sitting, thinking, at the chessboard. 'Come on, Nigel!' he shouted. 'Play the move! God, he's so slow! Knight F5 check! Play the move! It's a killer!'

At first I thought this was Nigel's idea of a joke. But then I noticed that he was shaking with excitement. 'At last!' he yelled, as his *alter ego* played the winning move. Rea smiled. 'If you think that seemed like an agonizing wait, you should try being in the theatre watching the game.'

'No thanks,' Nigel said. Then he remembered something. 'Did you notice what happened just before I played the winning move? Kasparov suddenly saw what he had allowed, and he just slumped right back in his chair, with his arms by his side. It was like he was saying "Okay, do it now. Please finish me off!"'

It had been almost cruel of Nigel to sit there for two minutes, before playing the final blow, which he had planned and could have executed instantly. But it was a moment he wanted to savour, and, as with the matador delivering the *coup de grâce*, the drama is only enhanced by the delay of deliberation.

202

It was an hour or so later, while we were enjoying some of Rea's best home cooking, that Nigel began fully to savour the victory, his first against Kasparov for seven years. He jumped up repeatedly from the table, almost between mouthfuls, and clenched his fists together in front of his chest, like a footballer after scoring a goal. 'Wuurgh! Wuurgh!'

When he had finally finished this victory jig and chant, Nigel looked for his guitar. But he had left it at the Savoy. So instead he just sang the words of the Led Zeppelin song: 'It's been a long . . . a long . . . a long . . . a long . . . a lonely . . . lonely . . . lonely time.'

CHAPTER THIRTEEN

On the night after Nigel Short's victory, another part of Britain's sporting empire was faring less well. The English soccer eleven lost two–nil to Holland, effectively putting an end to the team's World Cup campaign and causing national misery in the way that losses at football seem peculiarly able to evoke in the British public. The newspapers, of course, blamed the referee. He was a German.

The next afternoon Garri Kasparov and Nigel Short were in their usual positions just before the start of a game at the Savoy Theatre: off-stage and waiting for the signal from the Channel Four technicians that the cameras were ready for them. At such times the players would exchange a few words behind the curtains, usually at Kasparov's instigation. On this occasion the world champion opened with a new gambit. 'So,' he said, 'you're out of the World Cup, too.' It was a clever little dig, with a subtext – you've got no hope in the world chess championship either – well judged to infuriate.

Short managed to come up with an immediate response to Kasparov's tricky opening, in a way he had not always achieved at the board during the match. 'Yes, Garri,' he snapped back, 'we're going to declare war on Germany.' And with that he walked on-stage. As usual, Kasparov followed after about thirty seconds, and as usual the players fixed smiles and shook hands across the board as if they were seeing each other for the very first time that day.

Short and Kasparov always performed this harmless charade for the public: chess aficionados are almost as insistent as Japanese Sumo wrestling fans on ritual. Once the game is in progress almost any sort of low trick or deception is allowed, but the players must always shake hands at the start of the game and at the end, no matter how much the one dislikes the other, no matter how reluctant the one is to resign to the other. It makes the game seem civilized, even when it isn't; and that in turn makes the chess fans feel they are participants in a civilized pursuit, even when they aren't.

There was only one world championship match in which, halfway through, one of the players decided he could no longer bear to shake hands with his opponent: that was the Soviet defector Viktor Korchnoi in Merano, 1981, against Anatoly Karpov. Shocked chess followers across the world suddenly switched their allegiance from the underdog Korchnoi to the hitherto unpopular Karpov: there are some things that are simply not done, even in the murky world of championship chess.

Kasparov's cutting aside to Short just before the start of the seventeenth match-game was, however, quite within the strange rules of grandmasterly etiquette. And, besides, the world champion probably felt that Short had earned the jibe, after the Englishman's remark of the previous day that he had been twice as quick as Kasparov to win a game in a world championship match.

This mutual provocation continued over the board. In two earlier games as Black, the eleventh and the thirteenth, Short had deliberately mutilated his own pawn structure. The idea was to activate his pieces through the wide-open spaces he had created in his own position. It was a most unconventional strategy; but in neither game could Kasparov prove it to be bad. After the second of these games the world champion seemed aesthetically outraged, telling the *Times* chess correspondent, 'I don't want to argue publicly with Short about pawn structure, but I am really surprised that he doesn't care about pawn weaknesses in his own position.'

Nigel was duly amused and provoked: in the seventeenth game he voluntarily saddled himself, right out of the opening, with a pawn structure so ugly that it reduced visiting grandmasters to shudders of disgust. What they, and perhaps Kasparov, had not realized was that Short had been experimenting with his seconds for days on just such a provocation. He would set up positions with horribly fractured pawn structures, and then dare Hübner and Speelman, jointly and severally, to try to beat him. I never saw them win. It was like seeing a boxing champion take on two sparring partners, by ducking and parrying, but never actually throwing a punch.

The idea, in practice, was that Kasparov might be so outraged that he would try too hard to win against a position that was not as bad as it looked and overreach himself. In the seventeenth game, that is exactly what happened. On move twenty-four the champion plunged headlong into an exorbitant trap that Short had laid two moves earlier. It was, in fact, a very well-camouflaged trick, resting on a spectacular geometric sequence of moves which was peculiarly hard for the human eye to anticipate, but, once seen, was completely obvious, and, somehow, very funny.

Something, not human, had seen the trick in advance. In the press room the moves of the game had been fed into a new 'talking' chess computer programme endorsed by the world champion, called 'Kasparov's Gambit'. 'Kasparov's Gambit' indicated that it had seen Short's trap and warned the player of the White pieces to 'Watch out!' When Short played the first move of the trap the machine's screen flashed out, 'Well done.'

The real Kasparov, however, had completely missed the sequence in advance. But as soon as Short played his twenty-fourth move, a bishop sacrifice, the champion instantly realized that his own previous move had been a terrible oversight. It was a beautiful chessboard joke by Short – he called it 'a wonderful cheap trick' – the equivalent, perhaps, of the banana-skin in slapstick comedy. But Kasparov was as unamused as the victim of the banana-skin gag is meant to be.

He jumped back in his chair and began shaking his head violently from side to side as if trying to clear his head. Nigel savoured just a few seconds of this before getting up. As he walked off-stage he shot me one of his toothiest grins, and then, making absolutely sure that he was on the blind side of the Channel Four cameras, made a little triumphant gesture with his fist.

(Long after the game was over Nigel was still giggling at the outrageousness of his trick and at Kasparov's astonished reaction on falling into it. 'You should have seen his face!' he kept saying. 'You should have seen his face!')

The main reason Short left the stage at the time, as he explained to me later, was to calm down in the quiet of his rest room while the theatre was still buzzing with astonishment. His 'wonderful cheap trick' had won a pawn and wiped out most of Kasparov's kingside: in his first spasm of excitement at the denouement, Nigel thought he might be winning. That would be two wins in a row for the challenger, and an extraordinarily rare loss with the White pieces by the world champion. Earlier on in the match, when Nigel was repeatedly drawing games which he might have won, he had told me that he felt that Kasparov was 'like a very imposing but very fragile dam. If I can just make one break in its structure then many cracks could suddenly appear all over the place.'

But as he surveyed the position on the closed-circuit screen in his rest room back-stage, Nigel gradually realized that the extra pawn his trick had so spectacularly won was probably not sufficient for a win. He had the advantage and could torment the champion for a couple of hours or so, but that would be about it.

Kasparov had come to a similar conclusion, and with his thirty-first move he offered a draw, in a slightly strained voice. This, unlike his jibe at Nigel just before the game, was a clear breach of etiquette. It is simply not done to offer a draw, a pawn down and with some suffering left to be undergone; Kasparov even had much less time left on his clock than Short. It is one of the unwritten rules of grandmaster chess that the side with the winning chances, however slight, is the only one with the moral right to offer to end hostilities: Boris Spassky always used to make a great point of this by saying, 'I offer a draw from a position of strength.'

Normally when Short turns down a draw against another grandmaster he responds with the stock phrase 'I would like to play on.' But in response to Kasparov's offer of a draw he simply arched his eyebrows, played his next move and left the board. Only an hour later, when Kasparov had reached the time control, did he concede the draw.

Afterwards, as Nigel talked over the game with Jon Speelman and Robert Hübner, he mentioned that Kasparov had offered a draw on move thirty-two 'while I still had some chances to torture him'. Speelman laughed incredulously; but Hübner, who has – in his usual thorough manner – made quite a study of the world champion's character, seemed completely unsurprised: 'Kasparov is not in emotional control at the board. Here he was, suffering, desperately wanting a draw, so he just blurted out what he wanted. He just can't help himself.'

The next day Raymond Keene, discussing the game with Kasparov, asked him why he had offered a draw to Short on move thirty-two. 'I never offered a draw in this game,' said the world champion. Keene persisted, saying that Speelman had told him about the draw offer. 'It never happened,' said Kaspasrov, and indicated that the matter should not be discussed again.

As I was in the front row of the stalls during the game and clearly heard Kasparov offer a draw, it would be tempting to say that the world champion is a bare-faced liar. But it is not quite as simple as that. As Short wrote in the *Spectator* about Kasparov back in 1989, 'He has the ability to manipulate a set of circumstances into a simplistic theory to suit his own emotional needs.' In this case Kasparov's emotional need was not to recognize that he had offered a draw in breach of etiquette. He was embarrassed about it, so he conveniently forgot what he had done. By the next day he would have been genuinely outraged at the suggestion that he had done anything untoward. When Garri Kasparov wrestles with his conscience, he always wins. It's what he's best at.

Kasparov also had a theory to explain how it was that he had blundered into Short's trap in the seventeenth game. He informed the press conference immediately afterwards that his errors in general, and his failure to win more than once in the second half of the match, were the results of being 'tired and emotionally exhausted'. Asked by one of the journalists to elaborate on the reasons for his 'emotional exhaustion', Kasparov said he would reveal them after the match. He never did, and it was left to others to wonder about the absence of his wife throughout the match.

Short, sitting next to Kasparov, as the world champion gave his excuses, just stared into the middle distance with a glassy expression. But afterwards he was exasperated: 'He just can't tolerate the fact that I have been playing on equal terms with him over the past eight games. He expected me to collapse, as I used to against him before this match. But something has changed. And he assumes that it must be something the matter with him, rather than that I have become stronger. He likes to believe that if he didn't have these personal worries – and I have some idea what they might be – he would beat me in every game. It's extremely arrogant, but normal for him.'

Perhaps this was unfair, but Short's exasperation was understandable. If he had won the seventeenth game, he would have had a glimmer of a hope of winning the match: Kasparov is a very moody man, and there was no telling how he would have reacted to a second loss in a row. But now Kasparov needed only one point – two draws or a win – from the remaining seven games to retain his title. A further half-point would win the match outright for the world champion and give him five-eighths of the £1.7 million prize fund.

The first of those half-points came in the next game, the eighteenth. Nigel adopted an extreme version of his occasional strategy of playing the world champion's own moves against their originator. He deliberately followed, for thirteen moves, one of Kasparov's most famous wins, played only six months earlier against the Belorussian number one, Boris Gelfand. The point was that Gelfand had played Kasparov's own defence against the world champion, making it possible for Short to plan this 'mirror' chess strategy in advance. After the game Kasparov conceded that he found it both strange and difficult 'to have to analyse the same position from the other side of the board'. But the champion proved as adept at playing against himself as he was at playing others. On move thirteen he introduced a notable improvement on the plan the Belorussian champion had played against him, and thereafter he was in no difficulties.

After playing his thirty-third move Kasparov offered a draw, and this time he had every right to do so. Short had two possible continuations. One, the simpler option, led immediately to a dead drawn position. The other was more tricky, but, with best play, would give an advantage to Kasparov. Reluctantly Nigel stretched out his hand to shake on the draw. The world champion was now only half a point away from retaining his title.

Late that night Nigel was still agonizing over whether he should have gambled, turned down the draw and risked a loss. 'Perhaps I should have pressed the hyperspace button,' he said. 'Earlier in the match I probably would have done so. But now . . .' and his voice tailed off. He didn't need to finish the sentence. He was almost too tired to say what was obvious: that exhaustion was preventing him from playing every game to the bitter end. And in any case, 'pressing the hyperspace button' – the video game equivalent of double or quits – had not worked on the one occasion Short had tried it in the match. Playing Black in the first game, with only ten seconds left on his clock, he had turned down Kasparov's panicky draw offer – and lost on time two moves later.

Those traumatic few moments began to weigh more and more heavily on Nigel's mind as the match drew to its close. On the day after the eighteenth game, we went for a wander around the Savoy Theatre, deserted and empty aside from the security guard who let us in.

'Let me show you why I lost the first game on time,' said Nigel. First he took me to the rest room marked 'White Player'. Inside the small windowless room was a white leather sofa which faced two closed-circuit television monitors, one showing the position on the board, the other the whole stage. Then Nigel took me up a winding flight of stairs to the room marked 'Black Player'. It looked identical to the other room, except that the leather sofa was black.

'Do you notice another difference?' asked Nigel. I didn't. 'Don't you see? This rest room for the Black Player is much further from the stage than the White room. It takes the best part of a minute to get to and from the board from here. I just hadn't appreciated that in the first game. Didn't you notice how, after that, I stayed at the board much more during my Black games than in my White ones?'

I said that it still seemed to me that he had disappeared off-stage at least every ten minutes, even when he had the Black pieces. 'That was unavoidable. That's how often I needed to go to the loo during every game,' Nigel replied.

I had not really learnt why Nigel had lost on time in the first game – and I don't think even he believed it could be blamed on anything other than mismanagement of his chess clock. I had discovered something more interesting: that not just at the start of the match, not just at the beginning of each game, but at every playing moment of every game throughout the whole match, the challenger was weak-bladdered with nervous tension. And this, more than anything else, explained why he was now, after eighteen games utterly drained.

If there had still been even a remote chance of victory in the match, adrenalin alone might have ensured that the challenger remained unaware of his own exhaustion. But the resolve of even the most determined marathon runner becomes depleted when he loses sight of his rival's heels.

And the day after the eighteenth game, it dawned on Nigel that the match could suddenly end with the next encounter. A win for Kasparov would give the world champion outright victory, and the pieces could be put back in the box for the last time.

But it wasn't the prospect of defeat which was depressing the challenger; it was just the sense of impending anticlimax, the anticlimax that accompanies the end of any struggle, however successful.

'I can feel the match ending. And it just makes me so sad. Because I know that if it doesn't end with the next game, it will probably end with the one after that. Or the one after that. I can only postpone the end. It's been such a long struggle: not just this match, but all the contests leading up to it. Three years of work, and now I can feel its end approaching. It's dominated my life for so long I can't imagine how things will be without this struggle. At the moment I feel like crying. I won't, but I feel like it.'

We were walking across Hyde Park, and Nigel suddenly noticed a musician soliciting small change. 'Perhaps I'll become a busker,' he said. 'I'm not so bad on the guitar.'

*

211

Nigel Short was not the only one to feel that the match could end with the very next game. Raymond Keene, who saw Garri Kasparov on most days of the week, reported to me that the world champion had stated his determination to win game nineteen with the White pieces and so end the match with a flourish. Above all, Kasparov was desperately anxious, not so much to re-establish a winning margin of six points, as to be the last one to win a game in the match. He absolutely did not want to wait months, until he and Short next played together in a tournament, to have a chance of revenge for his annihilation in the sixteenth game.

And the press was out in force for the nineteenth game, expecting to witness the match's final obsequies. As Rob the bodyguard came to Nigel's rooms to fetch him for the game, he listened to a colleague's words squawking out from a concealed walkie-talkie and then turned to us. 'He's just warned me that there are photographers jumping all over the joint today.'

'I wonder why,' said Nigel.

'Can't imagine,' said the bodyguard.

On the stage, and in front of almost as many photographers as there were for the first game, Kasparov speedily confirmed Keene's report of his intentions. He opened with his favourite Ruy Lopez, for the first time since the seventh game. Kasparov had employed the Anti-Marshall variation of the Ruy Lopez in the first, third and seventh games of the match and had won all three games, half his total number of wins in the entire contest.

The biggest mystery of the whole event, as far as Short and his analytical team were concerned, was why Kasparov had not repeated his devastating Anti-Marshall, since it had won so crushingly for him in the seventh game. Whatever the reason, it was not a mystery why the champion should return to the Ruy Lopez now. He was saying, in effect, that he had started the match with this opening and would end it in exactly the same way.

But Short and Hübner had been planning, ever since that seventh game, to try out a completely new defence to the Ruy Lopez – or rather a defence so out of fashion that it would come as a big shock to Kasparov. It was a variation on a theme invented by Wilhem Steinitz, world champion exactly a hundred years ago, and had not been seen in a match for the title since 1954. Better still, a swift perusal of the collected games of Garri Kasparov showed that he had faced this defence only once in his career, when he was fourteen years old.

The world champion managed to find a promising path through the thickets of ancient theory. But being forced to analyse obscure positions from a very early stage in the game had taken its toll of Kasparov's clock. He left himself with only a quarter of an hour for the last fifteen moves before the time-control.

At that point all the commentators, in the grandmaster analysis room, in the Savoy Theatre and on television seemed agreed that Kasparov's position was winning. But from the front row of the stalls it was clear that the champion had suddenly seen some diabolical resources for Short. He kept staring nervously at his clock and then at the board. Short meanwhile, for a man who was supposed to be losing the game – and the match outright – appeared remarkably unconcerned.

Then Kasparov played his twenty-sixth move and muttered something. Short suddenly sank into deep thought, clenching his legs around the sides of the table and shielding his eyes with his hands. He had only one decent move in the position, and yet he sat in that tortured position for a quarter of an hour. It was clear to me that Kasparov had offered a draw and that Nigel was desperately searching for a reason to play on. The position was very obscure, but it was impossible to find any variation in which Short had an advantage. Yet a draw meant that Kasparov would retain his title. A draw meant that the match was one game closer to its end.

Finally, Nigel stretched out his hand. 'Okay. Draw,' he said, and signed his scoresheet off as a shared point. At this point the commentators assumed that Short had resigned and that the match was over. They could not hear what passed between Short and Kasparov as they began their instant post-mortem. 'I don't know what's going on here: it's very complicated,' said the world champion, ten seconds after retaining his title. 'I don't know either, it's a complete mess,' said his opponent. 'Well, bugger me,' said Grandmaster Raymond Keene, live on television as it suddenly dawned on him that Short had not resigned, but had accepted yet another of Kasparov's draw offers.

As so often in the match, even very strong players were convinced that one side or another was 'clearly' winning, and hastened to inform the public of this fact. As so often, only Kasparov and Short were capable of analysing deeply enough to reach the conclusion that the very same position defied assessment. As Robert Hübner used to tell me on such occasions, 'Those who say they understand chess, understand nothing.'

I ran into Kasparov's manager, Andrew Page, just after the game and congratulated him on his client's retention of the title of world champion. Page shook his head: 'Garri's in a thunderous mood. He wanted to win the game, and finish the match today.' I pointed out that Kasparov had chosen to offer the draw; no one had been stopping him from playing on for a win. 'Are *you* going to tell him that?' said Page.

Normally Kasparov's saturnine features brighten immediately they come into contact with a television camera: he has a natural affinity with the limelight. But the once and future world champion was still looking distinctly unecstatic by the time the television people caught up with him. 'It's the fifth time I am world champion,' he shrugged. 'You get used to it.' And then, in what I imagine was a reference to his overall score in the match, he concluded gloomily, 'I expected it would be better.'

At about the same time, in a two-bedroom flat somewhere in West Hampstead, a man was stroking the head of his two-and-a-half-year-old daughter. 'Kyveli,' he said, 'your daddy is not going to be world champion.' The man's wife firmly corrected him. 'Not yet,' she said. 'Not yet.' I had the feeling that for Rea Short the next campaign to take Garri Kasparov's title had already begun. And for Kyveli anything else would be a break with normality: when her father started his last campaign for the world championship at the Fidé interzonal tournament, in Manila in 1990, she had not been conceived.

*

Kasparov's bleak mood could in large part be put down to sheer exhaustion. He confessed openly, now that he had achieved the twelve points necessary to retain his title, that he was 'really tired' and insisted that, in future, world chess championship matches 'should have a different number of games'.

It was strange to hear Kasparov speak in such a way. He has always prided himself on having a physique and constitution more commonly seen in less cerebral sports. Indeed he owed his world title to the fact that he ground down Anatoly Karpov into physical submission over six months' play, from September 1984 to February 1985. At that stage Karpov was still in the lead, but had no energy left to continue.

Yet now Kasparov was pleading exhaustion after a mere seven weeks' struggle. He was, admittedly, eight years older than the Kasparov who had challenged Karpov. And there were other reasons. Part of the problem was that under the London rules, for the first time in a world championship match, the players were not allowed to use the excuse of imaginary or actual illness to postpone a game. Tied to the brutal monotony of the television schedules, they were, as Nigel Short put it, 'prisoners in the same cell'.

There was also the matter of Short's own, controversial approach to the match. The challenger's conscious decision to play the sharpest, most critical lines in chess theory and to attempt, especially with the White pieces, to use the most violently aggressive tactics, backfired in a number of games. But, as Robert Hübner pointed out in one of his consoling talks with Nigel, no one had ever tried to treat Kasparov in this way before: in order to refute these brutally direct assaults, the world champion had had to put his own powers of calculation under unprecedented strain.

It was, after all, the first time that Kasparov had played a world championship match of any description against a player younger than himself; and he seemed almost confused by the apparently fresh appearance of his English opponent, even after he had handed out six beatings to him. Almost, that is, but not entirely. Late in the match Kasparov, when asked about this, remarked, 'I know Nigel Short does not appear to be as exhausted as I am. But I believe he is very tired, and just does not show it in his face.'

Not to his opponent, at any rate. But to his back-up team of Hübner and Speelman, who were themselves very tired after seven weeks of constant analysis, Nigel presented an almost abject appearance on the day before the twentieth game. In the past the three of them had sat round a board set up on a table, Hübner and Speelman on one side, Short, always with his back to the window, on the other.

Now, however, he seemed not to have the energy even to remain seated as the two grandmaster assistants took him through the variations they had prepared for the next game. Nigel lay on the sofa by the side of the table, with one hand over his eyes. The sofa was well below the level of the chess pieces, but it seemed that somehow, by the sound of them moving around and by what the analysts were muttering, Nigel was able to visualize what was going on. Occasionally he would say, 'That sounds more interesting,' and haul himself up to look at the board.

But on other occasions he would appear to sink into reveries of past battles. At one point Robert Hübner suggested that Short might consider playing an idea of the Hungarian Grand-master Honfi. 'Honfi, Honfi . . .' said Nigel dreamily. 'I played him in 1977, in the world cadet championship. I remember, during our game, this other kid came up and began giggling at our moves. I found out later that was Garri Kasparov, aged fourteen.'

Then Nigel leapt up from the posture of a psychiatrist's patient and rapidly set up a configuration of pieces on the board. 'That's the position I had with Honfi, when little Gazza came up and laughed.' Then Nigel played a couple of moves. 'I went here, and then Honfi went there. And Kasparov was quite right: those were two terrible blunders.'

No psychiatrist would have been surprised that at such a time Nigel Short's mind would turn to his first encounter, sixteen years before, with Garri Kasparov. But he would, per-haps, be amazed that Short was able to reconstruct on the chessboard a position he had not seen since he was twelve years old. I was simply reassured that the stupendous mainframe of Nigel's chess memory had not been impaired, even temporarily, by the wear and tear of two months' struggle and analysis.

Although the four-hour games themselves were tiring enough, the work the spectators never saw had also taken its toll. To spend eight hours constantly looking for new and unexpected moves in familiar positions, which is what the Short team were doing on every day between games, wrings the juices from even the most fertile minds. I was not contributing to these analyses, merely observing them. But, after a few hours of trying to follow the players' analyses, I could no longer follow the moves on the board without feeling giddy.

This might in part have been due to the strange analytical methods of Jon Speelman. Even though Speelman is well known to be one of the quickest analysts in the firmament of grandmasters, Robert Hübner told Nigel that he was continually amazed by the speed of Speelman's thought. The trouble was, Jon's physical and mental co-ordination were not harmoniously intertwined, and in his effort to move the pieces around the board to where he wanted them to go, he would constantly knock them over. The result was that there never seemed to be a single position on the board at any one time, but instead a heaving mass of agitated pieces. No wonder, by the end of two months of this, Nigel preferred to take such analysis lying down.

Nigel Short gave his analysts very specific instructions for the twentieth match-game. Although he needed to win it to keep the match alive, he knew he no longer had the energy even to attempt to blast Kasparov's Sicilian Defence off the board. Robert Hübner was commissioned to find some fresh twist which would give White small but nagging pressure against the champion's favourite opening. 'If only it was so simple,' said Robert, but by the later afternoon of the day before the twentieth game he had found an entirely new idea on White's fifteenth move against the main line of Kasparov's defence. It was a plan which looked as harmless as clear water; but it contained a drop of disguised poison.

'It's nothing very much,' said Hübner, in his usual self-deprecating way, as he showed the move to his boss.

'But it's definitely something,' said Nigel. 'Something annoying for Gazza to think about, when all he wants is for the match to end.'

'I don't like the sound of that *at all*,' said Rea Short. We were sitting next to each other on the sofa of her husband's sitting room at the Savoy. It was fifteen minutes before the start of the twentieth game. From the bathroom next door Nigel was belting out a song at a volume which would scatter pigeons. 'I don't know. He's not got such a terrible voice,' I said.

'That's not what I mean.'

I listened again and picked out some all too familiar lyrics: 'My friend, the end is near / and now I come to take / the final curtain . . .' The bathroom door swung open, and we got the full blast of Sinatra arr. Short, with full vibrato on the bit about having few regrets and doing it his way.

It wasn't just the choice of song which gave the game away, or rather told us that Nigel was not going to win, even though no other result would keep him in the match. As he emerged from the bathroom we could see that he was wearing exactly the same clothes as he had for the first game of the match: even that weirdly zigzagging tie with which fifty-five days earlier Nigel had hoped to hypnotize the world champion. Instead it was the challenger who had appeared hypnotized that day, by losing on time in a winning position. Now he clearly felt that his time had run out, even before he arrived at the board.

A hundred yards away, and a quarter of an hour later, the players went through all their usual rituals, for the twentieth time. Kasparov rapidly adjusted all his pieces on their original squares, muttering 'J'adoube' as he did so. Short scoured the board for stray specks of dust, and then turned the heads of his knights round to face the opponent. (Kasparov, like most other players, would leave his knights in the classic position, with their heads pointing left.)

And then, which absolutely could not have been predicted,

218

the world champion fell headlong into Robert Hübner's prepared variation. I felt a slight frisson as Nigel, on his fifteenth
move, unveiled the idea which had been invented less than
twelve hours earlier. Naturally all the grandmasters commenting
on the game instantly denounced the move as insipid. Equally
naturally, Kasparov alone sensed the poison in Hübner's harmless-
looking move. He spent longer over his reply -- three-quarters
of an hour -- than he had on any other move in the match.

His face looked thunderously angry: for the first time, but far
too late to make any difference, the world champion had been
badly hit by Short's opening preparation. In every other match-
game with Black he had brilliantly ducked and weaved. Finally,
in the twentieth game, by following a plan that he had played
twice before in the match, he had presented a stationary target.

While Kasparov fumed and fidgeted, Short disappeared into
his rest room. 'I watched Gazza twitching away on my monitor,'
Nigel mused the next day, 'and I thought, "Poor bastard! He's
really suffering."' After eight weeks and twenty games, something very unlikely had happened to Nigel Short. He had
become capable of feeling sympathy for his opponent.

In his unenviable position Kasparov conducted an immacu-
late defence, playing a whole series of what chess players call
'only' moves. But on the thirty-fifth move the world champion
finally slipped. It was painful to watch him, short of time,
agonize over the move. He reached out his hand to play, and
then, like a beginner, snatched it back. Kasparov again reached
out to play the same move, and again pulled his hand away at
the last second. The most decisive of all chessplayers seemed
suddenly to have developed the yips.

A third time the champion's right hand hovered over the
board, and this time it did not falter. But the move it made
allowed a vicious trick for Short, after which Kasparov would,
at best, have faced a further hour or two of unpleasant defence.

Perhaps it was some sixth sense of impending danger which
caused the Russian to hesitate so uncharacteristically. But Short
did not hesitate. He did something much worse. With almost
twenty minutes left on his clock for only five moves he bashed
out a reply which failed completely to exploit Kasparov's error.

219

It was a move which left the position dry as dust, devoid of possibilities for either side. And, in making the move, Nigel, for almost the first time in the match, offered Kasparov a draw.

After 1561 moves, spread over eight weeks, neither side had the desire to play a 1562nd. Or as the ex-challenger said to me, and perhaps he was speaking for both players, 'The suffering is over now.'

That night and the next day Nigel Short slept for sixteen hours.

But for one person at least the struggle continued. Rea Short was still magnificently implacable, still brooding over the fatalism she sensed in her husband at the outset of the final game. 'Why the bloody hell did Nigel agree a draw if he had chances on the board?' she asked me the next day. I reassured Rea that, although it was true that Nigel had missed a chance, the final position of the final game was indeed a draw, and he could not be blamed for offering it. 'Good,' she said, 'because I really felt a victory would have been vital psychologically.'

I remarked that even a victory would probably have meant no more than that the match would last one more game.

'I'm not thinking of this match,' said Rea. 'I'm thinking of the next one.'

CHAPTER FOURTEEN

Nigel, Rea, Kyveli and I travelled up together in the lift towards the sixth floor of the Savoy. It was only a few minutes after Short, on the stage of the Savoy Theatre, had collected his cheque for coming second, and Garri Kasparov had been formally declared the winner and still world chess champion.

On the first floor the lift stopped and a man stepped in without a word. He ignored the adults in the lift, but, as if seeking somewhere to direct his gaze, stared intently at Kyveli. The two-year-old stared back with equal intensity at the heavy-jawed stranger, in the way that children do. Then, at the fifth floor, still without exchanging a word, but with a last lingering look at the little girl, the man left the lift. Nigel said nothing, as we carried on up to the sixth floor. Rea gave an amused half-smile, like some Greek Mona Lisa.

The man was, of course, Garri Kasparov. I suppose, having sat less than two feet away from each other in complete silence for about 100 hours over the previous eight weeks, it was absolutely natural that the two men should continue in much the same manner. But I found the encounter in the lift slightly poignant. Kasparov seemed awkward and embarrassed in the company of the Short family, and he stared at Kyveli like a man who had never seen a child before.

This was odd, because Kasparov was himself the father of a six-month-old baby girl, Pauline. But, then again, perhaps his reaction was not so surprising. He had not seen his daughter, or his wife Masha, for at least eight weeks, certainly not since the London match began, and perhaps not for even longer, while he had been isolated in his Croatian training camp for several months before the encounter with Short.

My thoughts returned to the strange conversation I had had with Nigel while walking down the Strand with his seconds three hours before the first game of his match for the world chess championship. 'When I win this match,' he had said, 'Kasparov will like me for it. . . . He has a great burden, which he wants me to take on. . . . He just envies me my normal, happy family life. . . . it's something the world chess champion can never have.'

Nigel, of course, had wanted above anything else to assume the burden under which Kasparov laboured so mightily. It was hard to imagine what, otherwise, was the purpose of the previous three and a half years' work. But as I recall the faces of the two men in the Savoy lift, barely half an hour after the end of their match, I do not find it hard to say which revealed the greater contentment: it was the loser's.

This was not just because of differing personal circumstances, although marital contentment counts for a lot. In the match itself, Short had over-performed. Based on the world chess ratings of the two players, he was expected to score six points out of twenty games against Kasparov. In fact he scored 7½ points, which meant that, as a result of the London match, Short's international rating would increase; Kasparov's would diminish, though still leaving him far above any of his rivals. While the world champion professed himself to be greatly relieved at the retention of his title, he finished the twenty-game match unable to 'crush' Short, as he had promised to do before the event.

Five points in the lead after nine games, Kasparov must have thought he had the perfect chance to annihilate the man who had been insulting him for months, and ensure that the disrespectful Englishman was too psychologically damaged ever again to mount a challenge for his title. But Short had then displayed an extraordinary resilience at the time of greatest crisis, and over the last eleven games had held his own with the champion, and even won the last decisive game of the encounter.

Unlike Kasparov, and with very good reason, Short had never publicly claimed he would win the match. But, almost as soon as he had emerged from his sixteen-hour sleep after the last game, I reminded Nigel about his private words to me immediately before the match, when he had claimed that he was destined to win.

He looked sheepish. 'I had to believe something like that.

How else could I play against the guy? Remember that in my last ten tournament games against Gazza, before the match, I scored only fifteen per cent. In the first ten games of this match I scored twenty-five per cent. In the second ten games of the match I scored fifty per cent. Either he's getting weaker, or I'm getting stronger, or maybe it's a bit of both. Whatever, you can bet that our next match will be a lot closer, and Gazza knows it.'

Long before then, Kasparov is committed to playing a match against the world's strongest chessplaying computer, the 'Deep Blue' programme of Carnegie Mellon University. 'Deep Blue' scans and evaluates positions at a rate of about two million per second. Yet it is not a match for Kasparov, and, were the Englishman not opposed in principle to playing against computers, would almost certainly be shown to be no match for Short.

It is one of the most satisfying mysteries of the intellect that such a machine, dedicated, created and designed for chess alone, cannot outplay humans, whose brains are multi-faceted, for whom chess is merely part of a rich mixture of experiences and emotions.

Perhaps that distinction is truer of Nigel Short than it is of Garri Kasparov. The world champion is as dedicated to chess as any human ever has been. His wife Masha, speaking to her husband's most recent biographer, pointed out, with more than a trace of pathos, 'You have to understand that, for a person like Garri, to win is indispensable. If he loses, it is as if he loses part of himself. For this reason I cannot even bear to consider his losing the championship.'

But it is not just an unparalleled desire to win which motivates Garri Kasparov. That would be to underestimate the man. He also wants to win every argument about every game, to prove, even in those encounters which he failed to win, that he had had the best of the intellectual debate; that he saw, oh, so much more than his opponent (as indeed he probably had).

This was seen with amusing clarity in the pages of *The Times* throughout the match with Short. Both players were required to give their views and analyses of the games to the newspaper's chess correspondent. On the morning after every game Kasparov would furnish the *Times* man with an astonishingly detailed post-mortem of all the critical points of the game, with the principal objective of proving, if possible, that all his decisions were the best ones. Many of these analyses were far too complicated for even Kasparov to have seen at the board. The man had obviously been up much of the night going over the games in even greater detail.

Nigel Short, however, never once bothered to speak to the *Times* man about the games the day after they were played. Instead he would delegate one of his seconds, usually Jon Speelman, to give the newspaper some analysis to satisfy its readers, and it was this which would duly appear, masquerading as the unintermediated voice of Nigel Short. The point was that England's greatest ever chessplayer did not care so very much about his own games, *once they were over*.

During the actual struggle at the board, he was every bit as involved as Kasparov: indeed I noticed how Nigel's own score sheets of the games always left a blank where the date was meant to be filled in. As he explained to me, when he sat down to play he was so focused on the game that he didn't even know what day it was. But when the game was over, it was over. It was gone. It was the past. This is, I believe, the secret of Short's extraordinary resilience, not just in the match against Kasparov, but in all his matches on the way to the championship, every one of which he came from behind to win. Only a man who can genuinely blot out from his mind all thoughts of a game once it is over can suffer five, six defeats at the hands of a man like Kasparov, and carry on as if nothing had happened.

At times during the match for the world championship I found Nigel's detachment from the business in hand, from chess itself, even a little chilling. Unless provoked, he would never want to talk about the match. Politics, music, cricket, anything would seem to interest him more. I remembered how once, when we had been on holiday together, a week before an important tournament, Nigel had surprised me by not bothering to pack a chess set. That was one thing; but even during the match against Kasparov he never kept a chess set in his suite at the Savoy. Yet his guitar was always at the ready, and frequently in use, even at those times when I would most have expected a chessboard to appear.

I began to feel that perhaps there were two Nigel Shorts, two completely different people, who had absolutely nothing in common with each other. One was the world's second-greatest chess matchplayer, the man whom I saw on the stage of the Savoy Theatre with Garri Kasparov, engaging in intellectual battles of unparalleled complexity and stress. The other was a laid-back Lancastrian, a down-to-earth family man whose greatest interests were cricket and Neil Young.

I never felt this so strongly as when I saw Nigel watching himself on television, beating Kasparov in the sixteenth game. Whom did Nigel think he was shouting at, as he saw that pale, thin man in John Lennon spectacles giving the world chess champion the *coup de grâce*? He certainly gave the appearance of believing that he was cheering on another person.

On the night of the nineteenth match-game, as after every game, I went back with Nigel to his home in Hampstead, to share his dinner with Rea and Kyveli – Greek children stay up late. The game had had a particularly complex conclusion, with the players agreeing a draw in a very murky position which many grandmasters had wrongly assessed as being lost for Short. As soon as we got into the flat I asked Nigel if he could explain to me what was really going on in the final position. Wearily, he agreed. I said I would go and find a chess set, if he would tell me where he kept such a thing. 'Oh, I'm sorry,' said the Western world's leading Grandmaster, 'I don't think there's a chess set in the house.'

And there wasn't. The only chessboard in Nigel's home, or in his suite booked for two months in the Savoy, was the one in his head. This was Nigel Short's inner game.

THE GAMES
OF THE
1993 WORLD CHESS
CHAMPIONSHIP

MATCH SCORE

FIRST HALF

	1	2	3	4	5	6	7	8	9	10	Ttl
Kasparov	1	½	1	1	½	½	1	½	1	½	7½
Short	0	½	0	0	½	½	0	½	0	½	2½

SECOND HALF

	11	12	13	14	15	16	17	18	19	20	Ttl
Kasparov	½	½	½	½	1	0	½	½	½	½	5
Short	½	½	½	½	0	1	½	½	½	½	5

FINAL SCORE

Kasparov 12½   Short 7½

WORLD CHAMPIONSHIP – GAME 1
7 September 1993

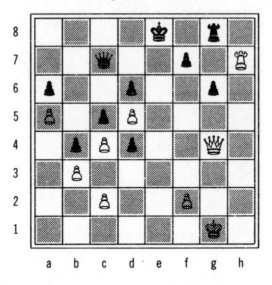

Knight = N   Bishop = B   Rook = R   Queen = Q   King = K
White: Kasparov   **Black**: Short

1	e4	e5		21	Re1	Bxc4
2	Nf3	Nc6		22	dxc4	h6
3	Bb5	a6		23	b3	c5
4	Ba4	Nf6		24	Bf4	Qd7
5	0-0	Be7		25	h3	Rd8
6	Re1	b5		26	Qe4	h5
7	Bb3	0-0		27	Re2	g6
8	a4	b4		28	Qf3	Bg7
9	d3	d6		29	Re4	Bf8
10	a5	Be6		30	Qe2	Qc7
11	Nbd2	Rb8		31	Bg5	Rc8
12	Bc4	Qc8		32	g4	hxg4
13	Nf1	Re8		33	Bf6	gxh3
14	Ne3	Nd4		34	Qg4	Ra8
15	Nxd4	exd4		35	Qxh3	Bg7
16	Nd5	Nxd5		36	Bxg7	Kxg7
17	exd5	Bd7		37	Rh4	Rg8
18	Bd2	Bf6		38	Rh7+	Kf8
19	Rxe8+	Bxe8		39	Qg4	Ke8
20	Qe2	Bb5		**Black lost on time**		

WORLD CHAMPIONSHIP – GAME 2
9 September 1993

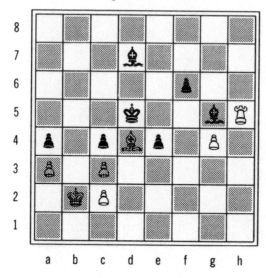

White: Short **Black**: Kasparov

1	e4	c5
2	Nf3	d6
3	d4	cxd4
4	Nxd4	Nf6
5	Nc3	a6
6	Bg5	Nc6
7	Qd2	e6
8	0-0-0	Bd7
9	f4	h6
10	Bh4	g5
11	fxg5	Ng4
12	Nf3	hxg5
13	Bg3	Be7
14	Be2	Nge5
15	Kb1	b5
16	Rdf1	Rc8
17	Nxe5	Nxe5
18	Rf2	f6

19	Rhf1	Bc6
20	a3	Bb7
21	h3	Nc4
22	Bxc4	Rxc4
23	Qd3	e5
24	Re2	Qc8
25	Rf5	Rxc3
26	bxc3	Qe6
27	Kb2	Kd7
28	Rf1	Qc4
29	Qxc4	bxc4
30	Ka2	Bc6
31	Rb1	Bd8
32	Rb8	Re8
33	Bf2	Ba5
34	Rxe8	Kxe8
35	Kb2	Kf7
36	Ba7	Ke6

37	g4	Bd8
38	Kc1	Be7
39	Re3	d5
40	exd5+	Kxd5
41	Kb2	Ke6
42	Bb6	Bd6
43	h4	gxh4
44	Rh3	e4
45	Rxh4	Bf4
46	Rh3	Bg5
47	Bd4	a5
48	Rh2	a4
49	Rh1	Bd7
50	Rh2	Kd5
51	Rh5	

Draw agreed

WORLD CHAMPIONSHIP – GAME 3
11 September 1993

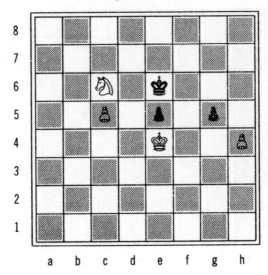

White: Kasparov **Black**: Short

1	e4	e5	21	Be3	Nh4	41	Nd2	Kf8
2	Nf3	Nc6	22	Ra2	Re6	42	Kf2	Ke7
3	Bb5	a6	23	d4	Rg6	43	Bb3	Bd7
4	Ba4	Nf6	24	Kh1	Re8	44	Nf3	Kf6
5	0-0	Be7	25	dxe5	Rxe5	45	c4	bxc4
6	Re1	b5	26	g4	Rf6	46	Bxc4	Be6
7	Bb3	0-0	27	Bd4	Ng3+	47	Be2	Bg4
8	a4	Bb7	28	hxg3	Nxf3	48	Bd1	g6
9	d3	Re8	29	Bxe5	Qxg4	49	Ba4	Bd7
10	Nbd2	Bf8	30	Rh2	Nxe1	50	Ne1	Ke6
11	c3	h6	31	Qxe1	dxe5	51	Bb3+	Ke7
12	Ba2	d6	32	Nd2	Rd6	52	Nd3	f6
13	Nh4	Qd7	33	Bc2	Be6	53	Nb4	f5
14	Ng6	Ne7	34	Kg1	Kg8	54	Ba4	fxe4
15	Nxf8	Kxf8	35	Nf1	Qg5	55	Bxc6	Bxc6
16	f3	Rad8	36	Qe3	Qd8	56	Nxc6+	Ke6
17	b4	Ng6	37	Rd2	c6	57	Ke3	g5
18	Nb3	Bc8	38	Rxd6	Qxd6	58	Kxe4	h4
19	Bb1	Nh5	39	Qc5	Qxc5	59	gxh4	
20	axb5	axb5	40	bxc5	h5		**Black resigned**	

WORLD CHAMPIONSHIP – GAME 4
14 September 1993

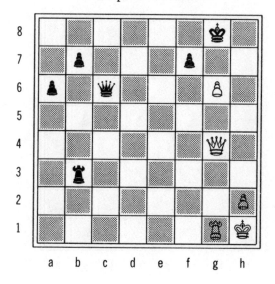

White: Short   **Black**: Kasparov

1	e4	c5		22	Bxc4	h4
2	Nf3	d6		23	Bd3	f5
3	d4	cxd4		24	Be2	Bg7
4	Nxd4	Nf6		25	c4	h3
5	Nc3	a6		26	g3	d5
6	Bg5	e6		27	Bf3	dxc4
7	f4	Qb6		28	Re3	c3
8	Qd2	Qxb2		29	Rxc3	Bxc3
9	Nb3	Qa3		30	Qxc3	0-0
10	Bxf6	gxf6		31	Rg1	Rc8
11	Be2	Nc6		32	Qf6	Bc6
12	0-0	Bd7		33	Bxc6	Rxc6
13	Kh1	h5		34	g4	Ng6
14	Nd1	Rc8		35	gxf5	exf5
15	Ne3	Qb4		36	Qxf5	Qxa2
16	c3	Qxe4		37	Qxh3	Qc2
17	Bd3	Qa4		38	f5	Rc3
18	Nc4	Rc7		39	Qg4	Rxb3
19	Nb6	Qa3		40	fxg6	Qc6+
20	Rae1	Ne7				
21	Nc4	Rxc4			**White resigned**	

WORLD CHAMPIONSHIP – GAME 5
16 September 1993

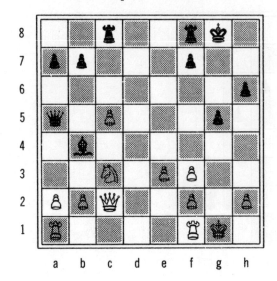

White: Kasparov   **Black**: Short

1	d4	Nf6	11	Be5	0-0
2	c4	e6	12	Bd3	Nc6
3	Nc3	Bb4	13	Bxe4	Nxe5
4	Qc2	d5	14	Bxd5	Bg4
5	cxd5	exd5	15	Nf3	Bxf3
6	Bg5	h6	16	Bxf3	Nxf3+
7	Bh4	c5	17	gxf3	Rac8
8	dxc5	g5	18	0-0	
9	Bg3	Ne4			
10	e3	Qa5		**Draw agreed**	

WORLD CHAMPIONSHIP – GAME 6
18 September 1993

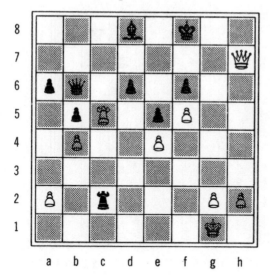

White: Short   **Black**: Kasparov

1	e4	c5	17	Nec3	Nf6
2	Nf3	d6	18	Rad1	Bxd5
3	d4	cxd4	19	Nxd5	Nxd5
4	Nxd4	Nf6	20	Rxd5	Rc8
5	Nc3	a6	21	Qg4	f6
6	Bc4	e6	22	Rf3	Rxc2
7	Bb3	Nbd7	23	Rh3	Rf7
8	f4	Nc5	24	Qh5	h6
9	f5	Be7	25	Qg6	Kf8
10	Qf3	0-0	26	Bxh6	gxh6
11	Be3	e5	27	Rxh6	Qb6+
12	Nde2	b5	28	Rc5	Bd8
13	Bd5	Rb8	29	Rh8+	Ke7
14	b4	Ncd7	30	Rh7	Rxh7
15	0-0	Nxd5	31	Qxh7+	Kf8
16	Nxd5	Bb7	**Draw agreed**		

WORLD CHAMPIONSHIP – GAME 7
21 September 1993

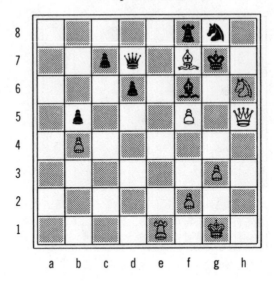

White: Kasparov   **Black**: Short

1	e4	e5	20	h5	Kh8
2	Nf3	Nc6	21	Nd5	g5
3	Bb5	a6	22	Ne3	Nf4
4	Ba4	Nf6	23	g3	Nxh5
5	0-0	Be7	24	Nf5	Bxf5
6	Re1	b5	25	exf5	Qd7
7	Bb3	0-0	26	Bxg5	h6
8	a4	Bb7	27	Nh4	Nf6
9	d3	d6	28	Bxf6	Bxf6
10	Nbd2	Nd7	29	Qh5	Kh7
11	c3	Nc5	30	Ng2	Ne7
12	axb5	axb5	31	Ne3	Ng8
13	Rxa8	Bxa8	32	d4	exd4
14	Bc2	Bf6	33	cxd4	Bxd4
15	b4	Ne6	34	Ng4	Kg7
16	Nf1	Bb7	35	Nxh6	Bf6
17	Ne3	g6	36	Bxf7	
18	Bb3	Bg7			
19	h4	Bc8		**Black resigned**	

WORLD CHAMPIONSHIP – GAME 8
23 September 1993

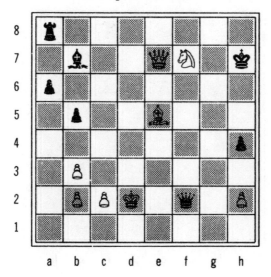

White: Short **Black:** Kasparov

1	e4	c5	15	0-0-0	Qe7	29	Qe6+	Kg7
2	Nf3	d6	16	Nc6	Nxb3+	30	Qf6+	Kg8
3	d4	cxd4	17	axb3	Qc5	31	Qe6+	Kg7
4	Nxd4	Nf6	18	Ne4	Qxc6	32	Bf6+	Kh6
5	Nc3	a6	19	Bxg5	Bb7	33	Nf7+	Kh7
6	Bc4	e6	20	Rd6	Bxd6	34	Ng5+	Kh6
7	Bb3	Nbd7	21	Nxd6+	Kf8	35	Bxh8+	Qg6
8	f4	Nc5	22	Rf1	Nxe5	36	Nf7+	Kh7
9	e5	dxe5	23	Qxe6	Qd5	37	Qe7	Qxg2
10	fxe5	Nfd7	24	Rxf7+	Nxf7	38	Be5	Qf1+
11	Bf4	b5	25	Be7+	Kg7	39	Kd2	Qf2+
12	Qg4	h5	26	Qf6+	Kh7	40	Kd3	Qf3+
13	Qg3	h4	27	Nxf7	Qh5	41	Kd2	Qf2+
14	Qg4	g5	28	Ng5+	Kg8	**Draw agreed**		

237

WORLD CHAMPIONSHIP – GAME 9
25 September 1993

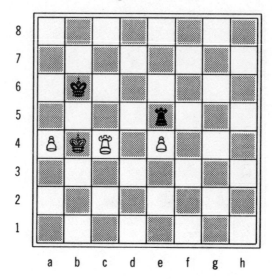

White: Kasparov **Black**: Short

1	d4	Nf6	19	Kxc2	Rc8	37	Rxa7	Kg5
2	c4	e6	20	h4	Nd7	38	Ra5+	Kf6
3	Nc3	Bb4	21	hxg5	Nxc5	39	Bc6	Rc2
4	Qc2	d5	22	gxh6	Ne4	40	Rf5+	Ke7
5	cxd5	exd5	23	c4	Nxf2	41	Bd5	Kd6
6	Bg5	h6	24	Rh4	f5	42	Rh5	Rd2
7	Bh4	c5	25	Rd4	dxc4	43	Rxh1	Rxd5
8	dxc5	g5	26	Bxc4+	Kh7	44	a4	Ra5
9	Bg3	Ne4	27	Rf1	Ng4	45	Ra1	Ke5
10	e3	Qa5	28	Kd2	Rab8	46	e4	Ke6
11	Nge2	Bf5	29	Rxf5	Rb2+	47	Ke3	Kd6
12	Be5	0-0	30	Kd3	Rxg2	48	Kd4	Kd7
13	Nd4	Bg6	31	Be6	Rc7	49	Kc4	Kc6
14	Nb3	Nxc3	32	Rxa5	Nf2+	50	Kb4	Re5
15	Bxc3	Bxc2	33	Ke2	Rh2	51	Rc1+	Kb6
16	Nxa5	Bxc3+	34	Kf3	Nh1	52	Rc4	
17	bxc3	b6	35	Rd7+	Rxd7			
18	Kd2	bxa5	36	Bxd7	Kxh6		**Black resigned**	

WORLD CHAMPIONSHIP – GAME 10
28 September 1993

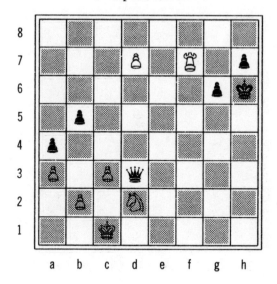

White: Short   **Black**: Kasparov

1	e4	c5	16	Nxe4	Rxf3	31	Nxd8+	Kg6
2	Nf3	d6	17	exd6	Nxb3+	32	Ne6	Qh2
3	d4	cxd4	18	Nxb3	Qf8	33	Nf4+	Kh6
4	Nxd4	Nf6	19	gxf3	Qxf3	34	Nd3	Qg1+
5	Nc3	a6	20	Nec5	Bc6	35	Re1	Qg5
6	Bc4	e6	21	Rhe1	e5	36	Ne5	g6
7	Bb3	Nbd7	22	d7	Rd8	37	Rf1	Be6
8	f4	Nc5	23	Rd6	a5	38	Nf7+	Bxf7
9	Qf3	b5	24	a3	a4	39	Rxf7	Qd5
10	f5	Bd7	25	Nd2	Qg2	40	Re7	Qd6
11	fxe6	fxe6	26	c3	Bd5	41	Rf7	Qd3
12	Bg5	Be7	27	Nd3	Bb3	42	Ne4	Qe3+
13	0-0-0	0-0	28	Nxe5	Qxh2	43	Nd2	Qd3
14	e5	Nfe4	29	Nc6	Qxd6			
15	Bxe7	Qxe7	30	Re8+	Kf7		**Draw agreed**	

239

WORLD CHAMPIONSHIP – GAME 11
30 September 1993

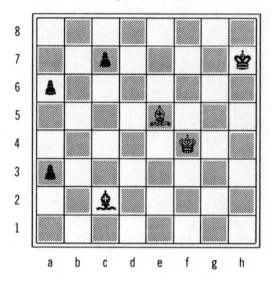

White: Kasparov   **Black**: Short

1	e4	e5	18	Bc5	Nb6	35	Bxf5	Rxe5
2	Nf3	Nc6	19	Rad1	Rxd1	36	Bd3	Bd5
3	d4	exd4	20	Rxd1	a6	37	Bd4	Rxe2
4	Nxd4	Bc5	21	f4	Nd7	38	Bxe2	Ke7
5	Nxc6	Qf6	22	Ba3	h5	39	Bxh5	Bxg2
6	Qd2	dxc6	23	Kf2	Rh6	40	Bd1	a3
7	Nc3	Be6	24	e5	c5	41	h4	Bd5
8	Na4	Rd8	25	Bf5	Rb6	42	h5	Ne5
9	Bd3	Bd4	26	Rd2	g6	43	h6	Bxa2
10	0-0	Ne7	27	Bc2	Re6	44	Bc5+	Kf7
11	c3	b5	28	Kg3	Nb6	45	Bc2	Bc4
12	cxd4	Qxd4	29	Bxc5	Nc4	46	h7	Kg7
13	Qc2	Qxa4	30	Rd5	Nxb2	47	Bf8+	Kh8
14	Qxa4	bxa4	31	f5	Bc6	48	Be7	Bd3
15	Bc2	Bc4	32	Rd2	gxf5	49	Bxf6+	Kxh7
16	Re1	Bb5	33	Kf4	Nc4	50	Bxe5	Bxc2
17	Be3	Nc8	34	Re2	f6	**Draw agreed**		

WORLD CHAMPIONSHIP – GAME 12
2 October 1993

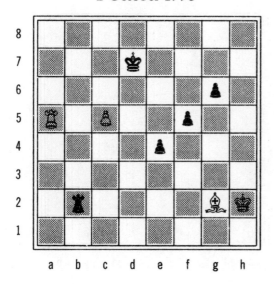

White: Short **Black**: Kasparov

1	e4	c5	22	Qxf4	exf4
2	Nf3	d6	23	Kf3	Rfd8
3	d4	cxd4	24	Rxd8	Rxd8
4	Nxd4	Nf6	25	Kxf4	Kf8
5	Nc3	a6	26	Ke3	Ke7
6	Bc4	e6	27	c4	h5
7	Bb3	Nc6	28	a4	bxa4
8	f4	Be7	29	Bxa4	h4
9	Be3	0-0	30	c5	Rh8
10	Qf3	Nxd4	31	Rc2	h3
11	Bxd4	b5	32	Bc6	c5
12	Bxf6	Bxf6	33	Kf2	h2
13	e5	Bh4+	34	Rc1	a5
14	g3	Rb8	35	Bd5	Rd8
15	gxh4	Bb7	36	Bg2	Rd2+
16	Ne4	dxe5	37	Kg3	Kd7
17	Rg1	g6	38	Ra1	f5
18	Rd1	Bxe4	39	Kxh2	Rxb2
19	Qxe4	Qxh4+	40	Rxa5	e4
20	Ke2	Qxh2+			
21	Rg2	Qxf4		**Draw agreed**	

241

WORLD CHAMPIONSHIP – GAME 13
5 October 1993

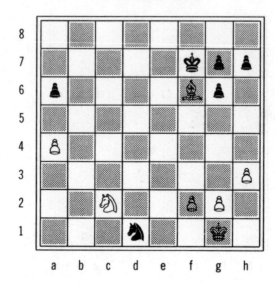

White: Kasparov   **Black**: Short

1	d4	d5	19	Rd1	Nxe5
2	c4	c6	20	Rxd4	Rb6
3	Nf3	Nf6	21	Rxd5	Rxd6
4	Nf3	dxc4	22	Rxd6	Bxd6
5	a4	Bf5	23	Bf4	Re8
6	e3	e6	24	Nd4	Bc5
7	Bxc4	Bb4	25	Nb3	Bb4
8	0-0	Nbd7	26	Be3	Nd3
9	Qe2	Bg6	27	Rb1	Rc8
10	e5	0-0	28	Bxa7	Rc2
11	Bd3	Qa5	29	Bd4	Kf7
12	e5	Nd5	30	h3	Be7
13	Bxg6	fxg6	31	Rd1	Nxb2
14	Ne4	c5	32	Na1	Nxd1
15	Nd6	Qa6	33	Nxc2	Bf6
16	Qxa6	bxa6	34	Bxf6	
17	Ng5	cxd4			
18	Nxe6	Rfb8		**Draw agreed**	

WORLD CHAMPIONSHIP – GAME 14
7 October 1993

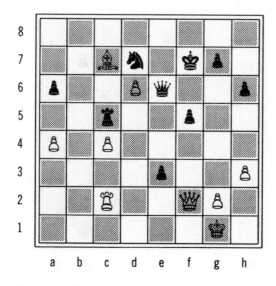

Knight = N Bishop = B Rook = R Queen = Q King = K
White: Short **Black**: Kasparov

1	e4	c5		21	Rxd5	Qe6
2	Nf3	d6		22	Rfd1	Rfc8
3	d4	cxd4		23	Ba5	Rc6
4	Nxd4	Nf6		24	b3	Rac8
5	Nc3	a6		25	Bc7	Re8
6	Bc4	e6		26	c4	bxc4
7	Bb3	Nc6		27	bxc4	f5
8	Be3	Be7		28	h3	h6
9	f4	0-0		29	Qc2	e4
10	0-0	Nxd4		30	Qa4	Rc5
11	Bxd4	b5		31	Rxc5	Nxc5
12	e5	dxe5		32	Qc6	Nd7
13	fxe5	Nd7		33	Qd5	Qg6
14	Nc4	Bb7		34	Qd2	Re5
15	Nd6	Bxd6		35	Qe3	Qe6
16	exd6	Qg5		36	Rc1	Rc5
17	Qe2	e5		37	Rc2	Kg8
18	Bc3	Qg6		38	a4	Kf7
19	Rad1	Kh8		39	Qf2	e3
20	Bd5	Bxd5		**Draw agreed**		

WORLD CHAMPIONSHIP – GAME 15
9 October 1993

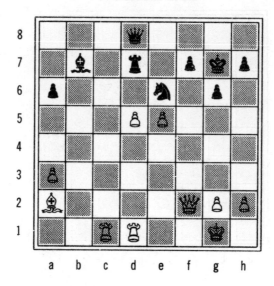

White: Kasparov   **Black**: Short

1	d4	d5	21	Nf4	Nxf4
2	c4	e6	22	Qxf4	Ne6
3	Nc3	Nf6	23	Qe5	Re7
4	cxd5	exd5	24	Qg3	Qc7
5	Bg5	Be7	25	Qh4	Ng7
6	e3	0-0	26	Rc1	Qd8
7	Bd3	Nbd7	27	Rfd1	Rcc7
8	Nge2	Re8	28	Na4	dxe4
9	0-0	Nf8	29	fxe4	Qe8
10	b4	a6	30	Nc3	Rcd7
11	a3	c6	31	Qf2	Ne6
12	Qc2	g6	32	e5	c5
13	f3	Ne6	33	bxc5	bxc5
14	Bh4	Nh5	34	d5	Nd4
15	Bxe7	Rxe7	35	Ne4	Qd8
16	Qd2	b6	36	Nf6+	Kg7
17	Rad1	Bb7	37	Nxd7	Rxd7
18	Bb1	Nhg7	38	Rxc5	Ne6
19	e4	Rc8	39	Rcc1	
20	Ba2	Rd7		**Black resigned**	

WORLD CHAMPIONSHIP – GAME 16
12 October 1993

White: Short   **Black**: Kasparov

1	e4	c5	21	Red1	Qc5
2	Nf3	d6	22	Qe3	Kg8
3	d4	cxd4	23	Kg1	Kf8
4	Nxd4	Nf6	24	Qf2	Ba8
5	Nc3	a6	25	Ne2	g6
6	Bc4	e6	26	Nd4	Qe5
7	Bb3	b5	27	Re1	g5
8	0-0	Be7	28	c3	Kg7
9	Qf3	Qc7	29	Bc2	Rg8
10	Qg3	Nc6	30	Nb3	Kf8
11	Nxc6	Qxc6	31	Rd4	Ke7
12	Re1	Bb7	32	a4	h5
13	a3	Rd8	33	axb5	axb5
14	f3	0-0	34	Rb4	h4
15	Bh6	Ne8	35	Nd4	g4
16	Kh1	Kh8	36	Rxb5	d5
17	Bg5	Bxg5	37	Qxh4	Qh5
18	Qxg5	Nf6	38	Nf5+	
19	Rad1	Rd7			
20	Rd3	Rfd8	**Black Resigned**		

WORLD CHAMPIONSHIP – GAME 17
14 October 1993

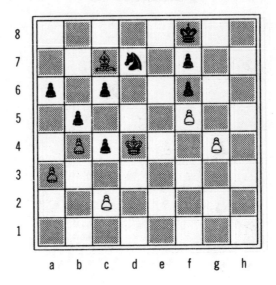

White: Kasparov **Black**: Short

1	e4	e5	15	Ng3	h5	29	b3	Rd7
2	Nf3	Nc6	16	Be2	h4	30	Rd2	Rxd2+
3	d4	exd4	17	Nf5	Bxf5	31	Bxd2	c5
4	Nxd4	Bc5	18	exf5	Ne5	32	Ke3	c6
5	Nxc6	Qf6	19	Re1	Kf8	33	Ke4	c4
6	Qd2	dxc6	20	Bf4	Rd4	34	b4	b5
7	Nc3	Be6	21	g3	Kg7	35	Bf4	Nd7
8	Na4	Rd8	22	Rad1	Re4	36	Kd4	Kf8
9	Bd3	Bd4	23	Kg2	hxg3	37	Bc7	Ke7
10	0-0	a6	24	fxg3	Bf2	38	g4	Kf8
11	Nc3	Ne7	25	Kxf2	Rxh2+	39	Bd6+	Kg7
12	Ne2	Bb6	26	Kf1	Rexc2	40	Bc7	Kf841
13	Qf4	Ng6	27	Rxe2	Rh1+	41	a3	
14	Qxf6	gxf6	28	Kf2	Rxd1	**Draw agreed**		

WORLD CHAMPIONSHIP – GAME 18
16 October 1993

White: Short **Black**: Kasparov

1	e4	c5	18	Be3	Be7
2	Nf3	d6	19	Nd2	Nf6
3	d4	cxd4	20	f3	Rfe8
4	Nxd4	Nf6	21	Kh1	Bc6
5	Nc3	a6	22	Rfe1	Rac8
6	Bc4	e6	23	Qf2	d5
7	Bb3	b5	24	Bb6	Qb8
8	0-0	Be7	25	Bc5	Bxc5
9	Qf3	Qc7	26	Nxc5	Nd4
10	Qg3	0-0	27	Nxe6	fxe6
11	Bh6	Ne8	28	exd5	Nxb3
12	Rad1	Bd7	29	Nxb3	exd5
13	Nf3	a5	30	Nxa5	Qa8
14	a4	b4	31	Nb3	Qxa4
15	Ne2	Nc6	32	Ra1	Qc6
16	Nf4	Bf6	33	Re2	
17	Nd3	e5		**Draw agreed**	

WORLD CHAMPIONSHIP – GAME 19
19 October 1993

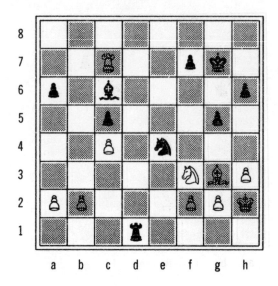

White: Kasparov   **Black**: Short

1	e4	e5		15	Nd2	Rfe8
2	Nf3	Nc6		16	h3	h6
3	Bb5	a6		17	Bh4	Rad8
4	Ba4	d6		18	Ndf3	g5
5	Bxc6+	bxc6		19	Bg3	Bd5
6	d4	exd4		20	Rad1	Kg7
7	Qxd4	Nf6		21	c4	Bb7
8	0-0	Be7		22	Rxd8	Rxd8
9	e5	c5		23	Nc6	Bxc6
10	Qd3	dxe5		24	Rxe7	Rd1+
11	Qxd8+	Bxd8		25	Kh2	Ne4
12	Nxe5	Be7		26	Rxc7	
13	Re1	0-0				
14	Bg5	Be6		**Draw agreed**		

WORLD CHAMPIONSHIP – GAME 20
21 October 1993

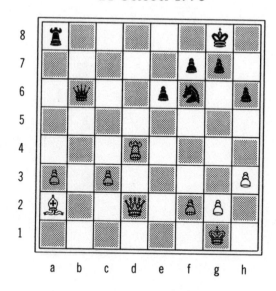

White: Short **Black**: Kasparov

1	e4	c5
2	Nf3	d6
3	d4	cxd4
4	Nxd4	Nf6
5	Nc3	a6
6	Bc4	e6
7	Bb3	b5
8	0-0	Be7
9	Qf3	Qc7
10	Qg3	0-0
11	Bh6	Ne8
12	Rad1	Bd7
13	a3	Nc6
14	Nxc6	Bxc6
15	Bf4	Qb7
16	Rfe1	a5
17	e5	dxe5
18	Bxe5	Bf6
19	Rd4	Rd8

20	Rxd8	Bxd8
21	Ne2	a4
22	Ba2	b4
23	axb4	Qxb4
24	Bc3	Qb7
25	Nd4	Nf6
26	Nxc6	Qxc6
27	Rd1	Be7
28	h3	Ra8
29	Rd4	Ne8
30	Qd3	Bf6
31	Rc4	Qa6
32	Bxf6	Nxf6
33	Qd2	h6
34	Rd4	Qb6
35	c3	a3
36	bxa3	

Draw agreed